A Short History
of Chinese Civilization

PLATE I

Female musicians. Section of a painting by K'iu Shï-chou (K'iu Ying).

A Short History of
Chinese Civilization

By Richard Wilhelm

Translated by
Joan Joshua

With an Introduction by
Lionel Giles M.A. D.Litt.

KENNIKAT PRESS
Port Washington, N. Y./London

A SHORT HISTORY OF CHINESE CIVILIZATION

First published in 1929
Reissued in 1970 by Kennikat Press
Library of Congress Catalog Card No: 77-115211
ISBN 0-8046-1104-1

Manufactured by Taylor Publishing Company   Dallas, Texas

PREFACE

THE works hitherto published on Chinese history may be divided into two classes: the one class—for the most part following the native Chinese annals—deals rather cursorily with the actual history of China, in order to come down as quickly as possible to modern times, which are usually dwelt upon at some length; the other class traces the origins of Chinese civilization in detail, with little regard for contemporary history. This book aims at a more comprehensive survey: no tedious enumeration of dates, wars, and sovereigns, but as clear an account as possible of the forces responsible for the various periods of Chinese civilization and culture, making the treatment of each subject more or less detailed in accordance with its cultural significance. The history is brought down to the time when Europeans first appear on the scene, when a change in China's civilization was effected. The story of this transformation is a theme in itself, and there is no lack of works that deal with it.

RICHARD WILHELM

FRANKFURT-AM-MAIN
May 1928

TRANSLATOR'S NOTE

I SHOULD like in the first place to express my deep indebtedness to Dr Lionel Giles, who has revised the translation throughout and given general help in matters of sinology. Without his editorial guidance through the labyrinths of Chinese history, religion, etc., and the sinological scholarship which he placed at my disposal in so wholehearted a manner, my translation must have suffered greatly in point of accuracy.

For the convenience of English readers I have followed Professor Bernhard Karlgren's system of Chinese transliteration as formulated in his pamphlet *The Romanization of Chinese* (China Society, London, 1928). This is based on the Wade orthography, with some modifications, and differs but slightly from the German transliteration of Professor Wilhelm.

The names of provinces and well-known towns are written in the spelling adopted by the Chinese Post Office, thus : Chekiang, Szechwan. Other place-names are transliterated according to Karlgren's system, with hyphens between the syllables—*e.g.*, Yün-kang.

In nearly all quotations from the Chinese Classics I have made use of Legge's translation, except in certain places where the author's interpretation differs from that of Legge, and I am indebted to the Oxford University Press for kind permission to employ Legge's work in this way. I have also to thank Mr John Murray for allowing me to quote Allen Upward's verse rendering of the prayer of King Ch'êng, from the *Shï King* (see p. 117), and the China Inland Mission for permission to use one of their publications as the basis of the map reproduced on the back endpapers.

J. JOSHUA

August 1929

INTRODUCTION

FAR too little attention has been paid hitherto to the place occupied by the Chinese in the history of the world. Universal histories, so called, concentrate for the most part on the Mediterranean civilization, beginning perhaps with the Egyptians and ancient Babylonians, continuing with Greece and Rome, and afterward dealing in great detail with the history of three or four European states. The Middle East—India, Persia, etc.—usually comes in for some notice, but China is either neglected altogether or dismissed in a chapter or two, the treatment accorded to her being necessarily superficial and generally inaccurate.

The reasons for this neglect are not far to seek. The various Western civilizations have points of contact with one another, and they all hang together to a certain extent. Egyptian culture influenced that of Crete and Greece, Greece in her turn influenced Rome, and the Roman Empire was the rootstock from which the civilization of modern Europe sprang. But until quite recent times there has been no such contact between China and the West. Her civilization is a curiously isolated phenomenon, developed internally and owing very little to foreign influences, while her own influence on the trend of Western history is practically negligible.

The remoteness of China from the Mediterranean basin has been an insurmountable obstacle to mutual intercourse and free exchange of ideas, though at certain periods a considerable trade was carried on with Europe both by land, across the vast deserts of Central Asia, and later by sea through the medium of the Arabs. But in spite of this trade the peoples of Europe remained in almost total ignorance of China (except as a shadowy region where

9

silk came from), which was fully equalled by the ignorance of the Chinese themselves concerning the nations of the West.

It is true that during the last three centuries our knowledge of contemporary China has greatly increased, though the process has been painfully slow. But even at the present day we have much to learn about the origin, development, and fundamental ideas of Chinese civilization. The chief stumbling-block in Chinese historical research is the difficulty of the written language. The material is there in plenty, but hardly any of it is accessible in translation. Few besides professed sinologists realize either the enormous extent of the historical literature existing in Chinese or the extremely small fraction of that literature which has been made easily available by translation. For instance, the dynastic histories alone total 3264 sections or chapters; yet only about a third of the first history, comprising forty-seven chapters, has been translated into French, and a few stray chapters are all that have been published in English. The comprehensive history *T'ung Kien Kang Mu* was utilized by De Mailla for his *Histoire générale de la Chine* some two hundred years ago; but as sinology was then in its infancy it goes without saying that the translation is neither complete nor wholly reliable.

Thanks to the imperishable labours of James Legge, the Confucian Classics have been open to English readers for over half a century, and it is from these invaluable documents of antiquity that much of the material presented to us in the following pages has been gathered. The fact that the Classics had all taken shape before the Christian era, and some of them long before the Han dynasty, goes to show at what an early date the civilization of the Chinese had begun to crystallize into the semblance of what it is to-day. For, as Hirth and other writers have pointed out, the Chou dynasty is the formative period of all Chinese culture, and in spite of its turbulence and feudal strife was of the utmost importance for the intellectual life of the nation.

Since those early times China has passed through many

terrific upheavals and convulsions; her soil has been laid waste time and again by monster rebellions, and more than once the whole country has been swept from end to end by a flood of invaders. Yet her civilization has never perished, but has always resumed its march forward, often absorbing the very foes who had been victorious in the field. What is the secret of this amazing vitality and endurance, possessed in like measure by no other nation?

One factor, no doubt, is the geographical position of China, separated as it is from the rest of the world by huge mountain barriers, trackless deserts, and wide seas. Thus the originally insignificant tribe on the banks of the Yellow River had leisure to expand very gradually and secure a firm hold on the country. From the dawn of history soon after the legendary emperors at least two thousand years elapsed before the whole of what is now known as China proper was occupied and brought under cultivation by the industrious Chinese farmer.

From the political point of view, Chinese civilization may be regarded as based on two social elements: (1) a class of peasant proprietors, firmly rooted to the soil; (2) a small oligarchy of intellect and culture. It is the harmonious combination of these two elements that has proved of such immense value to the Chinese. In ancient Greece we find intellect and culture in perhaps a higher degree and, relatively speaking, even more widely diffused; but the system of city-states was too unstable to endure very long. Under the Roman Empire the smallholders of Italy, forming the backbone of the country, were gradually wiped out, and their place taken by hordes of slaves who had little or no interest in the stability of the State. Slavery, it may be noted in passing, is an evil from which China has not been altogether exempt, but it has never reached alarming proportions: the majority of the population has always consisted of free village communities enjoying a large measure of self-government.

Civilization is ultimately based on morality, or the moral sense; and here we may certainly trace another cause making for the permanence of Chinese civilization. For the Chinese outlook on life, nay, their whole conception of the universe and its workings, is of an essentially moral order. The patriarchal system, a legacy from the distant past, was built up on the virtue of *hiao*, or filial piety, a word which in its written form is a ' son ' supporting ' old age.' Later on. it acquired a more comprehensive meaning, being extended to the relations between governors and governed, and thus becoming the very basis of the political structure.

Yet another ingredient which has acted as a potent preservative of Chinese civilization is the nature of the written language. If we regard civilization as a body of wisdom, moral and intellectual, comprising those arts and crafts which make for the elevation and refinement of life, it is clear that the means employed for transmitting this wisdom from generation to generation must be of no little importance. Now, Chinese writing, being fundamentally ideographic in character, and thus exempt from the changes which accompany the evolution of alphabetic languages, is an instrument peculiarly suited for the hiving of thought. Thanks to this immutable quality in the script, the sayings of Lao Tsï and Confucius, though committed to writing several centuries before the Christian era, can still be read by anyone who has learned the characters in use to-day.

It is interesting to speculate on the future that awaits this unique and wonderful Chinese civilization. Will it merge gradually into that of the world at large (contributing perhaps as much as it absorbs) or retain its own distinctive features? Contact with the West has already produced great results, such as the virtual disappearance of foot-binding; and it is likely that many of the changes which have revolutionized the conditions of life in Japan will be introduced, though much more slowly, into China. The patriarchal system is beginning to crumble, and is probably doomed to pass away; but economic necessities make it safe to predict that the country will remain predominantly agricultural, the peasantry continuing to form the overwhelming bulk of the population, though town-dwellers may also increase in numbers when new scientific methods of ensuring a constant food-supply have been adopted. Education and culture are bound to spread more widely amongst a people that has always held learning in such high esteem.

The future of the written language is a problem of which none can yet foresee the solution. The younger school of reformers lay much stress on its cumbrousness and the difficulty of mastering so many complex characters within a reasonably short time; but they have failed so far to suggest any practicable alternative. Romanization, or indeed any form of phonetic script, must be ruled out, unless the whole of existing Chinese literature is to be thrown on the scrap-heap. For, owing to the paucity of sounds in Chinese, nothing but the simplest colloquial language could be understood if phonetically reproduced in writing.

Moreover, an ideographic script possesses certain notable advantages: besides being, as we have seen, practically immune from decay in the sense that it does not become obsolete through change of pronunciation, it is equally intelligible to speakers of different dialects—an important consideration in a country where dialects differ so widely from one another. In this way it certainly forms a strong national bond of union.

It is significant that the progressive Japanese, whose books are written in Chinese characters with a certain admixture of their native *kana* (symbols from a phonetic syllabary), show no signs of discarding the Chinese element, though in their case the reform would be perfectly feasible. Professor B. H. Chamberlain, the acutest and most learned of all writers on Japan, goes so far as to say that " ideographic writing apparently possesses some inherent strength that makes it tend to triumph over (without entirely supplanting) phonetic writing, whenever the two are brought into competition in the same area. All the countries under Chinese influence exemplify this little-known fact in a striking manner."

We may take it, then, that Chinese literature will not be violently diverted into a new channel, but continue to run its own course. The existing characters will in

13

all probability be studied as long as Chinese civilization remains a distinct entity within the world system. Such simplification as may appear necessary for practical purposes will be effected, not by their abolition, but rather by a drastic reduction in the number of strokes required for writing them.

LIONEL GILES

CONTENTS

ILLUSTRATIONS

PLATES

17

ILLUSTRATIONS

ILLUSTRATIONS IN THE TEXT

A SHORT HISTORY
OF CHINESE CIVILIZATION

INTRODUCTION

SOURCES

I. CHINESE HISTORICAL RECORDS

THE historical literature on China is almost immeasurably vast, but there exists as yet no history of Chinese civilization. This literature, however, contains a number of indications and clues to the history of China's civilization which may be largely drawn upon, although they must of course be referred back to and supplemented from the original sources. It seems advisable, therefore, to cast a brief glance at ancient Chinese annals, in order to form an idea of available material.[1]

A traditional history naturally existed in China, as elsewhere, before there were any written records. We may assume that in China, as in the case of other civilizations, such tradition was, in the first instance, handed down orally and impressed on the hearer's memory in the form of rhymed verse. We find such verse frequently employed by Lao Tsï in his *Tao Tê King* and by Confucius in his commentary on the *Book of Changes*, and we may take for granted that this form, merely used by them in conjunction with a script already known for a long time, preceded the invention of writing as the chief medium of tradition.

We find in the *Book of Poetry* (*Shï King*) (the modern version of which was likewise edited by Confucius, but which is generally accepted as being of far earlier date) a mass of historical and cultural material which furnishes us with a picture of conditions during the period that gave

---

[1] See Liang K'i-ch'ao, *Chung Kuo Li Shï Yen Kiu Fa*, which appeared in 1922 as the first volume of a Chinese history of civilization.

birth to those odes.   The accidental quality of the allusions and the naïve way of writing are precisely what endow this work with special value as a source of the history of primitive civilization.

Actual historical chronicles are of very ancient date in China.   This fact is due to the existence in the country since the earliest times of the important office of scribe or script-magician,[1] who chronicled events and who, as astrologer and historian, possessed and handed on celestial and terrestrial knowledge and wisdom in the form of the written word. He was something more than an historian; he was the sage whose opinion was decisive, but whose task at the same time was to record events.   Already in the legendary time of Huang Ti we learn of the existence of these scribes, and the very earliest traditions abound in individual names— including, for instance, that of Lao Tsï—as well as in mention of the various offices concerned in the recording and handing down of the material.   Not only the Court of the suzerain, but those of the feudal states boasted these scribes, who as late as the Han period ranked before the first ministers as custodians of the records.

A number of the titles [2] of their chronicles have been preserved, but almost the whole of the actual works was destroyed in the " Burning of the Books " under Ts'in Shï Huang Ti.   Although the effects of this deed on ancient Chinese literature in general have been much exaggerated, they were certainly most disastrous as regards the historical literature of the states which had been striving for supremacy with Ts'in.   The victorious tyrant wanted to wipe out history in order to appear against an empty background as the superman with whom all history was to begin.[3]   Nevertheless, two of these works have been saved for posterity: one was the so-called *Annals of the Bamboo Books*, containing the official chronicles of the Wei state, disinterred from

[1] See O. Franke, " Der Ursprung der chinesischen Geschichtschreibung," in the *Sitzungsberichte der preussischen Akademie der Wissenschaften* (1925), p. 276 f., and A. Forke, *Der Ursprung der Chinesen* (Hamburg, 1925), p. 25.

[2] See Mencius.

[3] Hence the appellation he assumed : Ts'in Shï Huang Ti ('First Emperor from the House of Ts'in ').

the grave of one of the rulers of Wei ;[1] the other was the
Spring and Autumn Annals of the Lu state, on which
Confucius based his historical judgments, and which he
remodelled with that object in view. Both works are
remarkable for their brevity in recording chronologically
arranged events, and no greater prominence is accorded to
political measures than to astronomical and meteorological
phenomena. Apart from annals of this nature, there also
existed ancient documents concerned with the recording of
discourses. The relation between these two sources of
history is thus described : the scribe on the left chronicled
discourses, the scribe on the right chronicled events. Events
are in *Spring and Autumn*, discourses are in the *Records*.[2]

We possess among the Chinese Classics a book of these
ancient records, also edited, or at all events employed for
instruction, by Confucius, called the *Shu King*, or *Book of
History*. It is true that we are in a state of considerable
uncertainty regarding this book, which owing to its
historical character suffered badly in the " Burning of the
Books." It is said to have consisted originally of one
hundred sections. After the collapse of the Ts'in dynasty,
when the Han dynasty was again turning its attention to the
relics of antiquity, a recension of the work by one Fu Shêng
came to light. But it contained only twenty-eight sections.
Later a descendant of Confucius, K'ung An-kuo, discovered
a version in archaic script containing sixteen more sections.
It appears, however, that this version was again lost, and the
twenty-five sections in so-called archaic script contained in
the *Book of History* to-day were put together out of fragmentary quotations and similar material as late as the
Eastern Tsin dynasty. At the same time, some of the
genuine sections were divided, thus making up the total of
fifty-eight sections of which the work consists to-day.[3]
There is no doubt that the authentic portions of the *Book
of History* are founded on ancient tradition, and contain

[1] The *Bamboo Books* (*Chu Shu Ki Nien*) of to-day are not authentic throughout,
but doubtless contain some original matter. See the works of Wang Kuo-wei.
[2] See *Han Shu*, " I Wên Chï."
[3] See the various researches of Chinese scholars of the Ts'ing dynasty of the
Huang Ts'ing King Kie.

very vital material bearing on the state of civilization in the earliest times. It should, however, be used with great caution, as the oldest parts were transmitted by Confucius not as an historical work, but as a manual of political science, and were probably reconstituted by him to this end.

Besides the classical *Book of History*, valuable material exists in the form of records from the time of the Chou dynasty,[1] comprising later additions.

A number of other ancient works, not written as histories, but nevertheless containing material which affords an insight into olden days, calls for comment in a study of the history of civilization. The chief of these is the *Book of Changes*, in which not only do the oracles interpreting the various diagrams make reference to current events, such as the chastisement of the Devil's Country (Kuei Fang), the patriarchal method of procedure in the marriage of royal princesses, and various events at the end of the Yin and the beginning of the Chou dynasties, but a comprehensive survey is given in a chapter of the "Great Treatise"[2] of the development of civilization from the mythical days of Fu Hi to those of Yao and Shun, progress being represented as a revelation through the diagrams of the *Book of Changes*.

Mention may also be made of the works dealing with the customs of the Chou period—although considerable doubt exists as to their date of compilation—as well as of the many lost records cited by various authors in the time of Ts'in Shï Huang Ti, of which only a few remnants have been preserved.[3]

To the end of the Chou period belong the first two historical works which are really worthy of the name: the works of Tso K'iu[4] and the *Shï Pên*. The writings of Tso K'iu apparently comprised those political discourses (*Kuo*

---

[1] *I Chou Shu.*

[2] *Ta Chuan*, commonly but incorrectly called *Hi Tsï Chuan.*

[3] *E.g.*, in the *Tso Chuan* are cited *San Fên, Wu Tien, Pa So, Kiu Kiu*; in Chuang Tsï, *Kiu Pan, Liu T'ao*; in Mencius, *Chuan* or *Chï*, and so on. A book called *The Narrative of Mu, Son of Heaven*, describing his travels, which was found in the same tomb as the *Bamboo Books*, and other writings, the authenticity of which is, however, doubtful, are still extant.

[4] Thus according to the *Shï Ki*, although he is usually known as Tso-k'iu Ming. For the question of his authorship *cf.* O. Franke, *Beiträge zum Konfuzianischen*

PLATE 2

The three-tier Altar of Heaven in Peking. At the time of the winter solstice the Son of Heaven offered up the great sacrifice to heaven on the topmost terrace.

Yü) from which at a later date was compiled the so-called *Tso Chuan*, which was afterward ascribed to the pen of a disciple of Confucius as a commentary on the latter's *Chʻun Tsʻiu*. Tso Kʻiu's work differs from former records in that it does not depict history from the standpoint of a single state alone, but takes all the states into account, a course rendered necessary by the steady extension of the Chinese Empire; that it does not confine its scope to the mention of sovereign and State action, but elucidates social conditions; and, finally, that it substitutes coherent historical narrative for the chronicle form of former historians. In these respects this work represents, somewhere about the year 400 B.C., a revolution in the domain of Chinese historical writing.

We are unfortunately not so well informed regarding the other work, *Shï Pên*, which seems to have been lost during the disturbances that brought the Chou dynasty to an end. But we know that the famous historian Sï-ma Tsʻien, of whom more will be heard later, used it as a primary source, so in this way we learn something of its structure. It contained a record of the royal successions and the feudal houses, biographies of noteworthy men, chronological tables, tribal, family, and municipal histories, information about notable works and inventions. Through this classification an insight into history was afforded which enabled comparisons to be drawn between the various epochs; the work likewise gave greater attention to social conditions than former writings had done.

The next stage in the writing of history is reached by Sï-ma Tsʻien, who lived some three hundred years after Tso Kʻiu.[1] Great changes in the state of Chinese civilization had occurred in the intervening years. A united empire had taken the place of the feudal states; in the intellectual field creative activity had been superseded by the collection of ancient literature. China had extended her

Dogma, where the opinion of the Chinese scholar Kʻang Yu-wei is reproduced. It disposes finally of Grube's conjecture (*cf.* W. Grube, *Geschichte der chinesischen Literatur* (2nd ed., 1909), pp. 68 *et seq.*) that Confucius was the author of the *Tso Chuan*.

[1] About 140–80 B.C.

25

frontiers, and had acquired new colonies in the west. This was the time at which Sï-ma Ts'ien wrote the historical work which carried on his father's labours and became famous under the title *Shï Ki*, or *Historical Record*. Here vanish the last traces of the official historiographer. Although Sï-ma Ts'ien occupied this post, his history is the absolutely independent work of an historian who, as a free man, looks down the ages he has set himself to handle, and who, exercising his own practical judgment as to the laws governing the rise and fall of history, weaves his sources into an organic whole. Confucius was the first, in his *Spring and Autumn Annals*, to supply an historical survey in a private and not an official capacity. But in converting his work into a judgment of society he sacrificed actuality to this object; for he did not describe events and their causes, but asserted what should have happened and why. And only when his text is examined in conjunction with actual events does his hidden moral become clear. Sï-ma Ts'ien is himself conscious of the fact that in the capacity of a critical historian he is the spiritual descendant of Confucius. But he succeeded in converting apparently dry records into a vivid narrative and in pointing a moral by means of the events themselves without sacrificing fact. This achievement he owes to the work of all his predecessors, which he used most conscientiously. His contribution, however, is no mere mosaic of available material, but a completion of unfinished themes. Small wonder that he is honoured in China as the Father of History. The fact that in the records of the Han period only 191 volumes of historical literature are mentioned before Sï-ma Ts'ien, while several centuries later, in the Sui period, 16,585 are enumerated,[1] is the best demonstration of the influence he exerted on the writing of Chinese history.

Historical literature reached a very high level in the Tsin dynasty, which succeeded the period of the so-called Three Kingdoms and lasted until A.D. 420. The *History*

---

[1] See *Han Shu*, "I Wên Chï," under "Ch'un Ts'iu Kia" (425 volumes are mentioned, of which 191 are prior to Sï-ma Ts'ien), and *Sui Shu*, "King Tsi Chï," under "Shï Pu."

of the Three Kingdoms ranks among the best historical works, and must not be confused with the historical novel of a far later date dealing with the same period.

With the famous historiographer Pan Ku, who wrote the history of the Han period, a new style of historical writing was inaugurated. It was the avowed intention of his father, Pan Piao, to carry on the work of Sï-ma Ts'ien, and Pan Ku's own writings were the outcome, not of an official position, but purely of personal initiative. But he limited his work to recording the history of the Han dynasty.[1] There was this vital difference between the work of the two men: Sï-ma Ts'ien's chronicles were concerned with all historical happenings, and therefore with questions of social progress as well as political events; Pan Ku's book, on the other hand, was primarily a record of rulers. The advantage of keeping within the range of one dynasty was that it facilitated the lucid presentment of the material. Hence arose the custom of writing the histories of single dynasties as self-contained works. In the official collection of *The Twenty-four Historical Works* all but the *Record* of Sï-ma Ts'ien are dynastic histories. So it is easy to estimate Pan Ku's importance in the sphere of Chinese historiography. His influence cannot be pronounced, however, entirely favourable. The course of history, especially when regarded from the standpoint of cultural progress, is not governed by the divisions between dynasties, the rise and fall of which may frequently be ascribed to chance causes. When severed from their natural connexion events appear too spasmodic; on the one hand, a view of the background of civilization against which they are played is lost; on the other hand, the dynastic barrier shuts out all view of their later effect. Further, the writing of history from the standpoint of a single dynasty necessitates a certain bias; the enemies of the dynasty are displayed as rebels, the horizon is narrowed.

Historical literature underwent yet another reaction after the T'ang dynasty. We saw above how ever since the

[1] Pan Ku died in prison in A.D. 92. His sister Pan Chao, known by the name of Ts'ao Ta Ku, completed her brother's work.

time of Confucius the tendency had been for historical writing proper to pass from the hands of the official historian into those of the independent author, who quite consciously adopted a definite standpoint. The example set by Confucius had the effect of imbuing each of the great historians with a sense of the high dignity attaching to the office of the historical critic. Even those who happened to fill the post of historiographer wrote notwithstanding from a personal standpoint. Hence the value and the interest aroused by their works.

It was otherwise after the T'ang dynasty. The T'ang Emperor T'ai Tsung, who had high literary aspirations himself, deprived the independent author of the task of historical recording and entrusted it again to a college of officials. Thereafter it became customary for the history of each dynasty to be written after its downfall by a specially appointed body of scholars. The idea was to eliminate all possibility of a subjective viewpoint in favour of an objective one. This is, indeed, what happened. With the attainment of objectivity, however, vanished all feeling of personal responsibility. The histories became increasingly void of life and spirit, increasingly impersonal and dull. Even when great scholars formed a part of the staff they were but ciphers in the whole. Liang K'i-ch'ao has compared this method of writing history with the painting of a wall by a body of handicraftsmen. The result is mere decorators' work, not a work of art. Only quite a few notable masters, such as Ou-yang Siu, the Sung statesman and poet, who wrote the *History of the Five Dynasties* (907–960), were able to stamp the impress of their personalities on their work. Thus the appointment of historiographers in the early days endowed Chinese historical literature with vitality, and in the later days paralysed it.

In the composition of these dynastic histories it was the invariable practice to append to each new theme a note developing and explaining the content. There was also the annal or chronicle method, which in its most rigid form was the origin of Chinese historical writing. Neglected for a time, this method was reintroduced in a style adapted to the now more advanced form of historical literature. The *Tso Chuan* [1] is usually cited as the prototype of this style. But it has been proved pretty conclusively that the present chronological form of this work was assumed only when it came to be accepted as a commentary on the *Ch'un Ts'iu*. The oldest surviving work of this type is Sün Yüe's [2] revision of the history of the Han dynasty. Here the additional material is introduced by first recounting the events of the year in strictly chronological order, after which more detailed accounts of the main incidents are inserted as a commentary, in smaller script. The advantage of this kind of annotated chronology is that the commentary can be greatly enriched by the consideration of all sorts of cultural and sociological problems. The only drawback is that the connected course of events is interrupted by their being separated under different years, leading inevitably to repetition and confusion in time sequence. These disadvantages are the necessary result of making chronology instead of persons the basis of division. Nevertheless, Sün Yüe found many imitators, and the histories of a number of dynasties were treated in this 'extended chronicle' style. The custom was still retained, however, of making each dynasty the subject of a separate work. All the works which come under consideration here are dynastic histories.

Sï-ma Kuang [3] was the first historian bold enough to compile a comprehensive universal history again. Like the other famous Sï-ma, he was a man of abundant knowledge and markedly scientific turn of mind. It is not surprising, then, that his work, which covers the period 403 B.C.–A.D. 959, should also rank among the foremost Chinese histories. He made use of a quantity of material hitherto

---

[1] *Cf.* above, p. 24, *n.* 4.

[2] Sün Yüe, A.D. 148–209. The task was undertaken by order of the Emperor Hsien Ti, and Sün Yüe's work bore the title of *Han Ki* (*Han Annals*).

[3] Sï-ma Kuang (1019–86) held office for many years under the Sung dynasty. He was among the opponents of Wang An-shï, and withdrew into private life when the Court undertook to carry through the reforms of the latter. He then proceeded to write his historical work *Tsï Chï T'ung Kien* (*Universal Mirror of Aids to Government*).

neglected, and thus imparted extraordinary vitality and depth to the chronological form which he likewise retained. He assumed complete personal responsibility for this history. To him also history was no lifeless store of knowledge, but a living mirror, the right use of which would supply the basis for right government. Thus his "Mirror for Rulers," as we might call his work, became the basis, not only of historical writing, but of statesmanship. Chu Hi,[1] desirous of emulating the manner in which Confucius had compiled his universal history, laid special emphasis on these points in his rearrangement of the work.

Of greater importance than this work is one which inaugurated a new era in Chinese historical science: *Root Causes and Effects of Affairs recorded in the "Universal Mirror,"* by Yüan K'ü.[2] Like the *Han Ki*, this is no independent work, but rests throughout on the famous work by Sï-ma Kuang. But whereas Sün Yüe had divided up the Han history in the form of annals, Yüan K'ü set himself the task of arranging the events in the *T'ung Kien* under categories. He created 239 categories in all, within each of which the subjects were treated in historical sequence. He thus produced an historical encyclopædia, which later found many imitators. In accordance with the material he found to his hand, however, he confined himself to political and administrative matters and left cultural and social conditions untouched. Nor were his classifications always fortunate, and it is often difficult to trace any particular subject among the vast number of categories. His achievement was nevertheless taken as a model by many successors.

Besides political encyclopædias of this kind, dealing with the course of historical events, must be mentioned another class of works occupied with the description of institutions and social systems. To these belongs the work of Tu Yu,[3]

---

[1] Chu Hi (1130–1200) is the most prolific writer of Confucianist tendencies in the Sung period, and brought about a more or less pietistic reform of Confucianism. His revision of the *T'ung Kien* is entitled *Tsï Chï T'ung Kien Kang Mu*.

[2] *T'ung Kien Ki Shï Pên Mo.*

[3] Tu Yu, died 812. His work, *T'ung Tien*, is divided into "Political Economy," "The Examination System," "Government Offices," "Rites," "Music," "Military Science," "Geography," "National Defences."

of the Tʿang epoch, entitled *General Institutions*, which gives an account of the working and historical evolution in the various State institutions. This work was emulated by Ma Tuan-lin,[1] in his *Complete Antiquarian Researches*, whose fame has echoed down the centuries, though it does not quite equal the work of Tu Yu.

In the Sung dynasty Chêng Tsʿiao[2] compiled his *Complete Chronicles*, which run from the time of Fu Hi to the Tʿang dynasty. On the whole his attainment falls short of that of his great predecessor, Sï-ma Tsʿien, but the twenty chapters of compendiums in his work are of permanent value.

These three works, the *Universal Mirror*, the *Complete Antiquarian Researches*, and the *Complete Chronicles*, were afterward known collectively as the three comprehensive encyclopædias. Continuations were compiled for all three, and under the Manchus three further works of a comprehensive nature were produced on the political and social institutions of the ruling dynasty, bringing the total number of so-called comprehensive encyclopædias up to nine.

To these latter works must be added the great collective encyclopædias worthy of mention as historical and cultural works of reference. *The Great Institutions of the Yung-lo Period* (*Yung Lo Ta Tien*), dating from the beginning of the Ming dynasty, was so monumental that it was never printed; only one manuscript copy existed,[3] and this was consumed by fire during the Boxer Riots, the few volumes which were saved being now distributed all over the world. The illustrated encyclopædia, the *Tʿu Shu Tsi Chʿêng*, which appeared in the Kʿang-hi period, and of which various editions are contained in all the more important sinological libraries, is also worthy of mention.

---

[1] Ma Tuan-lin lived in the thirteenth century, at the end of the Sung and the beginning of the Yüan dynasty. When the latter arose he retired into private life and compiled his *Wên Hien Tʿung Kʿao*.

[2] Chêng Tsʿiao, 1108–66. His work, *Tʿung Chï*, was completed about 1149.

[3 According to "A Note on the *Yung Lo Ta Tien*," by Dr Lionel Giles (*The New China Review*, April, 1920), two manuscript copies were made from the original in the Ming period. The original and one copy perished by fire, and of the sole remaining copy, consisting originally of over ten thousand volumes, only about one hundred and sixty volumes have been traced in various libraries.—TRANSLATOR.]

Apart from the above-noted four classes of historical works—namely, the annotated, arranged by subject, the chronological, the encyclopædic, and the Government records—there exists a number of separate studies, of which some are noticeable chiefly as material for historical works, while others cover ground strictly limited as regards space and time. The first named mostly contain collected reports (such as local information or reports on constructions), biographies of selected categories of historical personages (such as noteworthy women or prominent scholars), family histories or individual biographies, travel descriptions and accounts of extraordinary occurrences and natural phenomena (such as, for example, the semi-fictitious *Hill and River Classic* and the account of the travels of King Mu), and collections of discourses and utterances. The other class of studies may be described as historical works in the stricter sense because they arrange material of various kinds on a uniform plan and are specialized only in a territorial sense. To this class belong chiefly the provincial, departmental, and district histories, which in China are an especially rich source of data bearing on social and cultural conditions, and many of which were compiled by famous scholars.

Finally, the development of auxiliary works was inevitable. Of these, one class was devoted to the elucidation of historical conditions, and resulted in extensive antiquarian researches; the other class occupied itself with criticism and the critical examination of undetermined problems. The critical works either examined existing historical writings critically or undertook the critical elucidation of history proper in its causes and effects. In time this led to a specialized branch of literature, that of historical investigations—which, however, have not always escaped the danger of discoursing elegantly without penetrating deeply; particularly was this the case after historical essays were included as subjects in the State examinations. At the same time, it should not be forgotten that the historical works of greatest note were precisely those which dealt critically with historic events.

SOURCES

A few very noteworthy critiques of the science of history have been produced. Of these, three deserve special mention : in the T͑ang period Liu Chï-ki wrote his *Comprehensive Survey of Historical Works*,[1] in the Sung period the already mentioned Chêng Ts͑iao produced a number of critical works on historical science, and, finally, in the Ts͑ing period comes the *Comprehensive Judgment of Literature and History*, by Chang Hüe-ch͑êng. As critiques and critical treatises on historical literature, these three works are sufficiently important to render permissible the statement that just as Tso K͑iu, Sï-ma Ts͑ien, Pan Ku, Sün Yüe, Tu Yu, Sï-ma Kuang, and Yüan Shu were the originators of Chinese history, so Liu Chï-ki, Chêng Ts͑iao, and Chang Hüe-ch͑êng were the founders of Chinese historical science.

In connexion with the work by Liang K͑i-ch͑ao noted above, and in order to give an idea of the quantity of historical literature in China and of its growth in the course of ages, a summary is herewith appended of lists of historical works in existence at various dates, showing incidentally that many of them must have been lost.

Period	Source	No. of Works	No. of Volumes
Han	*Han Shu*, "I Wên Chï"	11	425
Sui	*Sui Shu*, "King Tsi Chï"	817	13,264
T͑ang	*Kiu T͑ang* Shu, "King Tsi Chï"	884	17,946
Sung	*Sung Shï*, "I Wên Chï"	2,147	43,109
	T͑ung Chï, "I Wên Lüe" (Chêng Ts͑iao)	2,301	37,613 [2]
Yüan	*Wên Hien T͑ung K͑ao*, "King Tsi K͑ao" (Ma Tuan-lin)	1,036	24,096
Ming	*Ming Shï*, "I Wên Chï"	1,316	30,051 [3]
Ts͑ing	*Sï K͑u Shu Mu*	2,174	37,049

II. Direct Sources

(1) The position as regards the direct sources for a history of Chinese civilization differs essentially from that

---

[1] *Shï T͑ung*.   [2] Genealogical tables not included.
[3] Works of the Ming period only.

in the West. Probably the main reason is that in China we are concerned with a country the greater part of which has for thousands of years been the arena of incessant turmoil. The tide of history has never ebbed from this arena, destroying the continuity of tradition and leaving mere heaps of ruins for future historical research.

This has certain advantages, but likewise certain disadvantages. The chief of these advantages is the continuity of tradition. If we wish to obtain an idea of the ancient Sumerian or Mexican civilizations the conditions which we find to-day are very little guide. The old framework is perished, and even if the inhabitants of those countries still have some racial connexion with the people who formed part of and lived in those ancient civilizations, no trace of that life exists to-day. Other civilizations, with other customs, have swept across those places. Tradition has been interrupted, and the past must be skilfully pieced together from the remnants by science in much the same way that the bodily structure of a saurian is deduced from the remains of fossilized bones. It is otherwise in China. We are enabled to acquire some understanding of antiquity from the habits and customs of the modern Chinese people. Here too, of course, customs have altered as civilization has changed, but just as geological periods leave their traces, from which the expert can read the past, so have habits and customs from which the past is legible been preserved for thousands of years in China. For instance, the character denoting a family name still retains to-day the radical for ' woman,' and this, in conjunction with certain other facts, shows that Chinese culture, which in its later development became essentially patriarchal, was likewise based on matriarchal elements. One of the remarkable characteristics of Chinese civilization in this respect is that traces of all periods are found in the customs of the people, and that of China's bygone culture scarcely anything is entirely obliterated. Hence it comes that the spirit of China has bred unusually powerful traditions. True, the use of script to record historical events was known at a fairly early date in China, but it long remained only a makeshift, an aid to the memory, supplemented by oral tradition. Even Confucius is very brief in his chronicles (such as the *Ch'un Ts'iu* and the commentary on the *Book of Changes*) and makes his real disclosures by word of mouth. In China, as in other Oriental civilizations, this custom led to the evolution of tradition as something very solid and reliable. A striking example of the reliability of this tradition is the preservation by Fu Shêng of the genuine sections of the *Book of History*, which he brought to light in the reign of the Emperor Wên Ti, of the Han dynasty, after the work had apparently been given up as lost for decades subsequent to the "Burning of the Books" by Ts'in Shï Huang Ti. Other important books also possessed their schools of tradition, in which they were preserved and handed down with their traditional meaning.

This persistence of the collective memories of a civilization is also visible in other fields. As we shall see later on, the Chinese method of building with wood and tiles, coupled with the habit of neglecting repairs, is not conducive to the preservation of monuments of architecture for centuries. China is thus not in the fortunate position of possessing pre-Christian temple remains. Notwithstanding the impermanent nature of the wooden structure, however, we may feel certain that the method of construction in antiquity did not differ essentially from that of to-day. Occasional tomb finds confirm this assumption. The vital core of civilization is actually more stable than stone and bronze ; and this is of particular significance in relation to Chinese culture, since it enables us at the present day to acquire an intelligent grasp even of the most ancient Chinese civilization. Even at the present day ; but no man knows how long this germ of civilization will continue to live, for it is undeniable that the penetration of European and American customs is causing it rapidly to disintegrate. The machinery of European civilization is acting as a corrosive poison even on this ancient, deep-rooted civilization. The schools, formerly the fostering-places of the old civilization, have long since been Europeanized, and an ever increasing number of educated Chinese are to be found who have lost all touch with the old civilization and are less appreciative of it than is many a foreigner. This is one of the reasons why a survey of the history of Chinese civilization seemed to be called for.

(2) While the power of tradition is a great advantage, arising from the fact that China has been throughout the ages the scene of living history, there is, on the other hand, the consequent disadvantage that we find correspondingly few monuments of ancient date. Whereas interrupted civilizations left their monuments hidden under ruined mounds which, excavated at a later date, yielded undamaged material to historical research, the fluctuating life of China is responsible for circumstances unfavourable to the permanency of these historical treasure-houses. True, a few notable monuments have weathered the storms of time. The Great Wall, the foundations of which date back to the linking up of earlier isolated fortifications by Ts'in Shï Huang Ti in the third century B.C., and which was enlarged and extended as late as the fifteenth century A.D., still thrusts its ramparts, a mighty monument from the past, across the mountain chains dividing China from the northern steppes. The palaces and walls of Peking, taken over by the Manchus at the time of their conquest, were built between the years 1405 and 1420, and still furnish evidence of the well-nigh inconceivable power of a civilization such as the earlier Ming period represented. Isolated structures, especially pagodas, have also been preserved from ancient times; for instance, the pagoda of T'ienming Sï, near Peking, which certainly dates from the sixth century. The cave-temples of Yün-kang, near Ta-t'ung Fu, dating from the years 455 to 499, are likewise well known, as are the later grottos of Lung-mên, where the style of art displayed differs entirely from that of the earlier ones and may be rightly attributed to foreign influence.

Although further examples could be cited, the amount preserved intact down to the present day is on the whole alarmingly small for a civilization so old as that of China. Confucius is already complaining that he can find no extant memorials to confirm his knowledge of the state of civiliza-

PLATE 3

Tomb of Confucius at Kʻü-fou (Shantung). In front of the sepulchral mound, covered with plants and shaded by trees, stands an inscribed stone tablet forming a back to the stone sacrificial table with its candelabra and incense vessels.

tion existing five hundred years prior to his own time. How much more is this the case to-day! Even famous sanctuaries have undergone this fate. Si-ma Ts'ien gives an account of his visit to the home of Confucius at K'ü-fou, where he saw with his own eyes all manner of relics from the Master's day; but the waves of time have swept over those places too. The tomb itself is perhaps still undisturbed—although even that is not quite certain—but any buildings and monuments that remain are of far later date.

(3) We must not ignore the possibility, however, that scientifically conducted excavations may reveal much unsuspected material. Occasional discoveries of more or less importance have already been made, but excavation has never been carried on scientifically. A few years ago, for instance, an old city which had been submerged in 1108 by an inundation of the Yellow River was discovered near Ku-lü Hien, in the province of Chihli. Unfortunately, there was no authority on the spot to organize systematic excavation work, and so any objects of artistic or archæological interest were dug up indiscriminately, and found their way into the possession of antiquarian dealers. Other cities must also have disappeared into the Yellow River or in other ways, and there is now some hope that these treasures may be recovered, as a sinological institute has since been established at the Imperial University of Peking whose aim it is to rescue treasures of this nature for the benefit of science. I myself have seen the walls of a ruined city in Shantung, and there are remains of old gateways and walls near Ts'ing-chou Fu. Many similar remains are to be found elsewhere; but in places which attract attention or in well-known ancient tombs it is unlikely that much more will be found, as private ' connoisseurs ' have conducted independent searches in all ages. Confucius himself declared on one occasion that the inclusion of valuables in graves attracts grave-thieves, and this type of robbery was apparently carried on in China at a fairly early date.[1]

(4) Apart from such mass excavations, there are individual objects to be considered which have been preserved

[1] Compare analogous conditions in ancient Egypt.

by collectors and scholars on account of their artistic and antiquarian interest. Unfortunately, China has, until quite recently, been entirely lacking in public museums ; indeed, State supervision of antiquities and monuments is only a recent development.

It is well known that a number of wall-paintings were produced in the T'ang period. All the great masterpieces of the famous T'ang painters were frescoes. But in the remotest historical ages, too, in the Chou period and even earlier, frescoes are mentioned. It is related, for instance, what a deep impression Confucius received from the paintings in the Grand Temple at the capital, which he inspected on his journey there. That nothing more exists of the old Chou paintings is not surprising. They perished together with the buildings containing them. The discoveries at Tun-huang and Kao-ch'ang, which we shall discuss in another connexion, are sufficient proof, however, that fresco-painting was customary at a fairly early date. And although, of course, they were only the products of a somewhat crude provincial art, such memorials cannot be too highly valued for the light they throw on the civilization of the time. In contrast with these paintings, the frescoes in the T'ai Miao (the temple of the god of T'ai Shan) in Taianfu, two of which represent the departure of the god, are of lesser importance, for it is very questionable whether the tradition assigning these paintings to the T'ang period is correct. Even so, the pictures were certainly touched up and restored at a later date. Blocks sawn out of such frescoes from ancient temples have recently been making their appearance on the European market. The great majority of them are of late origin—certainly not earlier than the Ming dynasty. But even genuinely ancient specimens are quite valueless historically, as only exactly dated objects can be of any value for the history of Chinese civilization. In any case, there is little to be done with such fragmentary remains as mostly come into question. Here, too, foreign influence threatens to be a permanent danger to historical monuments in China.

(5) In addition to wall-paintings, pictures on paper and

silk are to be found in China. In European histories of art it has become customary to regard the Sung period as the zenith of Chinese painting, and this idea has promoted the search for T'ang and Sung pictures in the art market. In reality a great deception is being practised here. Pictures of the T'ang period [1] can scarcely be assumed to exist still in China, and even genuine Sung works are far more rare than joyful collectors, under the delusion that they possess a series of Sung pictures, usually think. Nevertheless, old pictures have a certain cultural value even in the case of copies, so long as the original painter can be ascertained. For the first consideration when passing a judgment on social conditions is to ascertain the garments, manners, and customs prevailing at definite dates, and this may also be done from copies, if intelligently executed. It is inadmissible, however, to adduce works of art bearing the signature of any given painter of olden times and showing, for instance, chairs and tables in a scene purporting to date from the Sung period.[2] In this connexion, the collections to be found in Japanese temples, containing authenticated Chinese paintings of early date, are of special importance. Such pictures, no doubt, were not ranked as masterpieces in contemporary China, either because they originated in schools which were not highly appreciated at the time or because they were the work of minor artists. But owing to the ravages of time and warfare from which these things suffered in China, even the objects of lesser account that we find in Japan are invaluable. Even here it is true that much irreplaceable material was destroyed in the earthquake that recently visited Tokyo. In China itself the former Imperial collections, now on exhibition in the Palace museum in Peking, also come into consideration. As these collections date back to the Ming emperors, and were added to later by the art-loving rulers of the Ts'ing dynasty, they contain objects of historical importance.

[1] The excavations in Central Asia, on the western boundaries of China, are a welcome addition in this respect, for, apart from old manuscripts, very ancient frescoes dating back to T'ang times have been brought to light.

[2] For chairs did not exist at that date in China. People sat on mats, as they do still in Japan.

I need mention only the collection of portraits representing emperors of past dynasties, which provides a mass of authentic material going back at least as far as the Sung dynasty. It is housed in the Tsï-kuang Ko, a part of the former Imperial Palace. It is to be hoped that the institution of museums, which are still in their infancy in China, will soon be developed ; for only in this way will it be possible for the valuable historical objects that still survive in China to be collated and preserved, sifted and arranged.

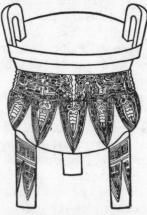

Fig. 1. Three-legged Bronze Sacrificial Vessel (*ting*) of the Shang Dynasty

The upper band of ornament shows the ogre mask (*t'ao-t'ie*) and dragon (*k'uei*), below which are cicadas, symbolical of the soul ; the whole on a ground of meander ornament representing thunder. From the catalogue of the bronze collection of the Emperor Hui Tsung (1101–25), of the Sung dynasty. The edition from which this figure is taken is dated 1528, and contains woodcuts made from blocks prepared between 1308 and 1312 (vol. i, p. 15).

(6) If circumstances are unfortunate in regard to pictures, still more is this the case with objects of general utility, such as clothes, furniture, and so forth, which have never excited the interest of Chinese collectors. Old fabrics from the K'ien-lung period are already rarities ; even mandarin robes of the Ts'ing time, which were still being worn scarcely more than a decade ago, are gradually disappearing from the market. Occasionally something of this kind comes to light; thus a short time ago some ancient garments belonging to the Ming dynasty, which had lain for centuries in the chests of the Imperial wardrobe, came into the market from the stocks of the Imperial house. Ancient fashions in dress are best preserved in actors' robes ; in Peking and in K'ü-fou, the home of Confucius's descendants, genuine costumes are sometimes worn at festive performances.

(7) Bronzes are more durable than all these things. As far back as Han times occasional finds of ancient bronze ritual vessels on mountain-slopes or in river-beds were reported. But after the final disappearance, during the disturbances accompanying the transition to the Ts'in dynasty,

of the great tripods of the Chou dynasty which were held in such high esteem as symbols of sovereignty, interest in antiquities of this nature waned for the time. Bronze-making in the Han period thus developed a style which, while continuing the Chou traditions, nevertheless struck out on original lines; hence it is not as a rule difficult to distinguish between objects of the Chou and Han periods.

Not until the time of the Sung dynasty was the interest of collectors first directed toward antique bronzes. The artist-emperor Hui Tsung owned a large personal collection of old ritual bronzes, which he had scientifically examined in the *Po Ku T'u*, a work which marks the beginning of the study of old bronzes. Other works followed, and interest then flagged again. But from that time onward spurious bronzes began to make their appearance, for the supply of such things always adjusts itself to the demand. The Manchu period, principally the reigns of Yung-chêng and K'ien-lung, experienced a fresh wave of collecting interest.

Fig. 2. Four-legged Sacrificial Vessel (*ting*) of the Shang Dynasty

The upper part of the ornament shows dragons, the lower a highly stylized ogre mask (*t'ao-t'ie*) on a ground of 'thunder' or meander pattern. The palmettes on the legs represent soul cicadas. The projecting dentated corner wings are characteristic of antiquity. From the same collection as Fig. 1.

A large collection of bronzes of all kinds came into the Imperial possession, and is still in the Palace museum in Peking. The historical significance of the inscriptions on these objects will be discussed later. For the moment we will merely note the historical valuation of these collections made by the scholar Wang Kuo-wei.

Besides the old sacrificial vessels in bronze, weapons of all kinds exist, and are still excavated from time to time. Of earliest date are the bronze axes, lance-heads, sword-blades, arrowheads, and so forth; in the Han and Tsin periods we find crossbow locks, and cooking vessels also occur; the latter are usually ascribed, though without any particular warrant, to the time of the general Chu-ko Liang ; so are the remarkable metal drums which apparently came from the extreme south of China.

Weights and measures from the Ts'in period onward also exist, and are of no small value in determining the units of measurement during the various dynasties. In addition, mention must be made of stamps and tallies—small tigers, bisected and fitting together, are found in the earlier days, but in the T'ang and Sung periods fishes were usually employed—as well as of letter-seals (some retaining their clay impressions), which were used to seal the leather or cloth strips enveloping the bamboo tablets which served as letters. Of special interest are the metal mirrors fairly frequently found, particularly in graves, from Ts'in and Han times onward. They were employed chiefly for purposes of magic, and behind their practical use, which certainly dates back as far as T'ang and Sung times, there persisted for a long time the semi-magical background of the wizard's mirror. The reliefs decorating the backs of the mirrors are of great cultural importance. They clearly show, not only styles of art prevailing at different periods, but foreign influence— the grape and animal patterns, for instance, occurring in the T'ang period—and the choice of design shows unmistakably how ideas changed in the course of time. These mirrors come right down to the days of the Yüan and Ming dynasties. In the Manchu period they are generally supplanted by other kinds of bronzes displaying increasing European influence.

Coins are likewise valuable as cultural landmarks. In China, after the end of the Chou dynasty, copper coins were cast (not struck), and this type of money persisted until early in the twentieth century. The oldest types are reminiscent of the objects of barter they represented (spades, combs, knives, etc.). Later appears the circular disc with a square hole in the centre, for stringing on cord. The style of casting, as well as the size and shape of the coins, furnishes an excellent indication of the condition of the State finances at the time of minting.[1]

[1] Paper money also existed at various dates. Old bank-notes have occasionally been found inside idols.

PLATE 4

The cave-temple at Yün-kang, near Ta-t'ung Fu (Shansi). The grottos with the stone Buddha relievos date from the Wei period. The buildings were renovated in the time of Wan Li.

All these bronze objects, then, supply material of great value to the history of Chinese civilization. Bronze-casting early reached in China a high standard of excellence, which was maintained for a long time. Iron occurs late, and never ousted bronze for certain purposes. Notwithstanding so much original material, however, we are not so well off as we might be. The majority of the antique Chinese bronzes on the market date no farther back than the nineteenth century. Liang K'i-ch'ao estimates that of the total amount of bronze objects in the Sung period barely 2 per cent. still survives. Bronze possesses a certain durability enabling it to withstand an underground sojourn under ordinarily favourable conditions without suffering any noteworthy damage. But all those objects that were the victims of fire, either of conflagrations or of wholesale melting down, are for all time irrecoverable. The archæologist P'an Tsu-yin enumerates six instances of the wholesale melting down of bronze articles.[1]

(*a*) Ts'in Shï Huang Ti had a number of bronze statues cast from weapons and sacrificial vessels collected throughout the empire.

(*b*) Toward the end of the Later Han dynasty Tung Cho had the bronze objects (ritual vessels, bells, etc.) of the two capitals Lo-yang and Ch'ang-an melted down for coining cash.

(*c*) During the ninth and eleventh years of the K'ai-huang period (581–601) of the Sui dynasty a number of bronze antiques were melted down for superstitious reasons.

(*d*) In the second year of the Hien-tê period (955), under the Later Chou dynasty, a decree ordered the smelting and surrender to the authorized *dépôts* within fifty days of all images and other bronze objects.

(*e*) In the third year (1158) of the Chêng-lung period of the Kin dynasty all the bronze objects seized in the Liao and Sung territories were melted down.

(*f*) In the sixth year (1136) of the Shao-hing period of the Southern Sung dynasty all bronze implements in the people's possession, and in the twenty-eighth year (1158) all

[1] See the introduction to his work, *Pan Ku Lou I K'i Kuan Shï*.

bronze implements whatsoever, except for fifteen hundred specimens in the Imperial collection, were recast into cash.

These instances do not include lesser losses through conflagrations, theft, etc., nor the wholesale destruction of old Chinese coins perpetrated during the World War.[1] Nor has account been taken of the considerable export to foreign art markets of the very pieces with historic interest.

(8) Stones are very important factors in China, where jade has always played a great part. Its prominence has been maintained here since the Stone Ages, and jade is still prized to-day as the most valuable of all precious stones, to a degree not always comprehensible even to the European connoisseur. In the earliest days jade was a vital feature of sacrificial ceremonies, and the archaic shapes have considerable historic interest and are met with fairly frequently. The presence of jade since the very beginning of Chinese history not only throws a light on the art of working this extremely hard and brittle stone, but enables conclusions to be drawn regarding the connexion of the Chinese even in prehistoric times with those districts in which jade is produced. In the middle course of the Yellow River, where many scholars would place the origins of Chinese civilization, cutting it off from all outside connexions and making it an autochthonous product, no jade occurs. On the evidence of the presence of jade and the high value placed on it in the remotest period of Chinese civilization, we must necessarily infer that China already enjoyed at that time comparatively close relations with Western regions.

While the use of jade is confined in the main to objects employed in the worship of gods and ancestors and articles of utility for the ruling classes, and it always retained its character as a valuable and comparatively rare precious stone, we find stone sculptures at a fairly early date too. Many inscriptions are naturally found on old stone monu-

[1] At Tsingtau Japanese furnaces were in action day and night for some years smelting the bronze coin purchased cheaply in the interior of China in order that it might be sold at great profit to the Allied Powers for munitions. Thus all the old Chinese coins within the radius of Japanese influence were totally destroyed. This not only meant a loss of metal to China, but resulted in a general increase in the cost of living.

ments. They will be dealt with elsewhere. Closer investigation has shown that the stone drums now displayed at the temple of Confucius in Peking, and long held to be products of the Chou dynasty and among the earliest stone memorials, are probably to be placed no earlier than the Ts'in period. There are, as a matter of fact, other monuments remaining to us from the Ts'in period, and the number increases

Fig. 3. Inscription in Archaic Script on one of the Old Stone Drums

considerably in Han times. The sepulchral reliefs from Shantung, dating back to the Han period and bearing representations of the greatest historic interest, have now become famous. Best known are the reliefs from Kia-siang in Shantung, several of which have been stolen and are in foreign museums. Some of the remaining reliefs are still at Kia-siang, some at Tsinan.[1]

The end of this form of sculpture coincides with the beginning of sculpture proper, which produced its most noted examples in the Yün-kang and Lung-mên grottos.

[1] See E. Chavannes, *Sculpture sur pierre en Chine* (Paris, 1893). It is noteworthy that most of the low reliefs in stone are in Shantung, apart from which they are confined almost entirely to Szechwan ; also that the employment of this technique gradually ceased in the Wei and Tsin times. It has begun to flourish anew only recently, with the widespread manufacture of forgeries.

Strange to say, most of these images originated in the Northern Wei and Northern Ts'i dynasties. The Sui dynasty is chiefly represented, apart from the Lung-mên examples, in the stone sculptures of Ts'ien-fu Shan, Yün-mên Shan, and Yü-han Shan, all of which are in Shantung, while most of the T'ang work is found at Süan-wei Shan and Nan-hiang-t'ang Shan, in the province of Chihli.[1]   The

Figs. 4 and 5. Rubbings from Stone Relievos in the Kia-siang Tombs

Fig. 4 represents the mythical inventor of agriculture, the Divine Husbandman, Shên Nung.
Fig. 5 represents the cruel tyrant Kie, the last ruler of the Hia dynasty, with a weapon in his hand, seated on two kneeling women.

T'ang period also produced the well-known equestrian reliefs on the tomb of the Emperor T'ai Tsung at Chao-ling. The Lohan sculptures of Ling-yen are Sung work.   In the Ming and Manchu periods sculpture naturally multiplied, right down to the time of the sculptures in the old Summer Palace near Peking, where the influence of European *baroque* art is evident; their destruction, on the other hand, is practical proof of the European attitude toward culture in China during the nineteenth century.

(9) The high standard early attained in China by pottery

[1] Some comprehensive publications on Chinese stone sculpture have recently appeared. See Sirén, *Chinese Sculpture from the Fifth to the Fourteenth Century* (4 vols., London, 1925), and Segalen-Gilbert de Voisins-Lartique, *Mission archéologique en Chine*, published by Paul Geuthner.

work is sufficient to account for the importance of this art as a contribution to the history of civilization. Pottery was made in the earliest historical times, and porcelain too was apparently a far older product than was long believed. A number of recent tomb finds brought to light has led to the conjecture that a type of painted porcelain was produced as early as the T'ang era. Extreme caution should be exercised, however, in forming judgments on porcelain especially, for no material is so destructible. The old porcelain extant to-day represents but an infinitesimal fraction of what once existed, and even if tomb finds have somewhat remedied the scarcity, it should not be forgotten that fakes and imitations of porcelain in particular have appeared in all ages, and especially during the last few centuries. In the reign period of K'ang-hi, Ming porcelain was copied and faked,[1] in that of Yung-chêng potters began to revert to the monochrome Sung glazes, while also continuing the manufacture of polychrome varieties, which were thenceforward augmented by the introduction of a new deep ruby-coloured enamel. Later still everything was imitated, even during the period about the middle of the nineteenth century when a dreadful deterioration in taste and technical skill set in, to make way once more toward the end of the century for a somewhat higher level of achievement. But with the foreign craze for porcelain collecting an ever increasing number of old pieces left China, and it is more difficult now to obtain good, authentic old pieces in Peking than on the international market.

Apart from actual porcelain, tiles and bricks are of interest as cultural landmarks when, for example, the way in which they are made—whether of good material and in large sizes, or small and poor—affords an unmistakable guide to the state of contemporary civilization and finance. Since these objects frequently bear date marks and, in addition, characteristic ornamentation, they supply valuable material for a

---

[1] Fakes differ from copies in that in the former the old marks indicating the period of manufacture are also reproduced. A number of K'ang-hi blue and white pieces bear marks of the Ming dynasty, but are far superior in quality to the originals.

history of styles.   The zeal of European collectors has for-
tunately, for the most part, left these objects untouched.[1]

A special branch of ceramics, of extreme value in a
history of civilization, is represented in sepulchral deposits.
Owing to the religious dread of graves, these deposits had
hitherto remained for the most part intact; they were
exhumed during railway construction, when for the first
time a mass disturbance of graves occurred.   These clay
articles represent all manner of everyday objects, placed
with the dead for their benefit in the next life, and thus afford
an excellent insight into contemporary customs.   A certain
caution must be exercised here, however.   In remote times
wooden models seem to have been employed, which Mencius
deplores as an apostasy from the ritual prohibiting the use
of naturalistic imitations of everyday articles and permitting
the burial only of symbolical objects.   Apart from a few
jade objects, none of these sepulchral deposits from remote
times exist to-day.   Occasional bronze finds, such as that
dating from the end of the Chou period recently brought to
light in Honan, the greater part of which was safely housed
in a Peking museum, show that valuable objects of everyday
life were nevertheless buried with the dead.   The custom
of including in the grave clay images of persons, animals,
and objects apparently began in Han times.   During the
T'ang period this custom resulted in the attainment of quite
a high artistic level, inspired in part, perhaps, by Hellenistic
art, the influence of which is likewise visible at that time in
Buddhist plastic art.   The custom was retained, and therefore we have no justification for classing all these sepulchral
deposits as T'ang work.   The practice of substituting for
the clay models paper ones which were burnt on the grave
seems to have originated in the Ts'ing period.   Tin implements on a miniature scale, mirrors, and cash are sometimes
found in more recent tombs.

These sepulchral deposits are of special cultural interest

---

[1] A certain interest in roof ornamentations has, as a matter of fact, recently been
displayed by collectors.   Visitors to the Summer Palace at Peking often succeed
in obtaining an ornamental tile as a souvenir—which the guide is careful to replace
for the next visitor !

PLATE 5

Temples on the summit of the sacred mountain, T'ai Shan. (From Boerschmann, *Baukunst und Landschaft in China*.)

because they so frequently throw a direct light on to the doings of everyday life. To avoid errors, however, it is of course best to confine oneself to finds which can be accurately dated. Here again it is very deplorable that most of the objects in the hands of art dealers should have been removed from their resting-place by unknown hands, so that nothing is known of their provenance. Of course there are also flourishing factories in Peking, and more especially in Japan, which provide for the continual satisfaction of the demand for T'ang plastic art.

In addition to these historic finds, brief mention should be made of certain prehistoric discoveries—namely, of the Stone period finds made during the last few years in the provinces of Fengtien, Honan, and Kansu by J. G. Andersson. They comprise various implements—viz., picks, axes, knives, chisels, arrowheads, as well as crucibles, pots, and rings. But it should be borne in mind that these remains should not be straightway assigned to a Chinese Stone Age. In the days of Confucius there were still ' barbaric ' tribes who used, among other things, stone arrowheads, and the story is related that Confucius knew, from the shape of an arrowhead of this nature lodged in the breast of a falling bird, the place where it must have been shot. I have myself acquired in Central Shantung stone arrowheads of various shapes which in all probability also came from some aboriginal tribe in touch with Chinese civilization. In the same way that so many things are different in China— running in parallel lines instead of following in vertical sequence—so the Bronze Age of the more advanced Chinese apparently marched side by side with the Stone Age of a more primitive race. The finds nevertheless show such characteristic variety, as well as similarity, that intercourse at a fairly early date (about the third millennium B.C.) between two nations at different levels of culture—the higher in the west, the more primitive in the north-east—must be assumed, from which the ' Chinese ' civilization was gradually developed.[1]

[1] See O. Franke, "Die prähistorischen Funde in Nordchina und die älteste chinesische Geschichte," in *Mitteilungen des Seminars für orientalische Sprachen* (Berlin, 1926), Part I, p. 99 *et seq.*

(10) Besides the material noted, actual inscriptions are naturally of great importance. The first to be considered are contemporary inscriptions on stone and metal. The custom of erecting inscribed stone tablets is of very ancient date in China. Such tablets have been in existence since Ts'in and Han times. These inscriptions serve a diversity of purposes. We find the Confucian Classics set out on stone tablets of various ages, and the value of the earliest among these for textual criticism is evident. Stone inscriptions are also known to Buddhism. Moreover, since early times, from as far back as the Sui dynasty at least,[1] Buddhists have inscribed their statues with personal notices concerning the pious donors, often containing interesting details of the expenses incurred.

A further category of inscribed tablets comprises those set up as memorials to illustrious personages. These particular records are not generally of great value. Where historical notabilities are concerned incidents of their careers can be ascertained with perfect confidence from historical works. Moreover, the eulogistic language in which records of this nature are usually couched is no suitable medium for commemorating strictly historical facts. Most of these inscriptions are composed in a definite literary form, sometimes at the cost of fact. They are occasionally useful, though, as corroborative documents.

Of greater value than all these are the records proper, in part boundary agreements, in part establishment records, found on stone tablets. The boundary agreements, in existence throughout the empire from the Han time downward, form a valuable addition to the standard histories, which so often disregard these very things. In this way, moreover, are effected the preservation and decipherment of foreign scripts, which would otherwise remain unknown and which furnish an entirely new picture of social conditions in innermost Asia in bygone days. Among establishment records may be mentioned the tablet recording the existence of the Nestorian church at Sianfu in A.D. 781, and bearing

---

[1] The Yün-kang sculptures lack all old inscription, and were therefore long neglected by Chinese scholars, whereas the tomb slabs of Kia-siang, belonging to the Han period, are precisely dated and bear long inscriptions.

Syrian characters as well as a Chinese inscription, and the tablet of 1511 at Kaifeng giving an account of the dissemination of the Jews throughout China.[1]   On a most

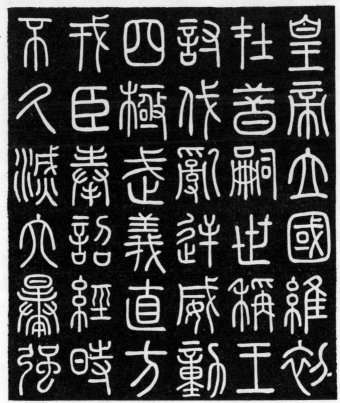

Fig. 6. Memorial Inscription of the Ts'in Period
The script is that introduced by the minister Li Sǐ.

interesting tablet dating from the Mongol dynasty[2] it is decreed in very curiously expressed Chinese that the Ho-shang (Buddhists), Ye-li-k'o-wên (Christians), Sien-shêng

[1] Two tablets are reported to have existed toward the middle of the nineteenth century at Kaifeng, bearing the information that the synagogue there was built in 1164 and restored in 1468.   No further mention is made of these tablets in after years, and Liang K'i-ch'ao assumes that they were lost.

[2] Cf. the Shêng Chǐ P'ai in the Yü Miao in Taianfu, mentioned in vol. iii of the Yü Shǐ.

(Taoists), and Ta-shï-man (Mohammedans) shall be exempted from taxation.

It would take too long to enumerate every category of these records, but they are quite worth studying, especially those hitherto neglected owing to their literary shortcomings.

Some of the ancient bronze objects also bear inscriptions which cover more than the mere date and are interesting if only for the archaic form of the script. Continual attempts have been made to establish the origins of Chinese civilization by reference to the forms of these archaic symbols and the manner in which they are built up. A few years ago bone remains were also found, and were assigned after close examination to the Yin dynasty. These remains, partly tortoiseshell, partly animal bone, served oracular purposes ; their varied inscriptions are of great cultural interest.[1]

(11) Attention must finally be drawn to the sources which are most numerous and at the same time most easily used : ancient and modern writings. Mention has already been made of historical literature and science in China. That this wealth of historical literature should form the main basis for a history of Chinese civilization is but natural. But it should be remembered that these works consist of historical material already arranged, and that frequently quite definite viewpoints have underlain this arrangement. The compilation of universal history as a judgment on society in general is an idea which has continually recurred ever since the *Ch'un Ts'iu* of Confucius. If it has undoubtedly kept history free from flattery in the case of powerful personalities, it has, on the other hand, often resulted in the adaptation of facts to meet the ethical codes of the day. The most valuable literary productions, therefore, do not always make the best sources. On the contrary, a more authentic record of facts may often be obtained from the more naïve accounts of clumsier writers.

The extent to which destiny has played havoc with historical literature in particular is well known. In China,

---

[1] See F. A. Chalfant, " Early Chinese Writing," in *Memoirs of the Carnegie Museum*, vol. iv, No. 1, September, 1906, and especially the detailed investigations of Lo Chên-yü. The bones came from Siao-tun, near An-yang Hien, in Honan.

when the fate of literature and the paucity of its remains are discussed, the blame is usually laid on the "Burning of the Books" under Ts'in Shï Huang Ti. In this holocaust, instituted by Li Sï in 213 B.C., it was doubtless the early historical works that suffered most, but there was no question of any extermination of literature. On the contrary, scholars were appointed in connexion with various branches of literature who also gave instruction in that branch. Far worse was the destruction of works of literature and art at the fall of the Ts'in dynasty, when the capital, Hien-yang, with all its great buildings and libraries, was devoured by flames, and for decades the new rulers were governed by interests far from literary. True, the Han dynasty later became ardent patrons of literature, and all ancient works procurable were collected and issued. Notwithstanding the discovery of numerous books of doubtful authenticity and of many palpable forgeries, the literary relics were ultimately reduced to some kind of order. But when a further conflagration of palaces ensued at the overthrow of the usurper Wang Mang in A.D. 23, literature experienced a fresh catastrophe. Once more endeavours were made by the rulers of the Later Han dynasty to seek out all available works of antiquity, and again rich treasure was collected. But when the general Tung Cho, who held the last puppet emperor of the Han dynasty in his power, moved his headquarters hastily to the west, in the tumult of migration the silk of manuscript rolls and paintings was used by the Court servitors to make sacks and curtains; and when the new capital was taken by the enemy the last remnants of books and valuables again went up in flames (A.D. 208). Twice more were great collections of books utterly destroyed: once under the Wei dynasty, and again when the last emperor of the Liang surrounded himself with valuable books, which were burnt with him at his downfall. These are the so-called five literary catastrophes, which caused such untold damage to ancient Chinese literature.[1] But they have not been the

[1] See the enumeration of these catastrophes in the memorial inscription of Niu Hung in the K'ai-huang period (quoted in *Wên Hien T'ung K'ao*, section "King Tsi K'ao").

only ones. The last irreplaceable loss of a monumental Chinese work extant only in one manuscript copy was the destruction of the *Yung Lo Ta Tien*, already mentioned above, during the Boxer rising.

The disasters of the olden days, when works existed in comparatively few manuscript copies, were naturally much more serious than when, later on, printing made most works available in fairly large editions. Particularly harmful in this respect was the collecting mania which impelled many rulers to amass books in one place, only to be destroyed subsequently in bulk.

(12) In addition to historical works, manuscripts and public documents form especially valuable sources. The fact that calligraphy is regarded as a fine art in China, and that manuscripts are much coveted by collectors, has exerted a favourable influence here. In this way numerous manuscripts were preserved right down to the Sung and T'ang periods. But just because the script has artistic value these documents are artistic rather than historic in character. And here, too, damage by moth, climate, and fire and the carelessness of ignorant owners have made considerable inroads on ancient stocks.

A glimpse of the State documents of past ages would be of great value. Other than the records on stone and bronze mentioned above, however, there is little to hope for. In China it was not the habit to preserve these documents carefully. Confucius furnished an example of this—at all events if it is true that out of the 3200 early pieces stated to have been extant in his day he deemed only 100 worth handing down to posterity. If the *Bamboo Books* may be believed, he considerably altered and idealized the earliest histories. For the stories of bloodshed and murder in those old times told in the *Bamboo Books* differ substantially from the calm wisdom of princes and counsellors which meets our eye in the *Book of History* to-day. That the statements in this work do not square with historic fact is proved by the excavations already mentioned, which have revealed conditions very different from the ideal standards placed before us in the *Shu King*.

PLATE 6

Tomb of Yo Fei and his son at Hangchow (province of Chekiang). (From Boerschmann, *Baukunst und Landschaft in China.*)

SOURCES

As regards the historical notes contained in State documents, which since Han times have supplied the basis for the official histories, fresh discoveries can hardly be anticipated there, as it was customary to destroy these documents as soon as the official history relating to them was finished. Only for the Ts'ing dynasty—that is to say, for the last three hundred years—are genuine State documents still available in addition to archival notes of this kind. Even some of these have gone astray during the disorders of the last few years; but the Sinological Institute of the Imperial University of Peking has succeeded in acquiring the remainder, and is about to publish them in scientific fashion.

In reality all Chinese literature, or, at all events, the greater part of it, supplies material for a history of civilization. The Classics, the philosophical and mathematical works, the medical, botanical, and geographical writings, the poems of a K'ü Yüan, a Tu Fu, or a Po Kü-i, all contain allusions and details of immediate value, in the same way that in the popular literature of plays, novels, and stories may be found cultural matter of great worth. Not only literary works, but daily notes, letters, household accounts, memoirs, and diaries are all useful.

In this respect our times have witnessed an enrichment of original material not experienced since the famous discovery of the *Bamboo Books* and of a mass of other writings found in the tomb of Ki in the Tsin period, which caused such a sensation at the time. In the western dominion of Sinkiang, in Kansu—especially at Tun-huang—Han and T'ang finds have been made by a number of scholars, M. A. Stein, Sven Hedin, Grünwedel, von Le Coq, Pelliot, and others, the examination of which is likely to throw quite a new light on events in Central Asia as well as on the state of contemporary civilization in China.[1]

It would be extremely helpful if we could learn something of Chinese history from external sources. They could be

---

[1] In China Wang Kuo-wei and Lo Chên-yü chiefly have busied themselves with the scientific examination of these finds, and, in Europe, apart from the scholars already mentioned, E. Chavannes and F. Herrmann in particular.

employed to supplement and emend Chinese material. In regard to the whole of the earlier period, unfortunately, such sources do not exist. Only in the Mongol period did they commence, with Marco Polo's account, followed later by others. Especially do we feel the lack of accounts from India telling us how Buddhism was introduced into China. The travels of the Chinese pilgrims Fa Hien and Hüan Tsang, on the other hand, to which may now be added the narrative of Hui-chao, recovered from Tun-huang after being lost since the end of the T'ang period, provide valuable sources for contemporary Indian history and culture.

For recent Chinese history since the Ming and Ts'ing times the accounts of the Jesuit missionaries from Peking are valuable; they acquired fame at the time throughout Europe, and exercised a powerful influence over European civilization. The same cannot, unfortunately, be said of the European literature about China which appeared during the nineteenth century. The number of published works is not the slightest index to their real value for a history of Chinese civilization. Only since sinology has become a science has the material lying to hand in Chinese sources been touched and some notable work been done. A comprehensive history of Chinese civilization is, however, still lacking.

CHAPTER I

ANTIQUITY

THERE has been much dispute as to whether Chinese civilization was an autochthonous product or immigrated, together with the inhabitants, from outside. This is a vain controversy, for we know to-day that a civilization is no ready-made article of export, capable of transfer from one country to another. It appears ever more probable, on the other hand, that the conception of an autochthonous civilization, arising out of itself, will prove equally untenable. Civilizations spring, like all life, from an intermingling of races and of their souls. So is the higher civilization of China a product of the mingling of several primitive civilizations.

The excavations along the great Central Asian strategic route in the extreme west of Kansu on the one hand, and along China's eastern sea-boundary in Manchuria on the other, date from the Later Stone Age, and reveal the fact that two separate centres of civilization existed in China at that period. The one points to the South Russian and Baltic districts in the west—to the assumption, therefore, of a continental civilization; the Manchurian mat-marked pottery indicates relationship with Japanese finds, and therefore a maritime civilization.

This agrees quite well with the theory that the area of the earliest Chinese civilization was the middle course of the Yellow River. The great plain, with its essentially continental climate, formed out of huge masses of loess, in which the rivers have in places carved out deep valleys, is the home of the earliest Chinese. There is apparently one movement, from west to east along the river courses. The ridges between the stretches of arable land in the hollows were probably covered for the most part with forest or jungle, against which the ancient settlers had to wage war with fire. No wonder the Divine Husbandman, to whom one tradition assigns the beginning of agriculture, is likewise the Lord of Fire.[1] As to whether the Chinese found the districts into which they migrated uninhabited or whether other settlers were already there, no definite opinion can be given, but encounters with other settlers seem to have occurred fairly early. There are various theories in regard to these settlers. According to one they are connected with the sea. Their totem animals are sea-animals and sea-monsters, and winged creatures are mentioned.[2] This might indicate a maritime civilization. These tribes, who harassed the Chinese, were at an early date known by the name of the Miao. They were, it appears, gradually driven toward the south and south-west, where their descendants are still living as the ' semi-civilized ' tribes of the southern provinces. These Miao, who proved inferior to the advancing Chinese, were at all events no more a nomad race than were the Chinese themselves. The nomads of the north-west supply a third element, which does not affect Chinese history until later. The Miao were apparently forced, in the first place, into the basin of the Yangtse, while the Chinese occupied the reaches of the Yellow River. In this way were laid the foundations of contrasting civilizations, afterward to prove so fruitful.

It would seem that the cultural elements which ultimately united to form the Chinese civilization also differed from one another in their matriarchal and patriarchal aspects. Tradition makes the matriarchal stage at its inception a state of chaotic disorder. The *Po Hu T'ung*, a work from the Han period, says:

> In the legendary days there was no moral or social order. Men knew only their mother, not their father. When hungry they hunted for food, when replete they threw away what was left. They devoured their food without removing fur or skin, they drank up the blood, and wrapped themselves in rushes and skins.

[1] Shên Nung, or Yen Ti (' the Fiery Ruler ').

[2] Kun, the father of Yü, who was banished to the Feather Mountain, was a mythical being of this description ; so were the remaining three of the four great ' criminals,' who were expelled by the ' Inspired Rulers.'

ANTIQUITY

Even in later times many traces still point to the fact that the matriarchate was not unknown in the China of remote antiquity. The character for surnames[1] is still formed to-day with the radical 'woman,' and the oldest clan names proper all contained this radical. Marriage customs still survive from which it would appear that the man was formerly married into the woman's family. Down to the present day the wife is still the acknowledged ruler of the house. While the man rules outside the home and sees to the farming and the food-supply, the woman spins and weaves clothes indoors; this is her well-defined sphere. Here we see one of the innate peculiarities of Chinese civilization, that no olden custom ever dies out altogether, but is always retained in some modified form.

While there are distinct indications of the existence of a matriarchate—apparently driven, along with the Miao, to the south and south-west, where it may still be traced—there are, on the other hand, signs just as evident, not only of the existence of confederacies, but of the patriarchal family too. These traces, however, suggest rather derivation from the surrounding tribes in the north and west, and, as a matter of fact, the fully developed patriarchal system did penetrate into China with the Chou tribes from the west somewhere about 1000 B.C. The process must not be imagined as a sudden one. Transition between the maritime and continental forms of civilization proceeds slowly and by stages.

The Third Appendix ("Great Treatise") to the *Book of Changes* contains a description of the manner in which the material products of civilization gradually came to man.[2] It is difficult to assign a date to this historical sketch. It contains only two points of interest. Firstly, a primitive period is distinguished, with a gradual transition from hunting and fishing to agriculture; no mention of a nomadic

[1] *Sing*, composed of 'woman' and 'to be born.'
[2] See *I Ging*, the *Book of Changes*, translated into German and elucidated by Richard Wilhelm (Jena, 1924, vol. i, p. 251 *et seq.*). [See also, in the "Sacred Books of the East," the *I King*, translated into English by James Legge (Clarendon Press, Oxford, 1899, p. 382 *et seq.*).—TRANSLATOR.]

stage is made—which conforms with other evidence.[1] Then follows a stage of progressive civilization. Secondly, the devising of the various tools of civilization is not ascribed to inventive thought; they are all descended from cosmic primeval states, and are regarded as religious objects, as the hexagrams of the *Book of Changes* show. Thus the religious origin of civilization is emphasized. A passage runs:

> Anciently, when Pao Hi had come to the rule of all under heaven, looking up, he contemplated the brilliant forms exhibited in the sky, and looking down he surveyed the patterns shown on the earth. He contemplated the ornamental appearances of birds and beasts and their suitabilities to different places. Near at hand, in his own person, he found things for consideration, and the same at a distance, in things in general. On this he devised the eight hexagrams to harmonize with the secret powers of the spirit-like intelligences, and to classify the qualities of the myriads of things.

This personality, Pao Hi or Fu Hi, represents the hunter, or inventor of cooking. Chinese works usually assign to him the first place in Chinese culture. He does not denote a personality, of course, but a period. The next passage runs:

> He invented the making of nets of various kinds by knitting strings, both for hunting and fishing. The idea of this was taken, probably, from the hexagram *li* ['the inhering'].

This figure *li* denotes the (oceanic?) sun-bird. It likewise denotes adhesion to (as fire adheres to the wood it is burning). The net is therefore not in the first place a practical invention, but a sacrificial object, subsequently profaned. The Appendix continues:

> On the death of Pao Hi, there arose Shên Nung in his place. He fashioned wood to form the ploughshare, and bent wood to make the plough-handle. The advantages of ploughing and weeding were then taught to all under heaven. The idea of this was taken, probably, from the hexagram *i* ['nourishment'].

The Divine Husbandman is the Lord of Fire, who clears the thicket with fire in order to obtain arable land, and

---

[1] Cow's milk is not usually partaken of in China even to-day, nor is beef eaten. In some sort of way it is still taboo.

PLATE 7

Main hall and bell-tower in the temple of Confucius at Wanhsien (province of Szechwan). (From Boerschmann, *Baukunst und Landschaft in China*.)

then employs as an agricultural implement the plough with which the tearing up of the earth was performed in olden days as a sacred rite. The figure *i* is composed of 'the eldest son' (*chên*, 'exciting power') below and 'the eldest daughter' (*sun*, 'penetration') above.

> He caused markets to be held at midday, thus bringing together all the people, and assembling in one place all their wares. They made their exchanges and retired, and everything came into its proper place. The idea of this was taken, probably, from the hexagram *i* ['gnawing through'].

The sun above and the activity below denote the sacred assembly at sacrifices, from which evolved the markets, with their primitive form of barter. These markets—in contrast to the later towns—are a characteristic of the primitive rural stage of civilization.

Next is described the first stage of a higher civilization, known under the names of the rulers Huang Ti, Yao, and Shun. Huang Ti, the Lord of the Yellow Earth, is represented in Chinese literature as the Duke of the Hundred Clans (Po Sing) of the tribes of the Hia people.[1] He wages war with the Miao tribes. He is said to have led his clan, whose totem animals were tigers, panthers, bears, and grizzly bears, to battle in war-chariots.[2] Those among the Miao who did not retreat were presumably employed as agricultural workers; for we sometimes find the population classified into the nine tribes of the ruler, the Hundred Clans, and the myriad black-haired people.[3]

The *Book of Changes* ascribes to the three lords, Huang Ti, Yao, and Shun, in complete accordance with these facts, the following cultural achievements:

> Huang Ti, Yao, and Shun simply wore their upper and lower garments, and good order was secured all under heaven. The idea of all this was taken, probably, from the hexagrams *k'ien* ['the creative'] and *k'un* ['the receptive'].
> They hollowed out trees to form canoes; they hardened poles

[1] Hia must have been an old name for the whole of the proto-Chinese tribes, probably as opposed to the Miao.
[2] The name Hien-yüan, by which he is also known, denotes chariots.
[3] *Li min*; compare the Indian Çudras.

61

with fire to make oars. The benefit of canoes and oars consisted in the facilitation of intercourse. The idea of this was taken, probably, from the hexagram *huan* ['dissipation : wood over water'].

They tamed oxen (in carts) and yoked horses (to chariots), thus providing for the carriage of what was heavy, and for distant journeys, thereby benefiting all under the sky. The idea of this was taken, probably, from the hexagram *sui* ['following : cheerfulness over movement'].

According to the interpretation of the text, a transmission of sacred customs also underlies the invention of the canoe and the cart, or, rather, their profane use. The canoe was originally the sun-boat, the ghost of which still peers forth to-day at the Dragon-boat Festival in early summer; and the wheel, which may originally have possessed thirty spokes, to correspond with the thirty days in the month,[1] was the sun-wheel. The transference of these sacred objects to everyday use resulted in the making of conveyances for land and water. There were two kinds of cart : the slow, heavy ox-wagon and the swift, armoured war-chariot. Riding was not customary with the Chinese, as it was with their nomadic neighbours, and was a very late importation from the Turkic tribes in the west.

The *Book of Changes* continues :

They introduced double gates, and night-watchmen with clappers, to warn off robbers. The idea of this was taken, probably, from the hexagram *yü* ['enthusiasm'].

The custom of corybantic music played in the obscurity of the temple, which caused men to yield themselves up to a state of excitement—the diagram combines 'excitement' and 'abandonment'—has, in its transmission to everyday use, become a police institution. Even nowadays there may still be heard the rattle of the night-watchman as he paces his protective round from door to door.

The next paragraph shows a similar development :

They cut wood and fashioned it into pestles. They hollowed out the ground into mortars. Thus the myriads of the people

---

[1] *Cf.* Lao Tsï, *Tao Tê King*, Section 11.

received the benefit arising from the use of the pestle and the mortar. The idea of this was taken, probably, from the hexagram *siâo kuo* ['preponderance of the small '].

Evidently this is also some primitive vegetation rite of a phallic nature. The earth, the hollowed-out stone, origin-ally considered female, lies still below, while the wooden pestle is stirred in it from above. This instrument, being employed to pound the grain, thus represents the original form of the mill in China, for grain was pounded in mortars long before it was ground.

The account now deals with dwelling-places:

> In the highest antiquity men made their homes in caves and dwelt in the forests. In subsequent ages, for these the sages sub-stituted houses, with the ridge-beam above and the roof below, as a protection against wind and rain. The idea of this was taken, probably, from the hexagram *ta chuang* ['power of the great '].

Primeval conditions, when men lived in caves and nests (lake-dwellings), are personified in legend by Yu Ch'ao and Sui Jên (the ' Nest-dweller ' and the ' Fire-borer '). The house, represented by the sign *ta chuang*, is the temple: wood ('excitement') above and heaven below; that is to say, a mysterious, dark, enclosed space from which (religious) fervour emanates. The underground tendency of the Chinese religion seems to have found expression in other ways also—namely, in the worship of the deity in the dark, canopied space where the oracles are received. The dark, sacred grove, rising above the grave at the terrestrial altar, is based on a similar notion. The house is evolved by adapt-ing the sacred edifice to meet human needs.

The burial of the dead is similarly described:

> When the ancients buried their dead, they covered the body thickly with brushwood, having laid it in the open country. They raised no mound over it, nor planted trees around; nor had they any fixed period for mourning. The sages at a later age substituted for this the inner and the outer coffin. The idea of this was taken, probably, from the hexagram *ta kuo* ['preponderance of the great '].

We usually find in matriarchal communities a deep-rooted horror of the dead. The body is therefore covered up, concealed from view; it is strewn with brushwood, buried under stones, and put aside. In patriarchal communities, on the other hand, the dead are the guardian spirits which hover beneficently round the descendants, and which are in some sort resurrected in the grandson. They are revered, and provided with a dwelling-place; in short, they are the object of religious worship. The basic connexion of the patriarchate with ancestor-worship is perfectly comprehensible, and we see indicated here, therefore, a change in customs resultant on the steady progress of the patriarchal system in ancient China. The great, the paternal, achieves preponderance.

Finally the use of script is also arrived at:

> In the highest antiquity government was carried out by the use of knotted cords. In subsequent ages the sages substituted written documents, by means of which all the officers could be controlled and all the people supervised. The idea of this was taken, probably, from the figure *kuai* ['piercing'].

Here is indicated the ancient method of the quipu (knot-writing), met with in Mexico. As appears from Lao Tsï, it must once have been in use in China too. The priest, on the other hand, was capable of tracing symbolic characters fraught with magic power. The Grand Astrologer of later times is a relic of this ancient magicianship. Gradually these characters are employed as script, to record terrestrial events. Thus in time the task devolves on the Grand Astrologer of recording historical events and the decrees of the ruler. The magic power of the written character is an idea that has never been entirely obliterated in China by the use of script for profane purposes. Written paper must not be soiled and thrown away. It is collected in special boxes, and consigned at intervals to the flames. If Chinese writing has never become so mechanical in character as the European alphabetical writing, it is because the latter consists simply of conventionalized signs having a mere phonetic value, whereas the Chinese characters reproduce a direct image and idea.

Opinions differ regarding the date of the origin of writing in China. A number of scholars went so far as to assert that the invention of writing certainly did not long precede the time of Confucius. This statement has been disproved by facts, for finds of bone in Honan revealed inscribed specimens almost a thousand years older than the time of Confucius and showing Chinese script already in a very advanced stage. Chinese tradition assigns the invention of writing to the time of Huang Ti—that is, the twenty-sixth century B.C. To that period also is ascribed the invention of the cycle of the ten celestial stems and that of the twelve terrestrial branches, which are combined into the cycle of sixty. As these cyclical signs often appear on the oracular bones, this traditional statement should not be summarily rejected. It is quite possible, however, that a kind of picture-writing existed in those olden times. For us the world is no longer divided into so many watertight compartments, as was formerly assumed. There is nothing to prevent our supposing that in China, where we have unearthed Neolithic pottery and the like allied to that of Western Russia, the germs of pictorial writing and astral symbols were known at a time some 2500 years before Christ, since we know that writing already existed then in other places.

Nevertheless, we cannot determine more than general conditions and customs, cultural possessions and associations, for the period of highest antiquity in China. The more definite the information we get from later sources, the more is caution called for.

Not only in regard to the times of Huang Ti do opinions differ greatly, but scholars by no means agree about the rulers Yao, Shun, and Yü, usually assigned to the twenty-second century B.C.

We shall be best advised, therefore, to ignore the accounts relating to individual rulers. We know that the traditions concerning them embodied in the *Book of History*, in which they are represented as glorified prototypes of the wise rulers of antiquity, were subjected to the revision of the Confucian school. And, in view of the Confucian conception of history, this simply means that we are not dealing here with historical documents at all. Still less do we know the origin of the information contained in the *Bamboo Books*.

The really useful material that has been handed down, supplying us with a picture of the state of civilization in those times, reveals the institution of a sovereign-priest of an astral religion who is the mediator between mankind and the god enthroned in the North Pole, and who sacrifices himself for men and gives them repose. We also find in this religion the magic number four, present in other cults of solar origin. The conditions revealed here afford an excellent clue to the religious life of this prehistoric civilization.

The accounts of the astral calendar, and of sacred rites ensuring the orderly maintenance of the world and the times and seasons to which men must conform, give a clear picture of a primitive astral religion, and fit in admirably with the culture of a primitive agrarian folk.

The sovereign was assisted by the four magician families Hi and Ho, each of whom he assigned to one of the cardinal points in order that they might astronomically determine the four solar seasons on the one hand and on the other observe the manifestations of men and beasts corresponding to those periods.

> Thereupon Yao commanded Hi and Ho, in reverent accordance with their observation of the wide heavens, to calculate and delineate the movements and appearances of the sun, the moon, the stars, and the zodiacal spaces; and so to deliver respectfully the seasons to the people.
>
> He separately commanded the second brother Hi to reside at Yü-i, in what was called the Bright Valley, and there respectfully to receive as a guest the rising sun, and to adjust and arrange the labours of the east [spring]. The day is of medium length, and the star is in Niao[1] ['the Bird']. You may thus exactly determine mid-spring. The people begin to disperse; and birds and beasts breed and copulate.

[1] This constellation, or, to be more exact, the centre of the celestial quadrant, was identified by the Buddhist monk Chang I-hing (A.D. 713–756) with Cor Hydræ, which at that time would have culminated at sunset. Taking into account the precession of the equinoxes, this would give the date as approximately 2250 B.C., which roughly tallies with the Chinese chronological data. This fact tells heavily in favour of the reliability of Chinese records.

He further commanded the third brother Hi to reside in South Kiao and arrange the transformations of the summer, and respectfully to observe the extreme limit of the shadow. The day is at its longest, and the star is Huo ['Fire']. You may thus exactly determine midsummer. The people are more dispersed; and birds and beasts have their feathers and hair thin and change their coats.

He separately commanded the second brother Ho to reside in the west,[1] in what was called the Dark Valley, and there respectfully to escort the setting sun, and to adjust and arrange the completing labours of the autumn. The night is of medium length, and the star is Hü ['Emptiness']. You may thus exactly determine midautumn. The people begin to feel at ease; and birds and beasts have their coats in good condition.

He further commanded the third brother Ho to reside in the northern region, in what was called the Sombre Capital, and there to adjust and examine the changes of the winter. The day is at its shortest, and the star is Mao ['Pleiades']. Thus you may exactly determine midwinter. The people keep their cosy corners; and the coats of birds and beasts are downy and thick.

Here we find the solar year divided into the four seasons, corresponding with the four cardinal points. From other sources we learn the figures and colours assigned to the four quadrants : to the east the green dragon,[2] to the south the vermilion bird, to the west the white tiger, to the north the sombre (black) warrior (the tortoise). Later the centre is added, with yellow as its colour.

A most interesting counterpart of this quadruple division is the octuple division, also without doubt of very ancient origin, appended to the eight diagrams of the *Book of Changes*; here the intermediate points of the compass are included, and the cardinal points and the seasons of the year are again correlated. But the enumeration of the signs

[1] The places where the brothers Hi and Ho reside are certainly not, as the commentaries would have it, at the corners of the earth, but before the four gates. A parallel exists in the four astral altars which still stand before the four gates of Peking : before the eastern gate the sun altar, before the southern gate the altar of heaven, before the western gate the moon altar, in the north the altar of earth. The manner in which earth and heaven occupy here the north and south, while sun and moon are relegated to the east and west, tallies with the order of the eight diagrams (trigrams) in the plan of the former heaven (*sien t'ien*).

[2] At that time blue and green were not yet differentiated ; the word for both is *ts'ing*, which denotes the colour of the sky as well as that of sprouting plants.

67

composing the yearly cycle of life takes the form of an incantation. It runs :

> God [1] comes forth in the sign of excitement [east, spring]. He makes all things complete in the sign of flexibility [south-east]. He causes his creatures to behold one another in the sign of light [south, summer]. He makes them labour in the sign of the receptive [south-west]. He makes them rejoice in the sign of cheerfulness [west, autumn]. He struggles against them in the sign of the creative [north-west]. He rewards their toil in the sign of the abyss [north, winter]. He perfects them in the sign of repose [north-east].

The course of the year and the course of the day are here brought into unison. It is the delineation of the harmony existing in those ancient times between nature and human life. Spring bestirs itself, and in nature a germination and a sprouting begin. It is the morning of the year. The exciting agent is electric force (thunder), setting life in motion again. Then come the gentle breezes, to aid growth in the plant world. The sign of flexibility applies equally to the wind, which breaks up the stubborn winter ice, and to wood, with its organic development. All things flow into their proper moulds. The perfect form develops out of the germ. Then comes the culminating point of the year, midsummer. Now do beings behold one another. It is light, bright light streaming outward, luring human beings ever farther from the isolation of their homes toward the centres of collective activity in the open fields. Then comes the ripening of fruits produced by the sign of the receptive. It is harvesting, the time of mutual service. The men are outside in the fields, the women bring out food to them. Then comes mid-autumn, in the sign of merriment and harvest rejoicing. Then the rigorous time of late autumn. Judgment is in the air. In the heavens the white tiger is dominant. The sign of creation fights against its creatures. That which has no resistance must perish. Then winter comes in the sign of the abyss. The barns are filled. The people return to their homes. The women work, while the men rest. The sign of rest, personified by the mountain, is the boundary

---

[1] See *I King*, Appendix V, chapter v.

PLATE 8

Corner of a hall in the Shansi Club at Tse-liu-tsing (province of Szechwan).
(From Boerschmann, *Baukunst und Landschaft in China*.)

where life and death meet, where the seed is entrusted to the earth that it may sprout forth anew.

That life disappears into the holy mountain, to issue thence in a new form, appears to have been a very ancient religious belief. In later days the T'ai Shan in Shantung was the mountain chiefly worshipped in this connexion, but others have probably preceded it in the course of religious development.

Here also, then, we see the parallelism between the cosmic order of nature and the life of man which is characteristic of this solar type of culture. Furthermore, some African tribes have very similar, though far more primitive, forms of religious belief. What in China is now but a gleam from the dim past is enacted in all its barbarity in Africa. There the sovereign-priest is the god, who is, however, sacrificed as a holy rite. The idea of a sacrifice also underlies the ancient sovereign-priesthood in China. There is no right of succession; the new ruler is consecrated by the old one to the deity—that is to say, he is dedicated as a sacrifice, and the old ruler retires from his office.

This deity is designated as the ancestor. There are, in addition, other deities, called *tsung*. This symbol denotes something which reveals and manifests itself in the dark seclusion of the temple. These deities are plainly underground beings.

Already in very early times the sacrifice of the god-king was replaced by animal sacrifices, but the original idea is quite clear—when, for instance, the ruler in olden times cuts off his front hair during a drought, attaches it to the forehead of the black sacrificial bull, and at the slaughter addresses his father, saying that he, a little child, presents himself to his exalted lord and father with the request that the sins of the people may descend on his own head, so that the ban of tribulation may be removed.

We catch a glimpse, in this dim history, of primitive conditions of which the counterpart is found in a definite stage of civilization throughout the world. The title *Ti* (=*deus*) assigned by tradition to these old priest-kings is significant. The inference has been drawn that they were originally

69

gods, who were afterward converted by tradition into sacred rulers. This assumption is highly improbable. Quite apart from the fact that the idealistic representations of later times show Yao and Shun with normal human features, the expression *Ti*, 'god,' is very suitable to a priest-king who is both god and sacrifice. It would be quite incorrect, of course, to imagine a kind of autocracy in those days. Clearly no power accompanied the dignity of the priest-king. He possessed only the religious authority as regulator of the seasons. The scope of his influence depended on the attitude of the various clans who adhered to him and lived in accordance with the times and seasons he dictated to them. The ruler was assisted in his administration by the Four Mountains and the Twelve Pastors. Even in the *Book of History*, where the divine power of these rulers is mentioned, it is quite clear that the latter depended for their political power entirely on the co-operation of these princes (*hou*).

The period distinguished under the names of Yao, Shun, and Yü is represented in the *Book of History* as the creative period in regard to the various forms of religion, culture, and politics. This point calls for closer examination, as much material from later days may quite well have crept into the legends of these traditional times. One thing is certain—that the priest-king had as yet no capital, but moved from place to place according as his presence was required. This shifting was represented later as a regular succession of tours of inspection by the ruler and of journeys of homage by the princes. It goes without saying that this theory was only a later attempt at systematization. Itinerant priest-kings seem quite appropriate to primitive times.

It appears, moreover, that the Hia tribes comprising the Hundred Clans of the Chinese were by no means isolated. Though the heights were for the most part still covered with impenetrable bush, the people spread toward the river courses. The dark-skinned Miao were settled in between, and round about were other foreign tribes : in the east the I (the character is composed of the characters for 'great' and 'a bow'), in the north-east the Ti (written with the characters for ' dog ' and ' fire ' [1]), in the south the Man (who cultivated silkworms) and the Miao (rice-growers).

The unity of the Chinese was assured by a religion, a system of times and seasons, and a cultural basis which were common to all. They also appear to have combined on occasion for military and economic purposes.

It is worthy of note that whereas under Yao the numerical category of four is predominant, with Shun, who is supposed to have come from the east, other categories are introduced : first the category of six (*e.g.*, the Six Superior Powers) and of twelve (the division into twelve provinces, with twelve pastors); secondly the category of five (*e.g.*, the Five Gem Tokens, the Five Moral Powers, the Five Instruments, the Five Precepts, the Five Punishments, the Five Banishments, the quinquennial tour of inspection—*i.e.*, the four-years journey of the ruler to the four quarters of the empire, and the one-year assembly of the Princes of the Four Quarters of the Empire at the seat of the ruler). The intermingling of another cultural element with the proto-Chinese might be inferred here. Various other signs indicate that new cultural ideas arose with Shun. He is famous for his filial piety, a trait which points to patriarchal associations, as does the number (nine) of his chief ministers, namely :

1. Sï K'ung, Chancellor (held by Yü).
2. Hou Tsi, Lord of the Millet (held by K'i).
3. Sï T'u, Master of Schools (held by Sie).
4. Shï, Supreme Judge (held by Kao Yao).
5. Kung Kung, Director of Works (held by Chui).
6. Yü, Master of Forests (held by I).
7. Ch'ï Tsung, Master of Rites (held by Po I).
8. Tien Yo, Master of Music (held by K'uei).
9. Na Yen, Master of Communication (held by Lung).

The numerical categories of Shun differ in type from the primitive solar types of Yao on the one hand and also from the system under Yü, which was based throughout on a cycle of five, but reverted to the system of Yao in the

[1] Wieger infers from this that they were nomads, noted for their dogs and watch-fires.

division of the empire into nine provinces (instead of the twelve provinces of Shun).

The religious system, as described in the *Book of History*, confirms the primitive degree of civilization to be inferred from other evidence. Besides the glorified ancestor (*wên tsu*) before whom the presentation of the descendant takes place, the Seven Directors, probably representing the seven stars of the Great Bear, are also the object of worship. There at the North Pole of the heavens was the seat of the

Fig. 7. Jade Ring *pi*, Symbolical of Heaven

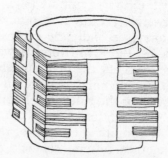

Fig. 8. Jade Tube *tsung*, Symbolical of the Earth

Supreme God, to whom the *lei* sacrifice was made. This *lei* sacrifice was probably offered up on a round hill at midnight of the New Year, and was a precursor of the later sacrifice to heaven. Apart from the worship of the Supreme God in the northern heavens, burnt-offerings were presented to the six *tsung* ('manifesting themselves in the dark'). The terrestrial objects of worship were the holy mountains, such as the T'ai Shan in the east, and the rivers, to which the *wang* sacrifice ('the far-off visible,' likewise probably a burnt-offering) was offered ; in addition, worship was paid to various local celestial and terrestrial deities. The use of sacred emblems made of jade (*yü*) imported from distant regions in the south-west is connected with sacrifices. These jade emblems were possibly symbolical of the six deities that were worshipped. They are :

(1) The flat (blue) ring *pi*, symbolical of heaven, 12 inches

in diameter, intended to represent the shape of heaven and the twelve months.

(2) The (yellow) tube *tsung*, symbolical of the earth, cylindrical within and cube-shaped without.

(3) The south was represented by a red *chang*. It was pointed at one side, with a hole bored through the

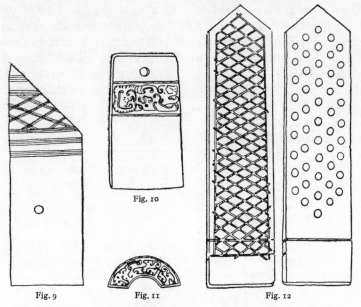

Fig. 10

Fig. 9   Fig. 11   Fig. 12

Fig. 9. Jade *chang*, Pointed at one Side, Symbolical of the South
Fig. 10. Jade *hu*, with Tiger Design, Symbolical of the West
Fig. 11. Jade *huang*, Semicircular, Symbolical of the North
Fig. 12. Jade *kuei*, Pointed at one End, Symbolical of the *ts'ing lung*

Two examples of the jade *kuei* are shown, one with reed pattern on the left, another with millet-seed pattern on the right.

lower half. The southern quadrant is named the vermilion bird (*chu niao*).

(4) The west was represented by a white *hu*. It bore a tiger design, as the western quadrant is named the white tiger (*pai hu*).

(5) The north was represented by a black *huang*. It was semicircular, and either plain or ornamented. The northern quadrant was *hüan wu*, the tortoise.

73

(6) The east was represented by a green *kuei*. It was rectangular in shape, pointed at one end. The eastern quadrant was *ts'ing lung*, the blue (or green) dragon.

To omit a mention of music would be to leave out a very vital feature of those ancient times. So impressive was the Shao music, which consisted of nine airs, that Confucius, after hearing it in the state of Ts'i, forgot to taste meat for three months while he practised its notes. Music in those times is something essentially magical. The tones so mysteriously reminiscent of the phenomena of nature, the rhythm which grips men and lifts them out of themselves, the pantomimic dances, all imbued with a deep cosmic significance, produce an unmistakable effect of something transcending the soul of man and directly influencing terrestrial events.

The music-master K'uei (the serpent-dragon) sings the praises of music in an expressive song, as follows:

> When I tap the sounding-stone or strike it strongly,
> When I gently touch the lute or zither to accompany
>   the singing,
> The spirits of ancestors come to the service;
> They take their places at the royal meal,
> The princes courtly virtue all reveal.
> In the courtyard below is heard the flute,
> Keeping tune with the beat of the drum.
> They mingle their music or hold their peace,
> As the rattle or stopper sounds;
> With the Pan-pipes and bells
> All filling up the intervals.
> Then birds and beasts crowd in,
> And to the tones of the sacred music
> The phœnix performs his measured gambols.

There is a remarkable legend to the effect that the Emperor Yao tests Shun, who is of the " lower people " (evidently, therefore, not of the clan of the priest-king [1]),

---

[1] Legend makes Shun the son of Ku Sou (' the Old Blind Man '; in later days the blind were the musicians; this would agree very well with the musical activities of Shun). It is possibly in this connexion that the *Bamboo Books* mention the coming of the Prince of Ku Sou as a guest—*i.e.*, in submission—to Yao (fifteenth year of Yao).

PLATE 9

Entrances to temples at Ningpo (province of Chekiang). (From Boerschmann, *Baukunst und Landschaft in China.*)

by ' wiving ' him—that is to say, by giving him his two daughters in marriage. The description of this marriage typifies an intermediate stage between the matriarchal system, in which the son-in-law was accepted into the wife's clan, and the later absolute patriarchate, in which the bride entered the man's family. In this case Shun becomes, as it were, the head of the house of Yao, and legend makes Yao send him his sons as well as his daughters. Intermediate customs of this kind ruled for some time longer. Even after some sort of right of succession had been established, this did not pass in a direct line, but to the brothers —a state of affairs which at a later date would have been regarded in China as a political offence. An express boast is made in the *Book of Changes* of the fact that T'ang, the founder of the Shang dynasty, gave his daughter in marriage. The expression ' to give in marriage ' (*kuei*) really means ' to send back.' This is probably connected with the customs following a marriage. After the bridegroom (who originally would have been assisted in the capture by his friends) had ' taken ' (*ts'ü*) his bride—a sure indication of an earlier practice of marriage by capture (possibly such marriages marked the transition stage between the matriarchal and patriarchal systems)—the young wife was permitted to return after three months to visit her parents. If the marriage had proved unsuitable, this was the stage at which it could be dissolved without any great formalities. As a rule, however—originally, no doubt, after she had given birth to her first son, and subsequently after a visit of some duration—she was sent back to her husband's house, and belonged to his family for life. But there persisted, for some time, a survival of the matriarchal system, whereby the brother was the legitimate protector of his sister if the husband treated her badly.[1]

Some natural phenomenon occurring in those remote times must have been responsible in the main for the closer alliance of several Chinese tribes with alien settlers. The great plain in the north of China, in the riverine valleys of which the majority of the settlers probably took up their

[1] Originally brothers were the heads of the family in external affairs.

75

abode, is, geographically speaking, the delta of the Yellow River. The Yellow River, descending from the mountains to flow through wide plains of loess, bears along in its rapid upper course a mass of silt, whence the name ' Yellow ' River seems to have been derived. As soon as the rapidity of the flow decreases, the silt serves to raise the river-bed, and even now, protected to the utmost as the river is by dikes, it is only a question of time until it overflows its banks at periods of spate and floods the plain far and wide. Thus, in the middle of the nineteenth century it altered its course, with the result that its estuary was shifted from the south to the north of the Shantung peninsula. A similar catastrophe occurred in the Mongol period, the change then being from north to south. This constitutes a permanent threat to the population which must have made itself felt more particularly when the Chinese began to expand across the plains, before any attempts had been made to regulate the course of these rivers in the northern plain the beds of which are in the winter almost dry, but which swell incredibly during the summer rains.

Meteorological catastrophes evidently played their part too, for it is often related in awestruck admiration of Yü how he maintained a calm and fearless demeanour in the face of the terrible storms which interrupted his sacrificial rites. In short, a deluge ensued, and lasted for a year. Various attempts to stem the disaster proved unavailing. Ultimately the combined energy of the people succeeded in subduing the elements and in draining the flood waters from the territory occupied by Chinese tribes. Legend has awarded the credit for this success to the clan hero of the Hia tribe, the great Yü. The *Book of History* contains an account of his achievement which in its primitive rendering is almost suggestive of Biblical utterances :

> The Emperor said, " Come, Yü !
> You also must have admirable words for me."
> Yü did obeisance, and said,
> " O Emperor, what can I say ?
> I can only think
> Of maintaining a daily assiduity."
> Kao Yao said, " Alas ! Will you describe it ? "

ANTIQUITY

Yü said:
" The inundating waters seemed to assail the heavens,
With roar and rush they embraced the mountains
And overtopped the hills;
So that the multitudes in the hollows
Were bewildered and overwhelmed.
But I forced ways through for myself
And hewed down the woods all along the hills;
I showed the people how to get flesh to eat.
I opened passages for the nine streams,
And conducted them to the four seas;
I deepened the channels and led them to the streams,
I showed the people how to procure
In addition to meat the food of toil.[1]
I urged them to make an exchange of goods;
Deficiency and excess were remedied.
In this way all the people had food,
And all the states began to acquire good rule." . . .
Yü said:
" From T'u Shan I took me a wife,
But I stayed with her only four days.
On my return I paid no heed
To the wailing of my son;
My thoughts and planning were all in my work.
The provinces demarcated by me
Extended far and wide;
To every one a pastor I gave;
Their rule extended to the seas.
The tutors appointed by me throughout
Proved worthy of their task.
Alone the obdurate people of Miao
Refused their duty to fulfil.
O Emperor, ponder this."

Let us cast a glance at peasant life as it must have been in those remote times, and as we still find it in the *Shï King*, notwithstanding the innumerable alterations these poems certainly underwent when they were collected under the auspices of feudal rulers. Ancient conditions are revealed throughout, and they held good, except for trifling changes, during the ensuing period.

As stated above, the Chinese were not the sole occupants of the middle reaches of the Yellow River. They dwelt, possibly in company with the remaining Miao, in scattered

[1] *I.e.*, grain.

settlements which were at the same time family communities. These settlements had a central point, where the village clustered round a well. The houses were either dug out of the loess (where the loess rose in steep cliffs) or built of mud. The house consisted of one room, facing south ; on the east was the door, on the west a window. In the centre of the roof was an open vent through which the smoke could escape and the rain-water enter and be collected. The name for this vent (*chung liu*, ' central inflow ') corresponds approximately to the ancient Roman *impluvium*. The dark southwest corner of the room, where the seed grain was stored and the sleeping mats were laid down, was the home of Ao, the most sacred deity in the house. Tsao, the hearth-god, who in the period of highest antiquity was probably female, abode on the hearth, where the family forgathered. This deity was less sacred than Ao, but more active, a more pronounced centre of interest.

The house was the woman's sphere. Here the wife reigned supreme, the husband's authority being confined to the outdoor world. In the winter the women span and wove ; spring-time was occupied with silkworm-breeding. Silkworm cultivation seems originally to have been indigenous to the south, while hemp, jute, and the fibre of the Pueraria (*ko*) served as yarn materials in the north. While the woman's chief work occupied the winter months, that of the man lay pre-eminently in the warmer seasons. At those seasons the men dispersed outside, in the fields which lay beyond the mulberry plantations surrounding the village. In the summer they dwelt there in open huts, where they remained at night, in order to keep guard over their crops. The women ventured into the fields only to bring the men food.

The village community was a family community. The inhabitants were divided up primarily according to generation, the relationship between fathers and sons being fairly intimate ; the oldest man in the family was the head. The men and the women, however, partly by reason of the different nature and times of their occupations, were fairly strictly segregated. This practice was possibly a survival

78

still of the early days of the matriarchate, which as time went on was eliminated more and more. For formerly, when the son left the clan to marry into another family, while the woman, who was ruled by the brother, carried on the family name, the exogamous patriarchal marriage was far more strictly enforced. The distinction between the sexes was probably widened by the men's houses, in which the men assembled in their free time for consultations and district celebrations, such as archery and drinking.

Outside the village was the sacred grove with its stream, where bathing took place in the spring and fresh air was enjoyed. This stream, through which it was considered beneficial to wade at ceremonial times,[1] flowed to the south of the grove, forming a protective boundary. There in spring and autumn took place the vegetation rites, in which human delight in revelry and fertilization spells for the soil intermingled in strangely dithyrambic fashion. These festivals had a wider significance than the narrow family association. Here the universal was manifested. Here the gods of the soil and of seeds dwelt, and here the emblems of social companionship assumed a wider meaning. Amid the wild, unbridled joy of religious celebrations was unconsciously effected a union of souls which extended beyond the village and embraced the universe at large. Dancing and singing took place here in the spring, when the young people celebrated together the festival of love's union. In the autumn there were eating and drinking and harvest festivals. Dances were performed in which masked figures took part, representing the beneficent animals (cats and tigers) which helped to destroy vermin. They were included in the eight sacrifices (*cha*). At the harvest festival, which was presided over by the old men, farewell was taken of the year and of the soil. Now all the people withdrew into their sheltered dwellings, to rest from their year's work while the women did their spinning and weaving.

With the autumn and spring festivals customs connected

[1] *Cf.* the frequently repeated oracle in the *Book of Changes*, " It will be advantageous to cross the great stream," indicating an original connexion with the boundary stream of the sacred grove.

with the fire on the domestic hearth seem to have been associated. In the autumn the fire was taken into the house; in
the spring it was brought out again. Certain rites relating
to ancestor-worship were evidently practised at the same
time. This was no mere individual worship relating to one
family, but a joint worship uniting the entire community
of the grove in common memory of the departed. Down
to the present day it is still customary to partake only of
cold food for a whole day during the spring celebrations.
And a general custom still prevails of setting graves in order
at this season, for which reason the presence at home of
as many members of the family as possible is considered
important.

The religious notions of those days are to be found in
old legends which have gradually become fables and myths
There is, for instance, the legend of the sun-bird and its eggs
found in a multitude of forms, the commonest of which
makes the progenitor of a clan issue from one of these eggs
that a swallow had brought a girl to eat. The legend of the
ox-herd and the weaving maiden is probably likewise of
solar-lunar origin. It is true that in the story which is
current to-day the weaving maiden does not, as in the mari
time form of civilization, represent the moon, but Vega
the ox-herd being Altair. Between them, keeping them
apart, flows the River of Heaven, across which, once a year
only, the auspicious magpies make a bridge by which the
maiden can join her lover. Of very ancient origin, without
a doubt, is the legend of the girl whose father was far away
and who promised herself in marriage to the horse in their
stable if he would take her to her father. In order to avoid
keeping her promise she had the horse put to death. But
the horse's hide, which had been spread out to dry, suddenly
rose up, seized the girl, and suspended itself with her on
a tree, where the girl turned into a silkworm. Dragons
whose magic power animates the waters of heaven and
earth, were also worshipped from the remotest times,[1] their
relations with women being frequently of a very dubious

---

[1] The Dragon-boat Festival, chiefly celebrated in the southern part of China
belonging to the maritime type of civilization, is certainly also a very ancient cult.

PLATE 10

Main entrance to the Imperial Palace in Peking.

nature. Snakes and bears have their share in popular superstitions, as well as the sly and cunning fox. Strangely ambiguous is the tortoise, which on the one hand is regarded as a cosmic emblem, and on the other is held in abhorrence as a loathsome symbol of unchastity. This circumstance is one of many which clearly indicate the dual origin of Chinese culture.

The further course of Chinese civilization seems to have run by no means so easily and smoothly as the *Book of History* represents. The priesthood-kingship, embracing the privilege of ruling the world by appointing the seasons, was established gradually, and not without difficulty, within the family of the ruler Yü. The time of the Hia dynasty, which is accepted as the first dynasty in China, is regarded as coincident with the establishment of the royal right of succession. This epoch may be taken as falling within the Neolithic period. Princes of other clans frequently came into power for longer or shorter periods, and it was not always easy, apparently, for the royal family to recover its suzerainty. The decisive factor was evidently recognition of the standard time-reckoning. Whoever followed that announced by the priest-king belonged to the Universal Order, but he who attempted to introduce other methods of reckoning was not only a political rebel, but a sacrilegious offender against the cosmic order of things. The speech at Kan, one of the most interesting things in the *Book of History*, and certainly of ancient date, illustrates this point. In this exhortation the ruler of Hu is accused of throwing the five cosmic elements into confusion by repudiating the calendar. The ban under which the army is placed is characteristic of those times.

The Exhortation of Kan

There was a great battle in Kan;
The Emperor called together the six leaders of his hosts
And addressed them, saying:
"Ah! all ye men in my six armies,
By this solemn oath I conjure you:
The ruler of Hu
Has done violence to the elements of nature,

And has idly abandoned all obligations.[1]
Therefore is heaven about to destroy his throne;
And I am reverently executing the punishment appointed
    by heaven.
If you, left-side men in the chariot,
Do not do your work on the left,
You are disregarding my orders!
If you, right-side men in the chariot,
Do not do your work on the right,
You are disregarding my orders!
If you, charioteers in the centre,
Do not guide your horses aright,
You are disregarding my orders !
Now you who obey my orders
Shall be rewarded before my great ancestors;
But you who disobey
Shall be put to death before the spirits of the dark earth;
Together with wife and child will I destroy you."

A similar spirit is manifested in the punishment toward the end of the dynasty of the princes of Hi and Ho, whose ancestors had been entrusted under Yao with the observation and determination of the seasons. It is said that they were punished by the majordomo Yin for permitting an uncalculated eclipse of the sun through neglect of their duties.[2] Here again, then, is a contravention of the astronomical regulations. The incident, it is true, seems to have occurred not long before the end of the dynasty. With the inaccuracy of the old astronomical observations, errors of calculation were bound to appear in the course of centuries. The celestial seasons no longer coincided with terrestrial phenomena. God had turned away from the ruling house. A new ruler was empowered to propitiate heaven by setting the world in order.[3]

Thus in connexion with the fall of the Hia dynasty there

---

[1] Literally, " has done violence to the five fundamental forces and idly abandoned the three fundamental regulations." The commentaries disagree on the interpretation of these crimes.

[2] At various times in the Hia dynasty a kind of secular shogunate seems to have shared the power of the priest-king, a state of affairs which continued later on, and which led to many difficulties over the right of succession.

[3] The section " Hia Siao Chêng " of the *Ta Tai Li* apparently contains a plan for the arrangement of the calendar. Confucius held it to be that of the Hia dynasty, which he esteemed most highly of all.

are recounted all sorts of celestial phenomena, clearly proving, according to the reports handed down by later rulers, that Kuei was rejected by heaven.

The new ruler, whose succession marked the advent of the house of Shang, was T'ang the Completer. It is now the middle of the second millennium before Christ. Light has not yet dawned upon the darkness of history; extant documents are but few, and underwent revision by the Court recorders of the next ruling house. We are nevertheless entering a period in which, even if exact details of the organization of cultural institutions are lacking, antique remains in bronze and bone at all events afford some guide to the intellectual life of that time.

The characteristic feature of this dynasty is the birth of the religious motive. Small wonder that the extant relics from those days are sacrificial vessels and oracular bones! From the first the house of Shang displayed the definite tendencies of a religious mission. The neighbouring state, which was attacked first, was accused of failing to perform the correct sacrificial rites for the gods. And the ruler of the house of Hia, named by posterity Kie ('the Murderer'), was likewise accused of sinning against the will of God, and it was asserted that it was God's will to deprive the sinner of his kingdom.

On closer inspection religion now assumes a more anthropomorphic and mythological character. If the astral religion of earlier times represented a more original and more rationalized type, the gods most worshipped now are the more intimate deities—on the one hand the ancestors, on the other the gods of the underworld. There are prayers to the ruler of heaven, to the great progenitor of the ruling race, which in form faintly resemble the Old Testament. The ancestors dwell up aloft and participate in human actions, which they accompany either with their blessing or their punishment. They are worshipped with burnt-offerings. They are besought for happiness and long life. Their origin, traced back to the dark bird (the swallow), which created the ancestor by commission of heaven,[1] is the subject of meditation.

History also abounds in portents and miracles. Mention

[1] See *Shï King*, IV, iii, 3.

is made of female mediums who prophesy future events. The mulberry-tree plays a remarkable *rôle*. According to one legend, I Yin, the counsellor of Prince T'ang, was born in a hollow mulberry. In the courtyard of T'ai Mou a sacred mulberry and a stalk of grain grew up together. Diviners prophesied the submission of seventy-six states, and they came from afar and paid homage ; their languages had to be interpreted through many stages before they could be translated into Chinese. Wu Ting, under whom the house of Shang flourished again, had a dream in which he saw his future assistant. He had a picture made of the vision, and by this means had search made for him throughout the empire. At last, among the feudal bondsmen, the man thus represented was found. It was Fu Yüe, under whom the empire enjoyed fresh prosperity. Even the transfer of the capital eastward, which followed under P'an Kêng [1]— undoubtedly in order to escape from the pressure of neigh-bours in the west—was ascribed to the command of God, the disregarding of which would bring danger and destruc-tion. All these things are evidence that life was thoroughly permeated by religious conceptions.

Apart from the bright gods on high, there were also the underground spirits of darkness, whom it was found wise to propitiate with live offerings burnt in pits. T'ang himself, after a drought lasting nine years, offered up a black bull, upon whose forehead he fastened hair from his own head. The sacrifices in the sacred grove seem also to have ac-quired an increasingly gloomy character. T'ang, for instance, covered in the sacred grove of the Hia, in order to exclude all light from heaven. The threats contained in the martial addresses, to slay in the sacred grove transgressors and their whole families, point to a custom providing for human sacrifices in those places. The manner in which Confucius shudderingly rebuffed an attempt on the part of one of his disciples to discuss the terrorizing effects of the grove under earlier royal houses plainly shows that he knew more about these proceedings than he cared to own.

[1] After the transfer to a new capital bearing the auspicious name of Yin the dynasty changed its name, and was thereafter called Yin instead of Shang.

PLATE 11

Colossal figure of the Buddha Amitabha, carved out of the rock. The side figure represents Kuan-yin. At Yün-kang (province of Shansi).

By a remarkable accident oracular bones have been re-covered from the ancient ruined capital at Yin which were in all probability buried there after the oracle had been con-sulted. These finds show us how one of the oracles—namely, divination by the tortoise—was worked. The bones were scraped smooth and notched on the back by means of red-hot sticks. This treatment produced cracks in front, the shape and number of which constituted the oracle. The oracular sentences were then scratched on the bones, and the latter were buried. In addition to divination by the tortoise (*pu*), the milfoil (*chan*), with which are con-nected the sixty-four hexagrams of the *Book of Changes*, was also consulted. The *Book of Changes* in the Yin period was not yet, however, the work now known by that name, but probably consisted of only sixty-four hexagrams, each of which had but one name. First came the figure *k'un*, 'the receptive,' and this was followed by the figure *k'ien*, ' the creative,' which arrangement, as already noted, was a remnant of the matriarchal system.

That remarkable document in the *Book of History*, " The Great Plan " (" Hung Fan "), which, notwithstanding its claims to have been handed down secretly from the highest antiquity, may in its present form be assigned with some confidence to the end of the Yin period, shows how vital a part the oracle, or in other words the religious motive, played in the whole system of government. This " Great Plan " describes the plan upon which the entire civilization of that time was erected, and is therefore sufficiently important to be reproduced in full :

THE GREAT PLAN

The Great Plan has nine divisions.

The first is called the five elements.

The second is called the reverent practice of the five businesses.

The third is called earnest devotion to the eight objects of government.

The fourth is called the harmonious use of the five time arrange-ments.

The fifth is called the establishment and use of sovereignty.

The sixth is called the correct use of the three virtues.

The seventh is called the intelligent use of the examination of doubts.

The eighth is called the thoughtful use of the various verifications.

The ninth is called the hortatory use of the five happinesses and the deterrent use of the six extremities.

(1) The five elements: the first is water; the second fire; the third wood; the fourth metal; the fifth earth. Water soaks as it descends, fire blazes as it ascends, wood is both bent and straight, metal adapts itself to change, the earth shows sowing and reaping. That which soaks and descends produces saltiness; that which blazes and ascends bitterness; that which is both bent and straight sourness; that which changes its shape pungency; that which shows sowing and reaping sweetness.

(2) The five businesses: the first is demeanour; the second speech; the third seeing; the fourth hearing; the fifth thinking. The virtue of demeanour is seriousness; of speech accordance; of seeing clearness; of hearing profundity; of thinking penetration. Seriousness is manifested in dignity, accordance in orderliness, clearness in wisdom, profundity in deliberation, penetration in godliness.

(3) The eight objects of government are: first, food; second, commodities; third, sacrifices; fourth, the provision of work; fifth, the provision of education; sixth, the punishment of crime; seventh, guests; eighth, the army.

(4) The five time arrangements are: first, the year (Jupiter); second, the moon; third, the day (the sun); fourth, the stars and constellations ; fifth, the calendaric calculations.

(5) Sovereignty: establish your hold on sovereignty. Collect the five happinesses, and distribute them among your people. If the people approve of your sovereignty they will give to you the preservation of it.

The multitudes of the people shall not have lawless confederacies, men (officers) shall not have self-seeking dispositions; only the sovereign shall be supreme.

Bear in mind any among the people who make proof of counsel or conduct or constancy. Suffer all who, while not actively helping the sovereign, yet do not fall into crime. And when their countenances proclaim their satisfaction, and they say, " We will love virtue," then confer favour on them. In this way will those men be assisting the perfection of the sovereign.[1]

---

[1] Here is clearly seen the powerlessness of the priest-king, who was entirely dependent on the good-will of the princes.

ANTIQUITY

Do not oppress the solitary and the friendless, nor fear the high and the illustrious.

When men show ability and energy, assist these qualities to develop, and the land will prosper through them. All right-minded men, if rewarded, will continue in their excellence. If you cannot offer them anything in your house [1] to love, such men will fall into crime.

If a man loves not virtue, though you confer favour on him, he will only cause you to be a participator in his evil ways.

> Without respect of person
> The royal right maintain,
> Without selfish desire
> The royal way maintain,
> Without a sign of aversion
> The royal path maintain.
> Without partiality and bias
> The royal path is even and smooth.
> Without bias and partiality
> The royal path is open and free,
> Without error and one-sidedness
> The royal path is straight and true.
> When they recognize the Pole Star of
> thy sovereignty
> They will all incline toward it.

What remains to be said of sovereignty concerns steadfastness and obedience, obedience unto God. If you obey and act in accordance with these remaining injunctions, all the people will come nearer to the light of the son of heaven and will say: "The son of heaven is the father and mother of the people, and is thus become the sovereign of the empire."

(6) The three virtues are: first, straightforward government; second, strong government; third, mild government. In peace and tranquillity the straightforward government must hold sway; when the powerful are unfriendly, strong government must hold sway; when they are friendly and in harmony, mild government may hold sway; for the underhand and the dissembler strong government must hold sway, for the illustrious and the wise mild government may hold sway. Only the ruler may confer favours, only the ruler may strike terror, only the ruler may receive jade food.[2] Those

[1] According to another interpretation, "in their home."

[2] The commentaries disagree about this expression. Some take it to mean the public revenues, others the royal viands at sacrifices and at the entertainments for the princes. The class privilege with regard to certain foods was maintained for a long time in China.

who serve may not confer favours, nor strike terror, nor partake of jade food. If this right be conferred on those who serve, then will harm befall your house and evil overcome your empire. Then will men (officers) become biased, wrongheaded, and perverse, and the people will become arrogant and commit excesses.

(7) The examination of doubts: select and appoint men for divining by the tortoise and by the milfoil, and let them consult the oracles of the tortoise and the milfoil.

The tortoise will show rain, clearing up, cloudiness, rifts, and crossings. The milfoil will show assiduity and repentance. The seven indications, of which five will be shown by the tortoise and two by the milfoil, will dissipate doubts. Appoint these men to consult the tortoise and the milfoil. Three men shall interpret the oracle; in the event of disagreement the majority shall be followed.

When, now, you have any grave doubt, consult your own heart, consult your counsellors, consult your people, consult the tortoise and the milfoil. If you, the tortoise, the milfoil, the counsellors, and the people are all in agreement, joint action will result. You will rejoice in health and strength; good fortune will befall your sons and grandsons.

If you, the tortoise, and the milfoil all agree, but the counsellors and the people disagree, the result will still be fortunate. If the counsellors, the tortoise, and the milfoil agree, but you and the people disagree, the result will still be fortunate. If the people, the tortoise, and the milfoil agree, but you and the counsellors disagree, the result will still be fortunate. If you and the tortoise agree, but the milfoil, the counsellors, and the people disagree, good fortune will attend internal affairs, but misfortune will accompany external operations. If the tortoise and the milfoil are both opposed to the views of men, there will be good fortune in stillness, but active operations will be unlucky.[1]

(8) The various verifications are: rain, sunshine, heat, cold, wind. When all five come in fullness, each in its proper season, all plants will thrive abundantly. If any one of them is excessive or entirely absent, complete misfortune will result.

Favourable verifications are: of gravity, when seasonable rain falls; of orderliness, when seasonable sunshine appears; of wisdom, when seasonable heat occurs; of deliberation, when seasonable cold prevails; of godliness, when a seasonable wind blows. Unfavourable verifications are: of wildness, when perpetual rain falls;

---

[1] The extraordinarily powerful influence of religion on political life, characteristic of the Yin dynasty, is visible here.

of arrogance, when perpetual sunshine appears; of carelessness, when perpetual heat prevails; of haste, when perpetual cold reigns; of foolishness, when a perpetual wind blows.

The king observes the year, the counsellors the month, the leaders of the people the day.

If throughout the year, the month, and the day seasonable weather continues without change, then will all the fruits of the field mature, government will be easy, the heroes among the people will acquire fame, families will enjoy peace and prosperity. If throughout the year, the month, and the day the weather be not seasonable, then will none of the fruits of the field mature, government will be confused and difficult, the heroes among the people will remain in obscurity, and unrest will prevail in the families.

The people are the stars. Among the stars are some which love the wind, some the rain; the course of the sun and the moon brings winter and summer; the wandering of the moon among the stars brings wind and rain.[1]

(9) The five happinesses are : first, long life; second, riches; third, good health and peace of mind; fourth, love of virtue; fifth, an end fulfilling the will of heaven.

The six extremities are: first, misfortune, which shortens life; second, sickness; third, sorrow; fourth, poverty; fifth, wickedness; sixth, weakness.

In addition to this summary of the principles of government, a very important section of the *Book of History* is that entitled " The Tribute of Yü." In its present form this section falls into two parts, the first of which describes the regulation of the rivers by the great Yü. In actual fact we seem to be confronted here with a geography dating from the end of the Yin dynasty, revealing the extent and physical character of the Chinese territory of that time. Of importance, also, are the lists of things sent to the capital as a tax from the various districts, for they show what the chief products were in those times of highest antiquity.[2]

[1] It is questionable whether this passage belongs to the verifications and not rather to the calendaric calculations (4).

[2] The first part of the " Yü Kung," on which Richthofen enlarges in detail, consists, as Chavannes clearly demonstrated, of two reports that have been woven together: the one is a geographical survey of China in remotest times, with tax-rolls and particulars of the most direct routes to the capital, to which the other supplies a framework in its account of the regulation of the waters by Yü. In the text only the economic-geographic portion is translated.

(1) The central province was called Ki Chou [= 'the Land between the Streams '—' Mesopotamia '].

The soil here is white and fine-grained.   The taxes are of the highest grade of the first class, with some exceptions.

The fields are of the medium grade of the middle class.   The island hunters [1] bring garments of skin.   Keeping to the right of the Kie rocks, they enter the Ho [Yellow River].

(2) Between the rivers Tsi and Ho lies Yen Chou.

The soil is black and rich.   The plant growth is luxuriant, and the trees are tall.   The fields are of the lowest grade of the middle class, and the taxes correspond.   After thirteen years' cultivation they are to equal those of the other provinces.

The special articles of tribute are varnish and silk.   The offerings sent in baskets are woven damasks.

The way lies down the river Tsi and the river T'a, when the Ho is reached.

(3) Between the sea and the Tai Mountain lies Ts'ing Chou.

The soil is white and rich.   Along the seashore are wide salt tracts.

The fields are of the lowest grade of the first class   The taxes are of the highest grade of the middle class.

The special articles of tribute are salt, grass-cloth, products of the sea, also grindstones.   From the valleys of the Tai come silk, hemp, lead, pine-trees, and curious stones.   The hunters of Lai breed cattle.   Their basket offerings are mountain silk.

The way lies down the river Wên, when the river Tsi is reached.

(4) Between the sea, the Tai Mountain, and the river Huai lies Sü Chou.

The soil is red, clayey, and rich.   The plants and trees are slow of growth.

The fields are of the medium grade of the first class.   The taxes are of the medium grade of the middle class.

The special article of tribute is earth of five colours.   From the valleys of the Yü come variegated pheasants.   From the southern slopes of the I Mountain come solitary dryandras, from the shores of the Sï river alluvial sounding-stones.   The hunters from the Huai river bring oyster-pearls and fish.   Their basket offerings are purple silks, patterned silks, and white silks.

The way lies down the river Huai or the river Sï, when the river Ho is reached.

---

[1] The " island hunters " are aboriginal inhabitants of the I tribe (barbarians from the east—the character I is composed of the characters for ' great ' and ' a bow ').

(5) Between the Huai river and the sea lies Yang Chou.

The soil is loamy and viscous.

The fields are of the lowest grade of the lowest class. The taxes are of the highest grade of the lowest class, with upward divergences in parts.

The special articles of tribute are three kinds of metal, *yao* and *k'un* stones, bamboos small and large, teeth, skins,[1] feathers, hair, and timber.

The island hunters bring clothing made from grass.

Their basket offerings are variegated silks. Their bundles contain oranges and pumelos, rendered when specially required.

The way lies down the Kiang [Yangtse] to the sea, whence the Huai and the Sï may be reached.

(6) Between Mount King and the south of Mount Hêng lies King Chou.

The soil is loamy and viscous.

The fields are of the medium grade of the lowest class. The taxes are of the lowest grade of the first class.

The special articles of tribute are feathers, hair, teeth, and hides;[1] also three kinds of metal, Cedrela-wood, wood for bows, cedars, cypresses, grindstones, whetstones, arrowhead stones, and cinnabar; also various species of bamboo and hardwood, of which especially notable kinds are found in the three provinces.

As bundle offerings, three-ribbed rushes are brought.

Their basket offerings are dark and purple silks, and strings of pearls.[2] When specially required, the great oracular tortoises are brought from the Nine Streams.

The way lies down the Kiang [Yangtse], then across the T'o and the Ts'ien to the Han river, then overland to the Lo river as far as the southern reaches of the Ho.

(7) Between Mount King and the Yellow River lies Yü Chou.

The soil is fine.   In the low-lying lands the soil is rich and black.

The fields are of the highest grade of the middle class.   The taxes are, with certain exceptions, of the medium grade of the first class.

The special articles of tribute are varnish, hides, fine hempen cloth, and jute.   The basket offerings are fine silks and floss-silk. Stones for polishing sounding-stones are rendered when required.

The way lies down the Lo river, when the Ho is reached.

---

[1] The " teeth " and " skins " are presumably ivory and rhinoceros hides. These animals must therefore have still been found in the Yangtse district.

[2] *Baroque* pearls—*i.e.*, pearls which are not quite round.

(8) Between the southern slope of Mount Hua and the Black Water lies Liang Chou.

The soil is a greenish black.

The fields are of the highest grade of the lowest class. The taxes are of the medium grade of the lowest class, in three gradings.

The special articles of tribute are jade musical stones,[1] iron, silver, steel, arrowhead stones, sounding-stones, bears large and small, foxes, jackals, and woven nets.

The way down from the western slope [Mount Si K'ing] lies across the Huan river. Thence the way lies down the Ts'ien river, then across country to the Mien river, then to the Wei river, which flows into the Ho.

(9) Between the Black Water and the western Ho lies Yung Chou.

The soil is yellow and light.

The fields are of the highest grade of the first class. The taxes are of the lowest grade of the middle class.

The special articles of tribute are *k'iu-lin* stones for sacrificial wands and green *lang-kan* stones.

The way down from Mount Tsi Shï lies through Lung-mên [the Dragon Gate] on the westerly Ho, when the northern bank of the Wei river is reached.

The K'un-lun, Si-chï, and Kü-sou tribes brought felt fabrics; the western Yung made submission to the central power.

The first half of the second part of this work contains another geographical survey of the labours connected with the regulation of the waters; the second half contains a Utopian picture of the world seen from the central dominion. We need not take these parts into account.

The general impression acquired is that as time went on some sort of political order gained ascendancy over the hitherto exclusively religious system. The population in the various territories which had declared their adherence to the central ruler seems certainly to have been of very unequal density. Round about, chiefly in the more inaccessible mountain regions, which had not yet been cleared for agriculture by fire, the indigenous hunting tribes still dwelt, and in the north-east there were apparently nomads as well. All the territories comprising the Chinese settlements, which

---

[1] This might possibly be translated " fine gold."

PLATE 12

Stone figures of warriors and officials lining the avenue leading to the tomb of the Emperor Hung-wu (Ming dynasty) at Nanking.

had from the very beginning been based on settled agriculture—as already mentioned, there is not the faintest indication of a nomadic stage among the Chinese, and many arguments against it—were linked up with the central domain by strictly defined routes. The taxes were probably determined with allowance for the quality of the soil, the density of the population, and the transport routes.

The special articles of tribute mentioned as coming from the different regions reveal a stage of social economy in which the requirements were already fairly extensive.

This is supplemented by the fact that we find, not only a well-organized army, whose needs are partly met by these special tributes, but also the clearly discernible beginnings of an urban civilization. The transfer of the capital eastward, mentioned in the *Book of History* as occurring under the ruler P'an Kêng, must have been a great and arduous undertaking, or he would never have been obliged to adduce so many religious and other reasons to persuade the people to go.

This shifting of the capital from west to east also furnishes a precedent for a proceeding which recurred frequently during the course of Chinese history. We know that it was chiefly fear of tribes pressing in from the west which compelled a collapsing dynasty to make way. The *Book of History* mentions on one occasion how the powerful ruler Wu Ting once chastised the Devil's Country. These tribes are the same as those which later, under the names of Huns and the Tu-küe, menaced the civilized territory of China. But this powerful ruler, who is extolled in a couple of very ancient odes in the *Book of Poetry*, could no longer avert the collapse.

Over-civilization and luxury became increasingly predominant in the capital. Shou Sin, the last ruler of the Yin dynasty, famous in history as the tyrant Chou, is described as a monster of debauchery, who was still further incited to commit all manner of inhuman atrocities by his notorious concubine T'a Ki. This description of course represents the dogmatic statements of the new ruling house, which was obliged to adduce religious reasons for overthrowing him. The exact agreement of the portrait of the tyrant Kie of the Hia dynasty with that of the tyrant Shou Sin of the house of Yin shows that a definite method was employed in such cases.

The state of over-civilization existing in the capital was evidently the cause of the breach between the Court and country. Although the Government was by no means weak, and could count on its side a number of eminent relatives and officers of the ruler, this social estrangement was probably the decisive factor. It is also quite possible that the bigoted religious policy of the dynasty may have veered round in the opposite direction.

Shou Sin is described as a man of almost superhuman strength, able to fell wild animals with a blow of his fist, and with such quick wits that he could always find sophistical reasons with which to refute the advice of his counsellors. A predilection for cruelty, combined with sensuality and a love of display, made him an object of hatred. Add to all this the pressure from the west and the collapse of social and economic order, and it is not surprising that the house of Yin approached its end accompanied by all manner of terrifying portents in the heavens and on earth.

CHAPTER II

THE FEUDAL PERIOD

THE rise of the house of Chou about 1150 B.C. brings us nearer to authentic history. With this dynasty we distinctly see the dawn of a new era in Chinese civilization. The stage now reached, indeed, is the beginning of the classic period of Chinese civilization, the foundation of all culture and all beauty, and has been regarded as a mighty prototype throughout the ages.

A combination of several factors accounts for the elevation of this house. The land of the Chou people was a colonial state just as were Austria, Saxony, and Prussia in the history of Germany. Settled in the extreme west, they founded a house, the extension of whose power was made possible by their very position as colonists in territories inhabited by foreign tribes—apparently by a Turkic race. At all events, they owed their power and civilization to an evidently happy racial mixture, which brought fresh blood and new ideas to the Chinese nation. Plainly recognizable here is the idea of a perfected patriarchate, combined with a feudal principle systematically carried out, making its entry on the stage of Chinese history. This is the result of the preponderating urban civilization, now visibly spreading. The towns were the centres of a power extending across the open country, where the old principle of kinship long continued to reign, side by side with the primitive agrarian-communistic ideas which had grown up during the development of the " great family." We find the state of society characterized by a distinction between town and country. In the country the combination of kinship and rural community still continued in force, the sacred grove still remained the spiritual centre of society. Domestic life comprised agriculture (for the men) and sartorial economy (sericulture and the cultivation and preparation of various textile plants by the women). Over these communities were the provincial towns, where the nobles resided ; over these again the feudal capitals with their feudal princes ; and the whole culminated in the capital

Fig. 13. Rubbing from a Stone Relievo at Kia-siang, representing King Wên and his Wife

(wherever it might be) of the great king, from whom a power emanated. This system also formed the basis of th military organization. The army was essentially a foot force ; the feudal vassals fought in chariots followed by light armed peasants. There was no cavalry. This was take over from neighbouring Turkic tribes later on. This stat of affairs, with its heroes and chariot warfare, its rivalr between the feudal lords, with their attempts to set themselves up as independent princes, developed on quite natural lines, and agrees with conditions in corresponding periods of other civilizations.

But, apart from these general resemblances to other civilizations—for instance, to those of the feudal period in Germanic Europe—those specific characteristics which differentiate the Chou period from other analogous periods must not be overlooked. No understanding of the Chou period and its significance in Chinese civilization can be acquired without taking into account the personalities of the founder of the house and his high *entourage*. The preceding dynasty had been, so to speak, a victim of the mechanical laws of a period of decline. Yet it had a number of able pillars. Its last ruler, Chou Sin,[1] was certainly a man of no mean intelligence. But his irresponsible attitude, his abandonment to sensual pleasures, and his seduction by a woman whose wickedness knew no bounds led him into paths where he merely abused power for personal ends. Thus he estranged not only the people and the princes, but even his best and most faithful counsellors, and the religious position he claimed as the Son of Heaven ceased to have any real justification. All groaned under the oppression of such a ruler. No wonder, then, that every kind of reproach was levelled at him, and that he was charged with all manner of wickedness and cruelty. He had trifled away his sovereignty, and that was all the more dangerous for the house of Yin because it had formerly based its right to dethrone its predecessors, the rulers of Hia, purely on grounds of morality and religion. If states are preserved only through the means by which they are founded, then Chou Sin pronounced his own doom when he trampled on those principles which had justified his ancestor in establishing his throne.

This places the house of Chou in a correspondingly favourable light. By this house were formulated the principles of statesmanship which thereafter for three millennia remained the standards for China and the whole of the East.

[1] This is the above-mentioned Shou Sin.

The Chou period marks the bright dawn of civilization, a sun whose rays lit up for a remarkable length of time the horizon of Eastern Asia.

The house of Chou is not of pure Chinese origin. The philosopher Mencius calls King Wên, the virtual founder of the world-power of Chou, a Western barbarian. The creation of a legend connecting the family tree of the house with the ancient rulers of China was not surprising, but such family trees are not historic. We find the real progenitor of the Chou in the person of the Duke Liu, who settled in the extreme north-west of China in the eighteenth century B.C. In the fourteenth century the pressure of the Hün-yü tribes, in whom one may discern the precursors of the Huns, compelled the hordes governed by the Chou to migrate further into China proper. The plain at the foot of Mount Kʻi (in the modern district of Fêng-siang) was the mother-country of the Chou.

The bond between the ruling house and its people was that of mutual understanding and mutual fidelity. The basic principle of the feudal system, the care of the feudal lord for his vassals and the fidelity of the vassals to their lord, formed from the outset the real strength of these intruders, whose civilization was at first of a very low order.[1]

The *Bamboo Books* disclose a quite consistent aim in the plans of the house of Chou. Their goal is the Chinese Empire, and into this great civilized community they penetrate. We see them procuring by means of successful military operations a position of considerable strength in the midst of conquered barbarian tribes. But these military operations are not the most vital factor. Both before and after them many kingdoms were welded together in those Central Asian regions which contributed very little to the civilization of China. The distinctive feature of the Chou rulers is their humanity toward their subjects, which they retained even in the hour of success. They held their

---

[1] A song in the *Book of Poetry* describes how the Princess Kiang followed her spouse to their new abode seated behind him on his horse. The wives of the early Chou rulers all play a distinctive part, and, in contrast to the bad Tʻa Ki, who ruined her consort Chou Sin, their influence is always good.

property in common with their vassals. The great supply system which a kingdom represents was in an ideal state of adjustment, whereby the whole and its parts obtained their rights in equal measure. The most famous example of this spirit is King Wên, who was the actual organizer of the power of Chou.

The selfish cruelty of the tyrant Chou Sin of the Shang dynasty made it inevitable that Wên should win men's hearts. Although his power was continually increasing, and he was even imprisoned for a time by the suspicious tyrant, he remained thoroughly loyal to the house of Shang. Two-thirds of the empire was under his sway, yet he conducted the neighbouring princes, who came to do him homage, to the Court of the sovereign ruler.

A remarkable state of affairs, resulting from the interplay of the following factors, existed for some time. On the one hand political wisdom demanded that the organization of the Chou territory should be continually improved and strengthened, while on the other hand the condition of rightful allegiance was steadily maintained. The ruler Wên was appointed Chieftain of the West, and was awarded by the sovereign ruler Chou Sin, who, in company with his evil genius, T'a Ki, was plunging ever deeper into vicious courses, the right to undertake independent wars and punitive expeditions. He already enjoyed *de facto*, therefore, the highest power in the kingdom.

He organized the power of his house by creating a western and an eastern administrative district, known as Shao and Chou respectively. One of these districts lay in reality outside China proper ; the other formed part of the feudal states. Understanding of this arrangement may be obtained by reference to the electorate of Brandenburg in Prussia and its relation to the Holy Roman Empire.

Another distinctive feature of the Chou period was that it embraced the most modern institutions of contemporary China. The tendency of the age favoured patriarchism, and as the Chou represented the purest patriarchism, their civilization was modern in this sense. The gloomy chthonian relics of the old religion came to be regarded more and more as superficial, and they gradually sank into obscurity. The heaven above was the abode of the Supreme God, who looked down on men, rewarding the virtuous and punishing the wicked. His representative on earth was the Son of Heaven, who now especially merited this name, since the ancestors of the race were associated with the Supreme Ruler at sacrifices—lived, as it were, in close proximity to God and conversed with him. Thus the whole of life assumes a brighter, more rational aspect. Morality and music are the forces employed to reach the hearts of men; fear and terror of earthly or future punishment no longer produces miserable outward docility. This state of mind, enlightened and free from superstition, was typical of the Chou period. This cheerful religion of the nobility naturally rested on a darker foundation, just as the Homeric Apollonian serenity, though sprung from dark underground spheres, made its home in the sunny outer world without freeing itself entirely, however, from the lower regions. At all events, so long as this enlightened, kindly, ethical religion could be followed without entering into problems of destiny, it endowed the lives of the nobility with freedom and harmony.

The life of the nobility was Court life. Just as the Chou soon relinquished the practice of riding mentioned in the old migratory days, and had, even before acquiring the throne, formed a strong army of war-chariots to serve as picked troops—supported, it is true, by other, lighter forces, presumably of foreign nationality—so we find them, at the time when their territorial power was extending, turning very marked attention to the building of fortified towns. The result was an increasing development of city and Court life, distinguished by great refinement in art and social customs, which was in marked contrast to the life of the common people in the country. The nobility who flocked round the ruler were attached to him by bonds of personal loyalty. They were ruled only by a fixed code of chivalry, and subjected to no penal laws. No legal judgment was passed on anyone belonging to this class who had committed a capital offence, but if his guilt was established he was given the opportunity of carrying out the death-penalty on

PLATE 13

Grave-spirit in terracotta, Tʻang period or earlier. (R.Wilhelm Collection.)

himself. The common people, on the other hand, were not bound by this code of chivalry, but, when guilty of transgressions, were subject to penal law. This might well be regarded as preferential treatment of the upper classes. And there is no doubt that this was the result when the vitality of this civilization ebbed. But at its zenith the power of morality was something thoroughly vital and strong, especially as it was supported by the ruler himself. The greatness of the first rulers of this house lay in the fact that they did not merely (as we should say to-day) set a good example to the people, but that they bore in their own persons the responsibility and inspired representation of their principles.

As already mentioned, the house of Chou marks the highest point in the development of patriarchism, not only because ancestor-worship was directly based on the worship of heaven—which had not been the case before—but because the right of succession in the ruling house strictly followed the direct line of descent. In the Shang period it was still customary for several brothers to succeed one another before the next generation acquired the sovereignty. This method of inheritance had naturally resulted in all sorts of contests for the throne. The house of Chou laid down as an inviolable law—the sanctity of which has been preserved throughout the centuries, in spite of occasional lapses—the strict right of succession from father to son. This law was soon to be tested. King Wu, son of King Wên, who, sword in hand, snatched the empire from the tyrant Chou, was already an elderly man when he ascended the throne, and at his death he left as his heir a minor, whom he entrusted to the guardianship of his younger brother, Duke Tan of Chou. This Duke of Chou is one of the most important figures in Chinese history. During the lifetime of his father Wên he had already played an extremely important and indispensable part in the regulation of the newly acquired territory. It would have been easy for him to assume the sovereignty after the death of his brother and to exclude his young nephew during his lifetime. This he did not do, but carried on the government as regent with the greatest discretion, side by side with the young King, whom he brought up with his own son Po K'in, contenting himself with allowing his own family to continue in possession of the small feudal state of Lu. To this attitude he remained faithful even when two other brothers, together with a descendant of the deposed dynasty, planned a rebellion. In all his actions the Duke of Chou showed himself entirely above suspicion, and he laid a new moral foundation for the house of Chou by his example of renunciation.

This strong spirit of morality, which had long since made family life a model of purity and affection, exercised a magical influence. In patriarchal society a type of family is sometimes found in which the father has unrestricted power over the entire household, the women finding themselves degraded to the position of slaves. Under the Chou dynasty a family life was introduced which at bottom, notwithstanding the rightful authority enjoyed by the head of the house, was based on the mutual affection of all members of the family. This happy state of affairs was guaranteed by ordering the family life in such harmonious fashion that each individual member had his appointed place assigned to him. On husband and wife devolved the duty of rearing and upbringing, which meant that just as the man's duty was to represent his family outside, so the mother had also her well-defined sphere of authority inside the house. Theoretically marriage was monogamous. The matron assisted the paterfamilias in the capacity of a helpmate, and she alone might perform her due share in the sacred rites of ancestor-worship. Another point was that marriage rested on a strictly exogamous basis. Even to-day the marriage of two persons bearing the same surname is a penal offence in China. The idea underlying this principle of exogamy is by no means the prevention of inbreeding, as families of different surnames may intermarry up to a very close degree of relationship. The reason seems rather to be that from the very outset girls are destined to enter another family. At birth they are not presented to their own ancestors, in order that they may not fall under the magic spell of family membership. On the other hand, they are solemnly presented at their marriage (which takes place in the home of the bridegroom) to the ancestors of the family they are about to enter, and it is the moral duty of the young wife to devote herself entirely to the new family which now claims her legally and not to continue selfishly to foster the ties of blood-relationship at the latter's expense. Here we see the great transformation which has gradually been accomplished in the family, and which, by very reason of its new morality, was supported by particularly strict religious sanctions. Even in the "great family" of the Chou days matrimony had naturally no independent significance. It was but a link in the family chain. The families concluded the marriage contract, and so far as ethical obligations were concerned the relationship of the young wife to her parents-in-law seriously rivalled that which bound her to her husband.

We stated just now that marriage in Chou times was theoretically monogamous. For the masses this principle has held good down to the present day. Among the ruling classes, on the other hand, through a desire for personal esteem, a relaxation of the rule became more and more the regular custom. Just because marriage was a family affair it was a matter of concern that the bride should not be handed over in isolation to the new family, but should take with her as helpers younger sisters and serving-maids. The number of women included in this way in the marriage contract was calculated in accordance with the rank of the bridegroom. Apart from this, if in the course of marriage the wife bore no children, she could give concubines access to her husband so that the race might be continued. For of all sins against the family the worst was to leave no male descendant to ensure its continuance and thus, through ancestor-worship, to enable the ancestors to keep in touch with the living. But in spite of these accretions, the essential character of monogamy was retained, for the children were all legitimate, and honoured in the first place their father's chief wife as their mother.

The effect of this peculiarity we have just noted—of bringing the several branches of a family together under one roof—was to prevent the evils of a harem system from creeping in so long as the sound morality of ancient days was maintained. Several passages in ancient literature sing the praises of the princesses of the house of Chou, who ministered in all unselfishness to their husbands while living in complete harmony with the sisters who accompanied them. The separation of the women's apartments from the rest of the household—they lay at the back of the courtyard, while those of the men were at the front—made this fairly easy to accomplish without undue constraint.

As upbringing was shared by husband and wife, so the relationship between father and son was that of paternal love on the one side and of filial respect on the other. It is true that here too natural feelings were glorified by custom, but they were not obscured or prejudiced by misguided educational zeal. Here also the principle held good that education cannot be reduced to a number of rules, but that the inspiring influence of the head of the family created an atmosphere to which all the members voluntarily adapted themselves through force of habit.

Further organization within the family system prescribed relations between elder and younger brothers involving affectionate care on the one hand and subordination on the other. In the " great family " it was inevitable that one of the brothers should occasionally assume the headship, and only if authority was unanimously conceded to him could the household be governed in the interests of all. This stress laid on brotherliness is also attributable to a natural senti-ment, which, however, when contrasted with other human tendencies, appears hallowed by morality and custom. The bond of union between the brothers in this " great family " is due to the fact that they all appertain to one father, and it is a sacred duty to hold these family ties high above any conflicting interests which might possibly arise out of the jealousy or quarrels of the brothers' wives coming from other families. In such a case it was a bounden duty to place the blood-tie above sex-relationship.

From the family to the national community is but a step. It is evident that the underlying spirit of the patriarchal family is of a more abstract nature than that of the earth-bound matriarchate, whose relationships (mother and child, wife and property) are all established on immediate realities. Paternity is a matter of trust, and all the duties within the paternal family, while intended to foster natural feelings of attachment between relatives, also aim at raising them to a higher level of obligation through the impelling power of a voluntary morality, when they first acquire religious value.

It was natural, therefore, that by a simple extension of the meaning of this obligation family relations should have their counterpart in the conditions obtaining in the state. When transferred to the prince, the natural attachment of the son to the father becomes the obligation of loyalty, just as paternal care becomes the duty of the prince to protect and intercede for his vassals.

A fifth relationship is still more abstract, and the moral obligation entailed still greater. This is the relation between friends. The constitution of the old confederacies may have accounted for this bond and for its inclusion among the fundamental relations of human society. In the district festivals, with their archery competitions and drinking-bouts and their custom of initiating the adolescent youth into the rank of manhood by presenting him with a man's cap, as well as in the retention of the masked dance to expel evil spirits—which had, it is true, degenerated into a mere masquerade—there exist most evident traces of those olden days. But, apart from this, we find developing out of the bond of friendship a human relationship which, by reason of the free adherence of the individual to the friend of his choice, makes possible a practical activity completing most satisfactorily the arrangements of nature in respect of other social relations.

The powerful influence exerted by the Chou was due in no small degree to the close touch between the rulers and the various classes of the people. It was a clever move when King Wu, immediately after his victory over the tyrant Chou Sin, confirmed some of the administrative conditions while he reorganized others. The liberality he displayed in the distribution of fiefs proclaimed him as a matter of course the feudal lord from whom all legal power emanated. The section on the music of Wu in the *Kia Yü* [1] has the following passage concerning this action of the King :

Have you not heard, then, the words from the pasture-ground ? [2] King Wu, after conquering the house of Yin [Shang] and restoring the good government of former days, before he descended from his chariot invested the descendants of Huang Ti with the territory of Ki and those of the ruler Shun with the territory of Ch'ên. When he had descended from it, he invested the descendants of the ruler of Hia with the territory of Ki [3] and those of the house of Yin with the territory of Sung. He raised a mound over the grave of the Prince Pi Kan and released the Viscount Ki from imprisonment. He sent for the Master of Ceremonies, Shang Yang, and restored him to his former office. The statute labours of the common people were lightened.

When on the homeward journey westward he had crossed the Yellow River, he set free the war-horses on the southern slope of the Hua Shan and dispersed the draught-oxen to pasture in the wilds of the Peach Forest, never to be yoked again. He had the chariots and coats of mail smeared with the blood of cattle and kept in the arsenals, to show that they were not to be used again. He had the shields and spears turned upside down and set on one side, wrapped in tiger-skins. He turned his generals and commanders into feudal princes, and commanded them to seal up the bows and arrows in quivers.

So was it known throughout the kingdom that King Wu would have recourse to weapons no more. Then the army was disbanded, and an archery practice was arranged. In the east shooting took place to the melody of the Wild Cat's Head, in the west to the song of the *k'i-lin*, and the military competitions, in which the archery consisted of piercing the leather targets, ceased. Court robes and gala caps were worn with broad girdles and audience tablets. The heroes with the strength of tigers put off their swords. At the meadow sacrifices the King associated his ancestor Hou Tsi with the Supreme God, and all the people learnt filial piety. He gave audiences, and made tours of inspection, and

[1] See *Kia Yü*, chapter xxxv, 3. The passage also occurs in the *Li Ki*.

[2] Mu Ye, the meadow near the old capital of the Shang dynasty in which the great decisive battle took place between King Wu and the tyrant Chou Sin.

[3] The two territories called Ki in the text are not the same. In Chinese they are written with different characters, but pronounced alike.

the princes knew whom they must serve. He guided the plough in the field set apart for sacrifices, and the people learnt to know their parents. These six things teach the greatest lessons in the world. He feasted the three classes of the aged and the five of the experienced ones in the great college, and the Son of Heaven himself with bared breast wielded the sacrificial knife. He handed them the liquor and waited on them, he held the cups while they rinsed their mouths after eating. He wore the royal cap, and, shield in hand, entered the ranks of the dancers who performed before them. Thus did he leave the feudal princes in a state of brotherly subordination.

In this manner were the regulations of the house of Chou spread far and wide, and the interaction of ceremonies and music established. How comprehensible, then, that the music of Wu has persisted for so long!

It is easy to understand how the kingdom was re-organized. Whereas the central power had hitherto been but loosely defined, and almost entirely dependent on the voluntary moral recognition of the feudal lords, the house of Chou distributed 'all the fiefs personally, and therefore, in spite of all its liberality, nay, by very reason of it, established its own supreme authority. Three principles were followed. The old legitimate dynasties were recognized by granting their descendants the tenure of particular territories. In this way they were drawn into the great sphere of civilization of the new ruling house. On the other hand, this inclusion was in itself a protection to the house against pretenders to the throne from these families, since they owed it feudal allegiance. Apart from the more or less formal recognition of legitimate rights, the claims of kinship were recognized. And not alone these claims: a similar consideration was given to worthy vassals. Relatives and vassals were invested with the most important territories in the empire. This impartial treatment of kinship and merit appeared to be one of the strongest props of the ruling house, and was so, indeed, so long as the central ruler was recognized as the first man in the empire.

The whole system was maintained by a wonderfully adjusted system of ritual. In the same way that the feudal lords were vassals of the sovereign, so was the latter subject to the Lord of Heaven, whom he worshipped in his capacity as Son of Heaven. The Son of Heaven always turned his face to the south when he received the feudal lords as guests. Only at the mysterious ceremony in which he approached the Sovereign on High with sacrifices did he turn to the north in order to express the dependence of all things terrestrial on the ruler of the cosmos. This sacrifice, presented to the Lord of Heaven in the south meadow outside the capital, expressed not only the communion of men with heaven, but also the fellowship of men with one another. Participation in the sacrifice was controlled by strict rules. These sacrifices combined the worship of celestial and terrestrial spirits, of nature, and of ancestors, and thus formed the religious basis of the human society united within the world empire. This great ceremony was the foundation of all morals ; no wonder Confucius declared at a later date that whoso understood the meaning of the Great Sacrifices could grasp the cosmic system as clearly as if it were lying on the palm of his hand.

This sacrifice was, so to speak, the metaphysical kernel of the civilization of Chou. Ceremonial and music were united here. The sacred pantomimic dances performed to the strains of impressive music were, with their mysterious symbolism, expressive of the connexion between the cosmic forces and the life of man. The company of sacrificial participants, the rites followed by them, the invocation, the presentation of the offering, the procession, were all imbued with a supernatural significance, whereby the invisible world was brought into effectual contact with human life at its most sacred spot. The sacrifice made to the Sovereign on High and to the dynastic ancestors, whom King Wên associated with the Supreme Ruler—an innovation which endowed the patriarchal system with its highest sanction— was encompassed by other sacrifices as with a variegated wreath. The right to act as high priest at the sacrifices to the Lord God was likewise the religious prerogative of the sovereign. For he alone was authorized to make the magnificent display worthy of the Sovereign on High. But alike for the feudal lords and the nobility the sacrifice

PLATE 14

Votive tablet of black marble, dated Wei dynasty, T'ien-p'ing (A.D.534–538).
Śakyamuṇi with Kaśyapa and Ananda, accompanied by two Bodhisattvas
and two guardian deities, with lions underneath. (Yi Yüan Collection.)

was the metaphysical act which represented their own supremacy. Each feudal state had its particular deities to which it sacrificed. Each feudal prince had to worship with offerings the deities of the mountains and streams that lay in his territory. Thus the right and duty of sacrifice was graded right away down to the man of the people, who worshipped only his own ancestors. Even ancestor-worship was graded: from the emperor, who had seven ancestral temples, to the duke with five, the marquis with three, and the Minister of State with one, down to the common man, who harboured his ancestors in his own house. The ancestors were divided according to generation. The highest ancestor occupied the most remote temple; the next in order, the bright and the dark ancestors respectively, dwelt alternately in the temples erected in the north and south. When the temples for the distant ancestors were full, the ancestral tablet of the highest ancestor but one was removed at the death of the next ruler. His spirit returned to the general group of family genii, and exercised no further individual influence. In this manner did the successive representatives of future generations replace one another in the temple to the right and left alternately. Only if a ruler had acquired especial merit were both his name (as *tsung*) and that of his highest ancestor (as *tsu*) permitted to remain and be the object of divine worship for the duration of the dynasty. But not only the number of generations to be worshipped, but also the grade of the sacrificial rites was made to correspond to the rank of the living representative of the family. Only the king might sacrifice to his ancestors with royal rites. The other descendants of a king, who enjoyed only princely rank, might sacrifice only with the rites corresponding to their rank. From those times dates the custom that every man is buried with the rites appropriate to his own rank, but is worshipped with the rites appertaining to the rank of his descendants. Thus the ancestors automatically participate in each rise in rank of succeeding generations.

We must not leave this field without devoting a few words at least to the subject of burial rites. Rites regarded as sacramental acts accompanied the whole course of a man's life. From birth, which was surrounded with all sorts of observances, onward to the declaration of manhood, when the youth was capped, while the girls put up their hair, and to the wedding, with its cheerful ceremonies and feasts, every age was encompassed with ritual. The men had their district festivals, with archery and drinking, while veneration was shown to the aged at feasts in the assembly halls. Guests were received and honoured in accordance with fixed rites, visits and gifts were exchanged at definite times—even war was accompanied by specific ceremonies and customs providing it too with a metaphysical background. Nor did ceremonies cease at death. The parting from the dead, the recalling of the soul from the roof of the house,[1] the dressing and encoffining of the body, the fasting, the loud lamenting, the placing of food with the dead, and, finally, when a suitable day had come, the burial and the various degrees of mourning as exhibited in dress, demeanour, and speech—all these were customs which became fixed at an early date.

The original customs of the Chou dynasty connected with the dead are not very easy to ascertain, as later on the Confucian school attached great importance to these particular customs and developed them accordingly. We must assume that in the early days far simpler forms were employed, which merely governed the general procedure in cases of mourning.

All the details contained in the descriptions of the ceremonies, for instance, are but the fruit of a thousand years of minute work on the part of the Confucian school. Thus we find that even the mourning period of three years after a father's death, which afterward became practically the basis of the entire system, was actually unknown to tradition even

[1] There is, of course, no question here of ignorance of the nature of death, as Conrady ("China," in *Ullsteins Weltgeschichte*, p. 496) seems to assume. Men very soon acquired enough experience to know that the dead cannot return. If, indeed, they did reappear, their apparent death was considered contrary to divine law, and they were placed under a ban. Rather have we here a strict religious custom, intended to demonstrate to the dead the sorrow of those left behind.

at the Courts of princes, such as that of T'êng.[1]   External
forms seem, on the whole, to have been simple ; it is almost
certain, for instance, that on the death of a ruler no human
sacrifices were offered, while in later times this practice was
punishable in the state of Ts'in.   The laying-out of tombs
seems likewise to have been quite simple.   It was all a
question of right sentiment.   As certain passages in the
Book of Poetry show, there was a certain quality of freedom
and brightness about these patriarchal customs.   The
memory of the dead was a blessing ; they were held in
remembrance, and perhaps a tree under which they had sat
was tended as a memorial for the future.[2]   Everything was
derived from the principle that the dead should not be a
burden to oppress the living.   At the sacrificial feast given
in their honour the dead were actually present—the ancestors were represented by the grandson, and shared in
the family's rejoicing.   This free association with the dead,
making of the family an organic entity which through the
blessing of ancestors and the piety of descendants was to
endure through time and eternity, we must assume to have
been the idea introduced by the ruling house.   And among
the nobles, too, it naturally continued to spread ever more
widely.

But just as in Greece superstitions in the form of gloomy
underground customs were maintained among the people
side by side with the serene, sunny philosophy of the
Homeric heroes, so here too the overshadowing fear of the
putrefying body, of the ghosts of long ago, continued to be
nursed alongside the patriarchal customs which regarded
the dead as spirits of light conferring blessings and good
fortune on their descendants.   This is the reason for the
peculiar contrasts that still prevail to-day in the Chinese
customs connected with the dead.   The Chinese know the
beneficent spirits, whom they mourn, whom they endeavour
to recall to life within themselves by a meditation period of

---

[1] See Mencius, Book III, chapter ii, for a description of the difficulties en-
countered by Mencius in T'êng when he tried to introduce this custom.   Confucius
met with similar opposition in Ts'i.

[2] Cf. *Shï King*, " Shao Nan," I, ii, 5.

three years, until the son makes the will of his deceased father his own and finally almost conjures up a vision of his father before his eyes. At the same time, however, customs still exist whose aim is to expel the dead, to prevent their return as ghosts, to intimidate them, and deter them from tormenting the living as spectres. An attempt was made later to reconcile these two conceptions by attributing to man two souls: the light, immaterial soul which ascends to heaven and as a divine spirit confers blessings on the worshipping descendant, and the inert, insensible, substantial soul which returns to the earth, and if awakened by some evil force haunts men as a ghost or demon. This attempt at elucidation is naturally of later date. Originally these contradictory customs and ideas existed side by side, no attempt being made to reconcile them; they were at most, perhaps, distinguished according to their acceptance by different strata of the population. There came at last the conception of a life beyond, in which, under the influence of Buddhism—as we may mention here by anticipation— the poor soul had to undergo great torment and must be assisted through the flames of Purgatory by the prayers and good works of the survivors. When this conception was embodied in the worship of the dead an extremely complex picture resulted.

Complete understanding of the overwhelming influence exerted by the Chou dynasty on the civilization of the future would be impossible without taking into account the relations existing between the rulers and the people. These rulers knew how to establish intimate contact with their subjects, satisfied their most deeply felt needs, and were always in sympathy with them. The clemency shown by this family was in marked contrast to the character of the previous dynasties, and was displayed, not only in a humane framing of the penal code, but especially in the consistent attention paid to the needs of the people. The people were, so to speak, the " great family " whose father was the prince. The proto-communist theories of Chinese society are still extant, though less in the form of an established system than as an ideal. Among the popular songs in the *Book of*

Poetry are a number that reveal the familiar relations between the people and their ruler. If a new palace was to be built, a park to be laid out, or any other plan appropriate to a capital to be executed, the people flocked to assist. For these palaces and parks were not regarded as strictly private property. Mencius gives quite a graphic account of King Wên's capacity for sharing enjoyments with his subjects.[1]

Similar conditions applied to the other activities on which the people were employed. Throughout may be found consideration for their own work and for their time. It is more than questionable whether the well system—that is to say, the rotatory distribution among eight families at a time of eight fields situated round a central area comprising the wells, the village, and the State domains—was ever introduced in the manner assumed in the *Ritual* of the Chou dynasty.[2] This picture is probably only a Utopian plan. There seems to be no doubt at all, however, that the peasants as yet enjoyed no rights over landed property, and that they had to surrender one-tenth of their produce, not as a tax, but as the outcome of the work to be performed for the community at large. They were permitted to retain just enough to meet the bare necessities of life for a peasant family. For this very reason it was found possible to raise the rate of taxation later on. No real increase in taxation was introduced, simply a different method of estimating the necessaries of life for these peasant families. Theoretically the proceeds always belonged to the community, or to the prince as its representative. But what counted for so much in the case of the Chou family was the liberality with which it permitted others to share in its benefits. A generosity similar to that displayed in the granting of fiefs was shown in the requisition of the people's services. This was in great part due to the essentially unwarlike character of this family. Nothing calmed the people more than the open disarmament effected after the

[1] See Mencius, Book I, Part I, chapter ii, where the contrast with the prohibitory regulations of the later military state is clearly shown. The difference is that of two distinct periods of civilization : the feudal, patriarchal period proper and the transition to the purely territorial state.

[2] See p. 155 *n.*

conquest of the kingdom. Thus stable conditions were restored, and peace took the place of the perpetual oppression under former dynasties.

Small causes often produce the greatest effects on men's minds, and it was the aid system introduced by the Chou which established their fame for all time. Care for the widows and orphans, the sick and the aged, was something the people could understand, and they never forgot it. Thus the house had the moral support of the people; and the influential classes, elders and heads of families especially, experienced a feeling of solidarity with a ruling house which knew so well how to give visible expression to its sentiments and how to let others share in the blessings which each man coveted.

The figures of King Wên and his two sons, Fa (later King Wu) and Tan (the Duke of Chou), have been preserved as patriarchal models among the people in exactly the same way as those of Abraham, Isaac, and Jacob among the people of Israel. King Wên, who at the time of the last ruler of the Yin dynasty was still a feudal prince, represented for them the man of noble and enduring heart and the embodiment of virtue in the midst of a corrupt generation. The more the tyrant Chou Sin gave vent to his fury and perverse cruelty, the more did men turn to the guardian of right, the Chief of the West, Wên, whose lustre was all the brighter for this dark setting. Two-thirds of the kingdom was under his rule, yet he paid homage to the ruler of the house of Yin. At one time the latter apparently planned to destroy King Wên. His imprisonment is recorded, during which time he occupied himself with elucidating the *Book of Changes*, that mysterious oracular document in which later the whole of the Chinese philosophy of life came to be centred. The *Bamboo Books* show that King Wên was by no means the man of passive endurance portrayed in orthodox tradition, but that he pursued very clear and definite aims with great consistency, and that his house did not acquire the rulership without active and purposeful co-operation on his part. Far more vital to the history of civilization, however, than the policy he pursued is the symbolic image he

PLATE 15

Female equestrian figure in clay from a tomb of the Tʻang period.
(Countess Sierstorpff Collection.)

left behind. This was steadily embellished, until finally, after his death, he was brought into communion with God himself, who conversed with him, ascending with him to heaven and descending with him to earth. Such an apotheosis of a human ruler was unknown in earlier days.

His son Fa, King Wu (which means 'the Military King'), had not his father's greatness. He reaped the ripe harvest and acquired the kingdom for his house. A later legend represents the conquest as the miraculous fulfilment, as it were, of a divine behest. Actually, however, certain traditions relate that terribly bloody battles were necessary to shake the foundations of the old kingdom, and we find accounts of the streams of blood which flowed in those contests. Mencius is confronted with the great difficulty of deciding between the theory demanding a smooth and easy fulfilment of a divine behest and tradition, which recorded sanguinary slaughters.[1] He decided in favour of the theory. Confucius took a still more impartial view. He stated on one occasion that the great musical rites with which King Wu celebrated his victory, although perfectly beautiful, were not perfectly good,[2] leaving a doubt as to whether ' good ' referred to a technical or to a moral point of view. The *Record of Rites*[3] contains a passage indicating that the ceremonies in question gave expression to a wrongful sentiment—namely, hatred of the enemy. There are also certain traditions showing that the actions of King Wu were not approved by all serious men. Thus Po I and Shu Ts'i, the two sons of the Prince of Ku-chu, who had sought refuge at the Court of King Wên, because they held him to be a worthy man, turned openly against him, and preferred a voluntary death to life under the new dynasty. But this betrayal of less ideal motives did not prevent the elevation of King Wu to the throne from being regarded as a fulfilment of the will of heaven.

The most potent factor, however, in the consolidation

---

[1] Mencius gives the *Book of History* as the source, but the passage is no longer there.

[2] See *Lun Yü*, III, 25, where it is contrasted with the Shao music of the ruler Shun, which Confucius pronounces to be perfectly good and perfectly beautiful.

[3] See *Li Ki*, " Yo Ki," XVII, § 16 *et seq.*, and *Kia Yü*.

of the new dynasty was the personality of Duke Tan of Chou, the brother of King Wu. He became the prototype of the loyal minister. Mention has already been made of the conduct by which he upheld the patriarchal right of succession. Already in the lifetime of his brother, King Wu, the story was told how, when the King was seriously ill, the Duke offered his own life to their ancestors as a ransom for his brother, and by this prayer saved him.[1]

After the death of King Wu, Tan carried on the government for King Ch'êng, who was still a minor. He was accused by his own brothers, in league with the descendant of the Yin dynasty who held a fief in Korea, of plotting to usurp the throne. He thereupon withdrew into voluntary exile, and it is during this period that he is reported to have carried on the work of his father, King Wên, on the *Book of Changes*.[2] A famine broke out, and the young King, in the course of a search for suitable expiatory measures which he had instituted in the Imperial archives, came across his uncle's prayer for the life of his father. The Duke's treacherous brothers were branded. A regular campaign was necessary, however, to quell the rising, which was apparently instigated by the old dynasty. The rebels were punished. In place of the last scion of the Yin dynasty, the noble lord of Wei, step-brother of the tyrant Chou Sin, was invested with the territory of Sung.

We must assume the entire administrative organization of the kingdom, which in its principal features remained a pattern for thousands of years, to have been planned by the Duke of Chou; and although the two works known to-day as the *Chou Ritual* and the *Ceremonial Customs* are, as we have already mentioned, certainly not the original works

---

[1] A very interesting point is the connexion between the Supreme Deity, who grants a house his mandate only in accordance with right and merit, and the ancestors, who are besought in times of stress for protection and help. The nature of God in an astral cosmogony is clearly visible here.

[2] The text relating to the individual lines of the hexagrams is attributed to the Duke of Chou and that relating to the hexagrams as a whole to King Wên. There is, in my opinion, no reason to doubt this attribution. The extant collection of sixty-four diagrams, which began with the figure *k'un* ('the receptive'), was certainly rearranged at the beginning of the Chou period. The text contains a number of passages which indicate the transition period between the two dynasties.

penned by the Duke of Chou—if, indeed, he left any written works at all, and was not rather the mere creator of the system itself, which is a moot point [1]—yet the kernel of the institutions recorded in those works is undoubtedly attributable to him.

The following ode from the *Book of Poetry*, containing a prayer by the young King Ch'êng, may serve as an example of the mentality of those times and the peculiar quality of their religious feeling (see *Shï King*, IV, i, 3):

> Let me be reverent, be reverent,
> Even as the way of heaven is evident,
> And its appointment easy is to mar.
>
> Let me not say " It is too high above ";
> Above us and below us doth it move,
> And daily watches wheresoe'er we are.
>
> It is but as a little child I ask,
> Without intelligence to do my task,
> Yet learning, month by month and day by day,
>
> I will hold fast some gleams of knowledge bright;
> Help me to bear my heavy burden right,
> And show me how to walk in wisdom's way.[2]

The whole spirit of the ode shows the close analogy between the state of civilization in China at this date and that of other countries at a similar stage of development—the pre-prophetic religion of Israel, for instance. This prayer is quite in the spirit of the prayer placed in the mouth of Solomon, the young King of Israel.

Examination of these institutions leaves us lost in admiration of the human essence that pervades them. They represent a complete system of human society organized on the basis of an hereditary grading by rank, and resting on the moral authority of the supreme feudal lord, who, as the Son of Heaven, is encircled with a sacred nimbus. But therein lies the inherent weakness of the system. Everything hinged on the magic influence of the sovereign. This

---

[1] The distinction drawn by Confucius between originating and transmitting supplies considerable food for thought in this connexion. See *Lun Yü*, VII, i.

[[2] By Allen Upward, from Legge's prose translation.—TRANSLATOR.]

influence was strengthened by the rich garland of dignities and honours which encompassed him, just as the grading by rank was protected by a similar grading of rights. The honours were merely in the nature of prerogatives in the performance of the religious ceremonies : only the ruler might offer the sacrifice to heaven, have a certain number of ancestral temples, and employ a certain number of dancers at the pantomimic performances, which were, in reality, of a religious nature. Everything depended ultimately, however, on the attitude of the ruler. If he lost his essential worthiness all these forms were but empty shams, devoid of virtue.

There is still another factor to be considered : the common people were not yet raised above the state of bare, plodding existence. The frequent descriptions of the many officers appointed to supervise the teaching of the people and to urge them on by rewards and punishments are apt to give the impression of a state organized on the model of a beehive. But the gulf existing between the people and the class of the Hundred Clans, though it might be concealed by the personal good-will of the sovereign, could not be lawfully bridged. The saying held good that " Ritual does not extend as far down as the people, nor the penal code as far up as the nobility." In times of high moral ideals this signified " *Noblesse oblige*." But when times changed it proved a convenient way for the nobility to evade the penalties which kept the common people in a state of fear and trembling.

Yet another point : knowledge remained the prerogative of the nobility. The higher school was a school for the nobles. The better children of the common people might attend only the county schools. In this way the power which in those times more than in any other lay in knowledge was reserved for the high nobility, who did not, except in case of necessity, surrender the secrets of government and administration, or even of reading and writing. Of the six liberal arts—ceremonies, music, archery, charioteering, mathematics, and writing—only so much was taught in the schools of the people as was essential to daily life. Furthermore, in view of the manner in which ranks were graded from the highest nobility, who held their own fiefs (*kung*, duke, *hou*, marquis, *po*, earl, *tsï*, viscount, *nan*, baron), through the various stages of official-dom, *bourgeoisie*, and peasantry, to the bondsmen and slaves, it is evident what possibilities of oppression existed if the inspiring example of the chief ruler failed to elevate, but allowed things to follow the natural course of routine.

In addition, very serious consequences might attend the inheritance of posts unless the best men were at the head of affairs. There were in the service of the feudal princes statesmen who, although not of the nobility, were a con-siderable asset to their masters by reason of their ability. Such officers were appointed from the earliest times. But their value was only individual. With their death their power ceased. Very different was the case of the noble families, most of whom were related to the princely house of the state and inherited the influential posts.[1] Possi-bilities of massed power were hereby afforded which must undermine the foundations of society if morals became lax.

The Chou had conquered the kingdom in the glow of the new patriarchal idea which they introduced. This idea endowed the house with the power to reorganize Chinese society. So long as this impetus endured, the forces which had created the kingdom could be relied upon. Under several successive rulers the kingdom enjoyed peace and prosperity. Outside, too, tranquillity reigned. Within were enforced the wise and salutary regulations instituted by the founders. The reverse side of the picture was never apparent. The inspiring influence of the chief ruler was, so report runs, so strong that, although penalties were instituted, they never had to be enforced. It was one of those periods in which human-development had attained an equilibrium and which were, unfortunately, always too brief.

---

[1] Thus in Lu, Confucius's native state, great power was enjoyed by the three families of Mêng, Shu, and Ki, which were descended from the junior branches of the family of Duke Huan ; the Tsin state had the six great families of Fan, Chung-hang, Chï, Han, Wei, and Chao. Similar conditions prevailed in other states.

CHAPTER III
THE DECLINE OF THE FEUDAL EMPIRE

THE Chou dynasty did not long maintain its power. As early as King Chao (1052–1002) the story is related how, on account of his ruthless manner of hunting, through which he incurred the displeasure of the people, this king perished in a campaign against the barbarians, having been provided, to cross the river, with a boat which sank midway across the stream. To the name of his successor, King Mu (1001–947), attaches the legend of far travels undertaken in the West. But reports are not sufficiently trustworthy to permit of conclusions being drawn regarding social relations between China and the West in those early days. Apart from a few remarkable animals and some chieftains who brought tribute—the chieftain of the Si Wang Mu,[1] for instance—there were no noticeable results from these journeys. With King Li begins the line of decadent rulers. He employed diviners to trace all those who reviled his government, thereby certainly producing momentary silence, which in 842 B.C., however, eased itself in a rebellion in which the King lost his throne. How precarious the position of the house of Chou must already have been at that time is evident from the fact that a kind of regency had to be established, called in history the period of Kung-ho[2]

---

[1] Si Wang Mu is almost certainly the Chinese transcription of a tribal name. As the characters mean, literally, ' Queen-Mother of the West,' a legend was built up round this figure, and even gave it a companion, Tung Wang Kung (' King-Father of the East '). The authorship of the *Mu T'ien Tsï Chuan*, which describes in detail the travels of the King, and was the forerunner of adventure books, is attributed by Chavannes (*Les Mémoires historiques de Se-ma Ts'ien*, vol. v, pp. 480–489) to Duke Mu of Ts'in.

[2] The dates of this period (841–828) agree in the various historical sources, whereas until this time the *Bamboo Books* have divergent figures. According to Sï-ma Ts'ien, this regency was conducted by the Dukes Chou and Shao, descendants of the dukes of the same names living at the beginning of the dynasty. According

(' General Harmony '). Although a temporary improvement was registered under King Süan (827–782), notably while the influence of the regency still prevailed, things were worse than ever under his son, King Yu (781–771). The latter was completely under the influence of Pao Sï, a lady of the harem, with whom he fell in love on account of her beauty. Whole pieces of valuable silks were destroyed because she liked the sound of tearing silk, and in order to make her smile—after all attempts to do so had failed—the King on his own initiative had all the beacons lighted as a signal for the feudal lords to come to his assistance against the Western barbarians. The appearance of all these armed vassals, and their dumbfounded expressions when they found the call was a hoax, did make the beautiful Pao Sï smile. But this merriment ended sadly. The father of the lawful queen joined hands with the Western barbarians and attacked the King. The beacons were now lighted in vain. Nobody appeared. The enemy took the capital, the beautiful Pao Sï was carried off, and King Yu was killed. Thus was fulfilled a popular belief which had long been presaged by terrifying signs and portents.[1]

The legitimate son of the murdered king was now placed on the throne with the dynastic title of P'ing (770–720). He transferred the seat of government finally to the " Eastern Metropolis " of Lo-yang, in the centre of the kingdom. From this time onward the ruling house ceased to have any importance in itself. It now occupied at most the position of a religious authority, and the territory around the capital was too small to furnish a stronghold for any kind of power. It lay—like the *patrimonium Petri* in the Early Middle Ages—squeezed between mighty territorial states. And although the Court was maintained with all its titles and

to the *Bamboo Books* and Chuang Tsï, on the other hand, a certain Baron Ho of Kung was at the head of the Government. This regency was taken as a model at the time of the Chinese revolution in 1911, and supplied the first name for the new Chinese Republic.

[1] An ode in the *Book of Poetry* mentions an evil omen to the kingdom in the shape of a precisely calculated eclipse of the sun. (See Legge, *Shï King*, p. 320.) This eclipse can be accurately dated. It occurred on August 29, 776 B.C., and is the earliest indisputable astronomical date in Chinese history. It would be going too far, however, to say that authentic Chinese history did not begin until this date.

dignities, the whole thing was but a phantom show. With the transfer in 770 B.C. to the new capital was inaugurated a new epoch in Chinese history : the Western Chou dynasty was succeeded by the Eastern Chou. But the period was known as "the Spring and Autumn period"—that is to say, the period of the rise and decline of the states.[1]

When we begin to search for the social causes of the fall of the house of Chou we are struck by the number of popular risings that occurred during its supremacy. King Chao perished through an act of sabotage on the part of the people, King Li was overthrown by a rebellion, and the death of King Yu was quite plainly due to the intentional passivity of the population in the face of the barbarian menace. The rulers are said to have treated the people with lack of consideration, to have caused much damage to the country by hunting, and to have been cruel and over-bearing. Even of the otherwise good King Süan it is related that he refused to guide the plough personally on the thousand-acre meadow, as the sovereign should do in his capacity as father of the people, and that by way of punishment he was made to lose a battle against the enemy.

All this may be quite correct, but it is not an adequate economic explanation of the collapse. The main cause must be sought in an economic overburdening of the peasant classes in the central territory. The numerous risings are sufficient indication of this. Conditions must be really unbearable before the people will rise in self-defence. The odes in the *Book of Poetry* dating from that period furnish some idea of what was going on in those

---

[1] This period is covered by the brief chronicle called the *Ch'un Ts'iu* (*Spring and Autumn Annals*), which Confucius probably compiled from historical records of the state of Lu. This chronicle contains in a veiled form a criticism by Confucius of the entire history of this period, a kind of universal history in the form of a judgment. He delivered the key to the text orally to his disciples. It is contained in the commentaries *Kung Yang* and *Ku Liang*. But while in these works we have not an historical account, but a text-book of history, pointing a moral, the work by Tso K'iu, which we may take to have been combined with the *Kuo Yü*, and which was afterward, in the Han period, metamorphosed into a commentary on the *Ch'un Ts'iu*, is an historical work which in importance probably has no equal in the literature of those times. Compare, apart from the works cited in the Introduction, the very interesting researches of Professor Karlgren on the text of the *Tso Chuan*.

PLATE 16

Buddhist Arhat imparting instruction. Woodcarving with draperies modelled in coloured plaster over cloth. Sung period. (R. Wilhelm Collection.)

times among the people. Those were warlike days. The barbarians from the north-west, who appear from time to time under the name of the Hien-yün or other appellations reminiscent of the name ' Huns,' were very troublesome, in the west the Jung were always attacking, and in the south tribes not yet regarded as belonging to China were consolidating themselves. Continual campaigns were therefore essential. The people had to bear the total burden of these wars. The picked troops consisted of armoured war-chariots, from which fighting was carried on by means of bows and arrows and long spears. But every chariot was surrounded by a division of foot-soldiers fighting with javelins, short swords, and bows and arrows. The implements of war were brought up in the rear in ox-wagons. The equipment and provisioning of the army was an extremely difficult matter, especially when fighting took place far from home, in the west or south. It was the peasants who had to bear the brunt of all the trouble and cost. The sovereign rulers, unable to maintain sympathetic relations with their feudal vassals, were entirely dependent on their own territory. To add to the troubles, this territory, which was frequently visited by all kinds of natural catastrophes, had now to meet in addition the high costs of the Court of the central ruler, for the tributes from the feudal states were steadily diminishing. The rulers also lacked all conception of the needs of the people. The great hunting expeditions laid waste the land, and the peasants were called upon for additional statute labour. Thus the demands on the agrarian folk were excessive. The original tithe required of them no longer proved sufficient. The greater the calls on the peasants to leave their homes for warring or hunting, the more heavily were they taxed. It was here that the system failed. The central territory was not sufficiently well developed economically to be equal to these burdens. Since the ruling house had removed to the east, it was certainly relieved of the obligation to defend the frontier, but it was also deprived of all possibility of expansion, and was from the outset condemned to a more or less parasitical existence.

The contested territory in the west abandoned by the Chou, which had to be protected against incursions on the part of the Jung as well as of the Hien-yün, was handed over to the family of a horse-dealer which had gradually worked its way up under the *ægis* of the ruling house. The newly established feudal state, upon which the obligation of frontier defence was now formally imposed, was given the name of Ts'in. This state was subsequently destined to unite the steadily disintegrating empire under its rule on a new basis.

The old feudal kingdom had now in effect ceased to exist. The hundreds of greater and smaller feudal states still in existence at the beginning of the Chou dynasty, remnants of the thousands of communities of olden days, had been steadily annexed by more powerful neighbours, a process which continued in the ensuing period. This was undoubtedly an abandonment of principle, but of course the times were to blame. Each prince was endeavouring to establish a Court with all the pomp of a central ruler. The prerogatives of kingship were being steadily usurped. On the other hand, the continuous warfare was depleting the populations, and each prince was therefore intent on acquiring as vast a population as possible, as a basis of power and wealth. In any case, the utmost diminution in the burdens which every Court entailed was in the interests of the population. On the whole, then, we find the people regarding with great equanimity the disappearance of superfluous ruling houses, provided they could hope for some alleviation of their burdens as a result.

Only fourteen states still counted as important in the Spring and Autumn period: (1) Wei, (2) Lu, (3) Ts'ai, (4) Ch'ên, (5) Wu and (6) Yüe, later on absorbed by (7) Ch'u, (8) Sung and (9) Ts'ao, annexed by (10) Ts'i, (11) Yen, (12) Tsin, later on subdivided into Chao, Wei (Liang), and Han, which latter state afterward annexed (13) Chêng, and, lastly, (14) Ts'in, which ultimately swallowed up all the other states.

A few of these states assumed in succession the leadership of the whole empire. It is usual to reckon five such hegemonies: the dukes Huan of Ts'i (685–643), Siang of Sung

(650–637), Wên of Tsin (636–628), Mu of Ts'in (659–621), and Chuang of Ch'u (613–591). This number is misleading, however, and is due merely to the use of the category of five, always employed in this kind of enumeration. In actual fact Duke Huan of Ts'i, together with his able minister Kuan I-wu (or Kuan Chung), first assumed responsibility for the administration of the empire; after him the chief rule was for several generations wielded by the state of Tsin, until finally the outlying states of Ch'u and Ts'in gradually acquired power. But before the state of Ch'u had risen to the height of its power the two states of Wu and Yüe, in the territory of the Lower Yangtse, were exerting considerable influence in the adjacent portions of the kingdom.

The two lords who wielded this supremacy most obviously, and united China into a kind of confederacy of states, were the dukes Huan of Ts'i and Wên of Tsin. Both had remarkable careers, and both figure prominently in the literature of the end of the Chou dynasty.

Within the individual feudal states nearly every change of ruler was accompanied by internal dissension caused by the prevailing harem system, whereby the son of any favourite concubine of a senile sensualist could be placed on the throne. Even the future chief ruler Huan gained his throne only by winning the race for it against his brother. Previously these two had both been obliged to take refuge outside the country. Huan had an able adviser in Pao Shu-ya, his brother an equally valuable confederate in Kuan Chung. In the course of the race Kuan Chung shot an arrow at his master's rival. It struck the clasp of his girdle and did no harm. With immediate presence of mind Pao Shu-ya called to Duke Huan to simulate death. His rivals thereupon slackened their speed, and Huan was able quietly to take possession of the throne. Acting on the advice of his minister Pao Shu-ya, Huan demanded the surrender of Kuan Chung by the people who had assisted him in his flight. He was handed over in chains. His end seemed imminent; but the Duke removed the chains with his own hands and made Kuan his chief minister.

Kuan Chung contributed greatly to the rise of the state of Ts'i. Economic provision was his first care. A financial basis was furnished by monopolies in iron and salt, both of which minerals occurred abundantly in Ts'i. The salt was extracted from salt-pans on the sea-coast, the iron from the very rich ore. In this way the State could acquire large revenues without oppressing the agrarian population. In addition, the iron could also be employed to renovate the armoury. By the introduction of iron parts the war-chariots became superior to the bronze-plated chariots in use. Thus began a form of State capitalism which in those times of barter was naturally a great advantage. Moreover, the Duke and his advisers displayed considerable broad-mindedness. It was no narrow home policy that they practised, but a disinterested national policy. By making sojourn in their own territory as pleasant as possible, and introducing far greater facilities for traffic and trade, they attracted large bodies of immigrants from other states. And as in those days of superfluity of land a large population was a decisive factor in the acquisition of power, the might of the state increased exceedingly. Even the surrounding states could rely on the support of Ts'i in times of great danger. When their north-easterly neighbour, the state of Yen (where Peking lies to-day), was invaded by the Jung moun-taineers, Ts'i came to the rescue, and in a destructive cam-paign over desert and primeval forest annihilated the enemies of civilization. Confucius thought very highly of this deed. "But for Kuan Chung we should now be wearing our garments buttoning on the side and our hair down our backs," he once said when one of his disciples spoke somewhat contemptuously of the opportunist Kuan Chung. Kuan Chung was, of course, primarily a politician in the technical sense—no moralizing theorist such as we find in the school of Lu, but an experienced practical politician. He is the real founder of the political school of thought in Chinese philosophy. The book that passes under his name is in its extant form a forgery. More detailed examination would be required to ascertain whether contains any reliable and authentic material. But Kuan

Chung's aims and his manner of accomplishing them are quite clear. Ku Hung-ming called Kuan Chung the Bismarck of his time. Comparisons of this sort are necessarily misleading. But it would not be far wrong to say that Kuan Chung had the good fortune to administer a state that had all it needed, and by reason thereof could tender his valuable diplomatic services in a disinterested manner.

The federal assemblies held with his assistance by Duke Huan may be regarded in a similar light. He sought to avoid as far as possible a military solution of the differences between the various Chinese states. These federal conferences were to establish the principles of joint action, royal succession, and political intercourse. Chiefly, however, they were to be the means of assembling the individual princes at a common board in order that pending affairs might be settled by negotiation. At these meetings the state of Ts'i naturally took the lead; it had in the background, moreover, the means of assuring the fulfilment of joint resolutions. But no usurpation of kingly rights was implied. On the contrary, Duke Huan's position as federal head had been expressly confirmed by the chief ruler, who also conferred on him the right to inflict punishment on insubordinate vassals. He once even exerted gentle pressure on the sovereign when, as a result of harem intrigues, the latter wished to set aside the heir to the throne, but the Duke of Ts'i begged that he should be sent to the next assembly. The King was obliged to give a grudging consent. The Duke had nevertheless done the royal house a service by this act. The new King honoured the old man in every way, and the latter remained loyal and respectful to the end. All the more remarkable is the fact that Duke Huan was wise and foolish almost in the same breath. So long as he was under the guidance of Kuan Chung he filled his position admirably. It is true that a campaign against the refractory ruler of Ch'u, who had usurped the royal title and made no further pretence to acknowledge his feudality by paying tribute, met with a comparatively meagre result, notwithstanding great preparations. A few words of apology on this ruler's part had to suffice. On the whole it must be acknowledged, however, that Huan faithfully guarded China's freedom and dignity. But from the moment of Kuan Chung's death the old man became a helpless prey to the lowest minions. Among them was a cook who had once killed his own child and served it up to his master, because the prince remarked in jest that he had never yet tasted human flesh. How right was the warning issued against him by the dying Kuan Chung, who said that the man who could bring himself to kill his own child to satisfy his master's whim would certainly not shrink from any infamy that might prove advantageous. Finally the old Duke perished miserably, amid a chaos of intrigues which this cook and a eunuch plotted together. He was immured in his palace and left to die of hunger. After his death his sons and their adherents fought like tigers for the throne. Not a thought was given to the dead man until finally the worms crawled out under the door of the death-chamber. Then he was interred according to the savage custom introduced into China from the barbarian states in the north and the west. Male and female retainers were buried alive in his tomb to be at the disposal of their master in the next life.

These events have been related in rather greater detail because they throw light on conditions in those early times, when heroism and intense cunning, generosity and cruelty, were so closely allied. We can well understand that later on the school of Confucius summarily condemned these times. Ideals were at best employed by the princes as pegs whereon to hang their own aims. Those princes borrowed a semblance of charity to cover their evil deeds. But after a long time a borrowed thing seems almost one's own.

A certain value must nevertheless be placed on these attempts, by means of federal assemblies and joint conferences, to promote general peace and to create, as it were a public opinion in China in order to enforce certain minimum requirements of justice. These were savage times Small value was placed on human life. Brutalities were indulged in, such as that of a noble using an enemy's skul

PLATE 17

Bronze sacrificial vessel in the form of an owl. Chou dynasty (?).
H. 210 mm. (Eumorfopoulos Collection.)

as a cup at drinking orgies. But it would also happen that in true loyalty a vassal laid down his life for his lord or friends went to their death together if Fate so willed it.

Duke Wên of Tsin had many troubles to overcome before he finally acquired the federal throne, left vacant by Duke Huan's untimely end. He had to pass nineteen years abroad, but, supported by the loyalty of his many friends and by the fidelity of the wives he was obliged to marry in his various harbours of refuge, he at last succeeded in reducing his chequered life to some kind of order. He was even less a stickler for convention than Duke Huan. Desiring the sovereign's presence for some reason at one of his assemblies, he simply sent to fetch him. Nevertheless, the state of Tsin, whose dynasty was related to the house of Chou, long exerted a very considerable influence. It owed this power not merely to fortunate economic conditions, but to the fact that, being a border territory, it could expand by annexing the territories of neighbouring barbarian tribes. On the other hand, its predominant civilization was Chinese, and it could therefore pose also as an upholder of civilization and religion.

As power was acquired by those states which in reality were foreign, conditions changed. To begin with, the districts situated along the course of the Yangtse were assuming increasing prominence. In those districts were taking place struggles for supremacy which involved the rest of China. Wu and Yüe, the territories round the estuary of the river, were naturally the first to dispute power with one another, with varying success. Finally, however, it was the centrally situated state of Ch'u, on the Middle Yangtse, which expanded by subjugating Chinese territory just as did Tsin by acquiring foreign lands. The manner in which Ch'u began to exercise its supremacy deprived the house of Chou of even the external semblance of kingship, which Ch'u had long ago usurped. This house now decided that the time had come openly to appropriate the insignia of suzerainty. In 606 B.C. Prince Chuang of Ch'u had undertaken a campaign against the Huns in the north-west. On the homeward journey he passed through the territory of

Chou. There he jokingly inquired how large the nine tripods really were and what they weighed. The bronze cauldrons in question were said to have been cast by Yü, and had been handed down from one dynasty to another. Like the sceptre and crown in Europe, they were emblematic of sovereignty. The ambassador who had come to bring the Prince of Ch'u thanks and greetings from the King of Chou gave a witty reply to this somewhat tactless question, and the matter dropped.

But the trend of circumstances was such that while Ts'in remained the leading power in the centre of the empire, in the south Ch'u was reaching out and forming a rival power. The victim of this pressure was the southern border of the kingdom. Here, on the other hand, we now find the civilization of the Miao tribes, which ages before had been forced back to the south by the Hia tribes, exerting a new influence on Chinese civilization. The political strife between north and south was but the external manifestation of very marked cultural differences, which will be dealt with in greater detail later on.

The state of Ts'in was expanding in the west. For a time, under the rulership of Duke Mu (659–621), it also interested itself in the hegemony of the Chinese federation of states. But it seems soon to have relinquished this policy deliberately and turned all its attention to home affairs, quite indifferent to the fate of the empire, which was being repeatedly laid waste by barbarian inroads. Not until Ts'in had placed its power, by various means, on a very secure basis did this state join in the contest for the heritage of the Chou.

Meanwhile, events pursued their course. As in Italy during the Renaissance period, so at the Courts of China material prosperity and intellectual vigour were habitually united with cold-blooded crime. Never was murder so rife as in those times. The catastrophe which all but wiped out the house of Chao, one of the great families of ministerial rank in Tsin, is perhaps most expressive of the whole atmosphere of those days. Chao Tun served Duke Ling, the nephew of the famous Duke Wên, and the old minister frequently reproached his master with his dissolute life. Various attempts on the part of the Duke to rid himself of the tiresome monitor by assassination miscarried. Chao Tun retired to a safe refuge. The Duke was murdered by one of Chao Tun's relatives, and the latter then returned to the state of Tsin, to remain there till his death.[1] His enemy T'u-an Ku, likewise a very powerful man, now tried to take his revenge and to exterminate the whole Chao family. Only one woman was saved, because she was related to the princely house. In the women's apartments of the new Duke's house she gave birth to a son. On hearing of this, T'u-an Ku had the apartments searched, but because the child did not cry it escaped discovery. Two faithful servants of the house now decided to sacrifice their own lives to save the Chao family. The one hid the heir in his house and gave out that it was his own child. The other took a strange child and fled with it to the mountains. According to a prearranged plan, the first retainer to all appearances now betrayed the fact that his friend had gone into hiding with the heir to the house of Chao. The friend was caught by police spies, and both he and the baby boy were killed. T'u-an Ku had no further suspicions, and the real heir grew up under the guardianship of his fatherly protector. The opportunity at last occurred of acquainting the Duke, who was ill, with the true state of affairs. The abominable T'u-an Ku was put to death, and the heir of the house of Chao was reinstated with every honour. And now, to conclude, the first retainer kills himself, that he may follow into the next life his friend who gave his life for the family, and there inform him of the boy's rescue.[2]

So things went on. Confucius once said that if the feudal princes usurped power, the ministers in the feudal states would soon follow suit, and disorder would then spread from rank to rank. This saying proved all too true. In various

---

[1] Since Chao Tun did not punish his relative for murdering the Duke, Confucius accuses him in the *Ch'un Ts'iu* of killing his master.

[2] This story was worked up during the Mongol period into rather more dramatic form in the well-known tragedy *The Orphan Boy of the House of Chao*. A French translation of it came to Goethe's notice, and may have influenced to a certain extent the composition of the fragment *Elpenor*.

places powerful vassals, relying on a fortified town, openly defied all State authority, and endeavoured to acquire rights over territory on their own initiative. The stability of the old kingdom was finally destroyed in the end by two events : the partition of the state of Tsin and the change of rulership in Ts'i.

In Tsin the three families of Chao (the very family of which we have just been speaking), Wei (whose capital was Liang),[1] and Han had annihilated the other three noble families. In the year 453 B.C. they divided among themselves the state of Tsin, the old ruling house of which had been wiped out in the recent disturbances. The notable point in this proceeding is that not only was this infringement of the old state system generally accepted—for annexations of smaller states by large ones had long been the order of the day—but that in the year 403 B.C. this act was officially confirmed by the King of Chou, who now admitted these three princely families into the family of feudal states.

In Ts'i the family of Ch'ên, who had settled in Ts'i under Duke Huan and changed their name to T'ien, had steadily been acquiring influence. A duke of Ts'i was deposed by the majordomo T'ien Ch'ang and the former's younger brother placed upon the throne. In 410 B.C. the remnants of princely authority were destroyed, and T'ien Ho usurped the dukedom and was officially recognized as duke by the King. The protest raised against the first step taken by the T'ien family—namely, the deposition of Duke Kien—was one of the last political acts of the aged Confucius. But in his native state of Lu he no longer found this regarded as a crime. Times had changed.

The trouble now, however, was not merely that the last remaining walls of the Chou dynasty were crumbling, but something infinitely greater. These events were but the external manifestations of much more far-reaching transformations. The whole ancient system of rank began to

---

[1] This state of Wei, which arose through the partition of the state of Tsin, must not be confused with the other Wei, which was one of the ancient feudal states. They are written in Chinese with quite different characters. In order to distinguish between them we shall call the former after the name of its capital, Liang-wei.

totter. The period of "the Warring States" which now commenced, and which is usually regarded as lasting from 403 to 221 B.C., was a time of continuous warfare between the remaining states. The only ancient Chinese feudal states still in existence were Yen, Wei, and Ts'i, together with the three successor states of Tsin: Chao, Han, and Liang-wei. At this time the chief power was already in the hands of the western state of Ts'in, which gradually withdrew from the confederacy in order to pursue its own policy in the west, and of the southern state of Ch'u, which was continually annexing land to the north and wished to bring the whole of China under its dominion. The wars carried on assumed a more and more sanguinary character, and steadily became wars of annihilation. Gone were the days when even in times of war sworn inter-state agreements safeguarded the trade and traffic of the peaceful population. History becomes a monotonous recital of the destruction of human lives following the capture of a town. Where formerly prisoners of war had their left ears cut off and were then set free, the practice now was to behead them. Especially appalling are the punctilious accounts of hundreds of thousands of decapitated bodies contained in the annals of the Ts'in state. Life had lost all security. Gone was the old pious belief in a God in heaven who looked down on men, protected the virtuous, and punished the wicked. In its place arose on the one hand gross materialism, which, good or bad, strove only for power and wealth, and on the other hand a crude belief in witchcraft, which erected beyond the world of reality a visionary world, to influence which by magic means was everybody's secret aim and endeavour.

In these struggles the old distinctions of rank almost ceased to exist. The princely houses of the many obliterated states were swallowed up among the common people. Hereditary princes could frequently be seen with their feet chopped off, serving as doorkeepers. New classes had risen in the scale, and in some cases families of alien blood and fugitives had climbed to the princely thrones. The princes themselves had lost almost the last remnants of respect for the King as head of the federation of states. The rulers of Ch'u had taken the title of king as early as 740 B.C., and were followed by Ts'i in 378, Liang-wei in 370, Yen and Han in 332, Chao in 329, and Sung simultaneously with Ts'in in 318 B.C.

The old system of rank was not the only thing to collapse. A complete revolution was taking place in economic conditions. Increasing importance had been acquired by the towns, the Courts in which were vying with one another in splendour. Since Confucius had started teaching his disciples privately the fine science of statecraft, hitherto the monopoly of the royal schools, private centres of instruction had sprung up like mushrooms. Not all of them followed such lofty aims as did Confucius in his Lu school. It was in keeping with the spirit of the times that a far higher value was placed on technical sciences with immediate practical utility. Not only were all manner of social theories evolved —those times produced innumerable social Utopias ranging from primitive agrarian communism to systematic, compulsory State control—but the principles of protective policy were mastered. These itinerant scholars moved from Court to Court, and it was considered a point of honour to gather as many of them together as possible. Thus thousands of these scholars were often assembled at the Tsi-hia Academy in the Ts'i state, and the state of Liang-wei sent written requests at various times to wandering scholars to place themselves at the disposal of the prince with advice and new ideas. A well-known representative of these itinerant scholars is the Confucianist Mêng K'o (Mencius), who has graphically described in his works the conversations he held with Prince Hui of Liang-wei. The works of Mencius in particular supply many an interesting glimpse of the innumerable other wandering philosophers, whose competition he did not always find agreeable. These itinerant politicians gave themselves great airs. They always appeared with a large following, and would sail up in dozens of carriages, surrounded by a host of pupils. The cost of entertaining such guests suitably must have been no light burden on the various states.

There is no more interesting tale than that which relates

PLATE 18

Wine vessel (*yu*) of the Chou period, with a large *tʿao-tʿie* mask.
H. 13 cm. (Verburgt Collection.)

how two of these itinerant politicians, Su Ts'in and Chang I, both of them disciples of the same master, Kuei-ku Tsï, the Philosopher of the Demon Gorge, kept the world agog for years with their diametrically opposed theories for amalgamating the states. While Chang I was representing the principles of imperialism at the Court of Ts'in—that is to say, wanted gradually to roll up the whole of the empire from west (Ts'in) to east—Su Ts'in, who had been unsuccessful in Ts'in, was busily advocating federation in several other states. As Ch'u was the principal state to come into question as federal head, federation took the form of a chain of alliances between the states running from south to north.[1] Politics were regarded as a form of sport. The power to manipulate the princes and their states at will was regarded as a subject for boasting.

Unfortunately, the sources at our disposal do not provide us with nearly so clear a picture of the economic and technical transformations in process. A great change had taken place in the military system. The fighting forces had become far more of a regular army. The border states in particular found in their barbarian population very useful auxiliary aid. A transformation in armaments seems also to have occurred at about this time. Whereas even in the military state of Ts'i, where iron was first employed under Kuan Chung, iron parts were at most used in the armouring of war-chariots, in Ch'u iron cutting weapons came into use. The stories found in contemporary literature of the marvellously sharp magic swords of Ch'u show the impression this new style of weapon made at the time. To this period, too, may be assigned the formation of a new body of troops in the north, in the state of Chao. The nucleus of the army had hitherto consisted of war-chariots, surrounded by light-armed foot-forces. In the fights against

---

[1] The imperialist theory—geographically speaking, the west to east federation— was called the *lien-hêng*, or horizontal union, while the federal idea of an alliance between the states running from south to north was called the *ho-tsung*, or perpendicular union. For obvious reasons, the unreliable nature of inter-state politics in those days, when alliances were formed or broken from one day to the next according to the mood of the ruler or the influence of favourites, was bound to result in a final victory for imperialism.

their barbarian neighbours, however, Chao instituted light cavalry, finding it a mobile weapon which many a time proved superior to the unwieldy formations of old. The theoretical study of tactics and strategy was also pursued. Besides a number of famous generals, we come across remains of a military science committed to writing.[1]

Not only is progress made in military technique, but technical science is beginning to be largely applied—for instance, in the rules governing state administration. The personal element is now increasingly overshadowed by mechanical rules. The bureaucracy of Ts'in Shï Huang Ti was not the creation of a moment; his methods were gradually developed in the course of time, and were applied more or less thoroughly in other states as well.

As towns grew in importance, so trade and industry naturally developed. Whereas formerly the large estate owners refrained, as a matter of honour, from industrial competition with the smaller people, a kind of manufacturing scheme was now evolved which, although it could not be labelled industrialism, nevertheless necessitated a considerable working capital, and was dependent upon the employment of cheap labour as the means of producing goods for larger fields of consumption. Trade began to acquire greater importance. It was no mere chance that a great merchant like Lü Pu-wei gradually acquired, through his capital and shrewd use of it, so much power that he became practically omnipotent as chief minister in the state of Ts'in.

Yet another transformation was of vast importance: the racial change in the Chinese people. We have already noted how the people suffered from the continuous warfare that raged in their midst. For, apart from the bloody work accomplished in battle by the sword, we cannot but reflect on the general distress brought about by these wars, as well as on their particular effect on the women and children. Mencius gives in one place a most vivid account of the prevailing

---

[1] Mention should here be made of the many military inventions described in the works of the philosopher Mo Ti. Most of them are weapons of defence against ingenious battering-engines.

136

state of things—how even in good years hunger and want were endemic, while in bad years the ditches of the country-side were filled with starving people ; how families were torn asunder, how father and son, husband and wife, had to part from each other for life, and how hunger and disease steadily accomplished their grim work. Terrible accounts constantly recur of the decimation of whole populations by war and adversity. In the taking of the town of Ch'ang-p'ing alone, after a forty-six days' famine, during which cases of cannibalism occurred among the besieged, four hundred thousand heads were cut off. Very similar figures occur in other instances. Destruction of the Chinese population was accompanied by an ever augmenting immi-gration of foreign elements, the chief of which, apart from the southern tribes of Ch'u, was the Tatars in the north-west. With them were introduced an increasing number of foreign manners and customs. Certain coarse features are definitely un-Chinese. Their origins are often easy to trace. Throughout several generations the princely house of Chao intermarried with foreign women. Small wonder, then, that we find one of its members indulging in the Scythian practice of having a drinking-cup made from the skull of his dead enemy, or that another exchanged the dignified old Chinese robe, with its wide sleeves and sweep-ing folds, for the more comfortable Tatar costume, and substituted short yellow leather boots for the shoes formerly worn.

All these things were signs of a disintegrating world. A new race, which ultimately was to represent Chinese civilization, was welded together out of much bloodshed and misery. Men and their works perished, but the great thoughts which the sages had preserved from antiquity remained. These thoughts were the sacred legacy which, saved from destruction through dark ages by a handful of loyal men, was in the future to prove the seed of new life. The ancient Chinese civilization had crumbled. It met its doom in the intensely imperialistic military state of Ts'in. Out of the ruins, however, new material had sprung, and it shows gross ignorance of facts to assert that everything that happened in China before Han times is of purely zoological interest.[1]

The period of political decline was a time of great fertility in mental development. It was as though the decay which was spreading through the land had liberated an all the more radiant spiritual power. Never again in the history of China do we find in such a short period so prolific a development of highly valuable ideas in all fields, so much free and unbiased searching, so many seeds of creative and effective thought. The clashing of the various civilizations and philosophies existing at that time on Chinese soil produced an awakening of the human consciousness which stands out clearly alongside the other great blossomings of culture sprung from similar clashings of competing civilizations—compare, for instance, the Greek philosophy born in the Ægean, on the borderland between Europe and Asia. It is this spiritual awakening which affords some consolation for the decay of the material envelope of Chinese civilization.

[1] See Spengler, *Der Untergang des Abendlandes*, vol. ii, pp. 58–59.

CHAPTER IV

INTELLECTUAL CURRENTS IN THE TIME
OF THE OLD EMPIRE

THE tremendous changes that occurred in the course of these many centuries in political and economic life, as well as in science, all combined to destroy the old civilization. The causes of these changes lay in the centuries of warfare conducted among the rival states with incredible loss of human life and economic products. No wonder the old naïve religion broke down under such stress. Already in the *Book of Poetry* the crisis is perceptible. The justice of the Lord on High who permits all these terrible things to happen is questioned; but threats are also directed at the great ones of the nation, who were the authors of the people's misery. Popular indignation is continually breaking out, and some prince deposed whose conduct has been particularly bad.

Another phenomenon noticeable is the emergence of private individuals from among the common people as rank ceases to count. In this connexion the following points are of particular interest: the private teaching instituted side by side with State instruction—the school of Confucius was but one of the many well-known schools during these centuries—and the fact that an ever increasing number of prominent personalities from among the people rose to the rank of statesmen, notwithstanding the existence of families whose official rank was inherited.

These schools busied themselves very actively with the needs of the times. They all formulated some kind of plan for assisting humanity, for alleviating the unspeakable suffering which was killing all joy in life, for creating conditions of human society that would render life more bearable. This universal search after truth arose, not merely to satisfy the requirements of the princes, who spared no expense in gathering men of knowledge about them, but chiefly from the needs of the times. It was these conditions that gave Chinese philosophy its specific stamp. It is clear why no time was found to study the objective side of cosmogony, and why all forces were concentrated on solving the practical problem of an ideal state of human society.

The chief schools of philosophy are grouped round three men, all of whom lived in the sixth and fifth centuries B.C.— namely, Confucius (K'ung Tsï), Lao Tsï, and Mo Tsï (Mo Ti).

(1) The *School of Confucius* is known in Chinese history as Ju-kia, the School of the Literati. Its seat was in the north of the empire, in the state of Lu, where the family of the great Duke Tan of Chou reigned and where many traditions of the Chou dynasty still survived. The school of Lu was accordingly an ardent supporter of the civilization of Chou, which it aimed at explaining and establishing more thoroughly. Since it thus modelled itself on the historical past, the preference of this school for scientific methods of historical research is easily to be understood.

Confucius was the most notable scholar of his day. He was indefatigable in the business of learning and teaching, and thus in the search for truth. The records of the school of Lu are the so-called classic writings which according to tradition Confucius edited, and which were interpreted in his spirit. Modern Chinese scholars, however, assign to Confucius a far smaller share in these works and their inception than was formerly attributed to him. The six Classics are : (a) the *Book of History*, (b) the *Book of Poetry*, (c) the *Book of Changes*, (d) the *Spring and Autumn Annals*, (e) the *Record of Rites*, (f) the *Record of Music*.

In regard to the two last named, the ancient forms of these works no longer exist. As already noted, the *Chou Li* (*Chou Ritual*) and the *I Li* (*Book of Ceremonial Customs*) are not as old as they seem. Neither work dates from pre-Confucian or even Confucian times. If permanent collections of customs and ceremonies of the Chou period were already available in Confucius's day—and certain passages of ancient date do point to their existence—they are now lost. The works in question represent the crystallizations of traditions from a later period. Moreover, the collection entitled the *Li Ki* (*Record of Rites*), or at all events its recension, is of still later date, having been made only in the Han period. This collection nevertheless contains much valuable material from earlier times, from which quite a good idea can be formed of the ritualistic teachings of the Confucian school. Confucius was noted for the remarkably high esteem in which he held music. Throughout his life he was interested not only in the theory, but in the practice of this art, which he regarded as all-important for the cultivation of the æsthetic side of human nature. In this art, as in ceremonial, however, his teaching was naturally confined in the main to direct, practical transmission. No records on music from his hand remain ; and even the ancient classical music of tradition which Confucius prized so highly has been almost entirely lost. The *Record of Rites* (*Li Ki*) contains a chapter entitled the " Record of Music " (" Yo Ki "), comprising a number of treatises on the theory of music dating from various times. Especially in regard to music does the great change in Chinese civilization discussed in the last chapter seem to have made itself felt, even in the lifetime of Confucius. He frequently laments the fact that the lascivious airs of Chêng and Wei are supplanting the serious music of the ancients. Time went on. In this very field, so dear to him, Confucius exercised least influence on the future ; for nowhere so much as in music does everything depend on continuity of tradition. Tradition, even when lost for a generation only, cannot be restored.

As regards the *Book of History*, opinions have undergone considerable modification in the course of time. In the accounts of Confucius and his school this book is continually cited as a kind of authoritative canon. It is no longer possible to-day to ascertain whether scattered political records are referred to here, or whether a permanent collection served as a kind of text-book in the Confucian school. This applies equally to the other problem—whether all available records from ancient times were employed, or whether the school of Lu used a selection made on the basis of expert knowledge by authorities on these times. In any case, the work known to-day as the *Book of History* (*Shu King*) was put together long after the time of Confucius, and this also applies to a great part of the records it contains, which were possibly compiled from quotations and other fragments surviving from olden days. There was a time when the *Book of History* was denied all historical value, because the systematized script known as the *Ta Chuan*, or Greater Seal character, which took form about 800 B.C., was held to be actually the first writing in China, doubt therefore being cast on the existence of older written records. Especially since the finding of the oracular bones of considerably earlier date, however, this hypercritical attitude has been abandoned. Chinese writing in all its forms is now known to derive from far earlier days; therefore the existence of written records from ancient times is by no means impossible. Nevertheless, it must not be forgotten that the Chinese works dating from the oldest times were entirely rechronicled after the invention of the Greater Seal character, which in turn was followed, after the old script of Ts'in Shï Huang Ti had been discarded, by a new method of transcription at the beginning of the Han dynasty. Both occasions naturally offered an opportunity for radical textual alterations, although the accuracy of the text was protected by the fact that it was not only read, but handed down orally as well.

The authenticity of the *Book of Poetry* is rather better established. It has suffered less from the ravages of time, and represents to-day, on the whole, the same text that was used for teaching purposes in the school of Lu. The share actually taken by Confucius in the editing of the three hundred or so odes of this book has recently again formed the subject of lively dispute.

The same applies to the *Book of Changes* (*I King*). This was an ancient book of oracles, to the sixty-four diagrams of which a text was appended which may in all probability be assigned to the beginning of the Chou period. This book was also employed in the school of Lu, not only for

PLATE 19

Bronze battleaxe (*wu-ts'i*) used in ceremonial dances. Chou period.
L. 195 mm. (Piek Collection, Bussum.)

purposes of divination, but as a philosophical work, and various passages in ancient literature show that Confucius himself was the first to make use of it, although it did not come to his notice as early as the other works.[1]   This does not imply, of course, that the appendices and commentaries to this book, entitled the " Ten Wings," all sprang from the pen of Confucius.   Many are certainly by another hand ; others, again, are records by disciples, and may be placed on a level with the records contained in the commentaries on the *Spring and Autumn Annals* by Kung-yang.

Although considerable diversity of opinion still exists regarding the extent of Confucius's personal share in the text, it is generally recognized to-day that the compiling of the *Spring and Autumn Annals* dates back to him.

As with other teachers of ancient times, so the literary work of Confucius is very difficult to identify.   Yet the chief points in his teachings have been very faithfully recorded in the *Conversations* (*Lun Yü*), compiled only a few decades after his death.[2]

During the period of the Warring States, the school of Lu boasted two exponents, Mêng K'o (Mencius), a native

---

[1] As against the assertion of Homer H. Dubs, in *T'oung Pao*, Nos. 1 and 2, 1927, we should like to point out that not only is Confucius's share in the *Book of Changes* taken for granted in the *Lun Yü* (vii, 16), but that the following tale from *Lü Shï Ch'un Ts'iu*, which is from a neutral source, and therefore entirely reliable, also assumes that the Master had a hand in the *Book of Changes*: The Master K'ung consulted the oracle, and drew the figure " Grace."   He regarded this as an evil omen.   Tsï Kung said, " But ' Grace' is a favourable sign.   Why should it portend evil ? "   The Master K'ung said, " White is white and black is black, but what can be favourable about ' Grace' ?   Thus, what the noble mind dislikes most is lack of definition in things.   What the world dislikes most is a man who is untrustworthy in his dealings.   Even robbers will not come to terms with an unreliable man, nor thieves have anything to do with him.   Robbers and thieves are great criminals, yet they can find confederates ; how much more does this apply to those who have great things to accomplish.   He who will accomplish great things must so demean himself that the world will be ready to help him ; to this end he must have men who are trustworthy."

[2] In contradistinction to the attitude toward the other Classics, Chinese scholars to-day take a very optimistic view of the *Lun Yü*.   It should not be forgotten that the Lu and Ts'i versions of the *Lun Yü*, which were evidently widely divergent, were not correlated until the Han period, by Chêng Hüan.   In addition, notwithstanding the general reliability of the text, some passages are palpably corrupt, while others undoubtedly originated in later tradition and do not agree with historical fact.

of Tsou (372–289 B.C.), and Sün K'uang (c. 312–230).[1] They held opposite views on many points, but both exerted great influence on the future development of its doctrines. The teaching of Confucius is based on the theory that human society is dependent upon the natural sympathy of men toward one another. This sympathy must primarily find expression within each man's immediate circle, and from there flow out with gradually decreasing intensity to those further removed. Thus its aim is wholly ethical: its goal is the highest good, as is once stated in the *Great Learning* (*Ta Hüe*). The path to this goal lies in the correct definition of names. The theory of the correct definition of names, which may be described as the central doctrine of Confucianism, is based on the notion that the name of a thing is no empty word, but is associated in the world of ideas with some well-defined meaning. Reality evolves out of chaos into cosmos through the very fact that accident causes reality to acquire, by means of the names of things, a fixed association. This theory is applicable not so much to cosmological questions as to concrete human relationships. The names which must be correctly defined are, for instance, those of father and son, husband and wife, prince and minister. Each of these names, if correctly defined, embraces a fixed field of duty, and only he is deserving of a name who is a real embodiment of its relevant duties. Only when the father is really a father and the son really a son are these names correctly applied, and only then may these individuals really enjoy the rights implied in these names.

The sum total of well-defined names, then, comprises a well-defined system of human society in general. And since every member of human society occupies the position corresponding to his name, each has an appropriate sphere of duties and rights within which he enjoys his own personal, inviolable dignity. The rules determining the behaviour proper to these positions are the rites. Neither compulsion nor persuasion is employed to exact their performance. The

---

[1] The works of Mencius are extant in seven volumes, those of Sün K'uang in thirty-two volumes, from which some idea of their teaching can be formed.

notion underlying the rites is that habit, based on free recognition of the justification for the appropriate ceremonies, will automatically ensure their fulfilment. The delimitation of the various degrees of rank in human society, fixed by virtue of an absolute moral authority, ensures the voluntary acquiescence of the individual members of society in their different positions and precludes all question of dispute between high and low.

This basic law for rational organization is centred within the individual and works outward in a graduated system, thus: cultivation of the individual self, organization of the family, administration of the state, pacification of the world. This law of rational organization, which demands of the individual what he expects of others, is the single thread which runs right through the teaching of Confucius.

In short, the aim of this school consists in recognizing as an obligation when transferred to the state that which is natural within the family by virtue of the blood tie. And the means whereby this organization of society is to be effected on a foundation of natural human sympathy is education.

Like all other schools of philosophy in contemporary China, the school of Lu also sought authority in the past. The rulers Yao and Shun in particular (who, by the way, do not appear in the *Book of Poetry* as handed down to us) were set up as models. The question is how far this appeal to antiquity is intrinsically justified. Probably, in the main, it was simply used as a means of finding an authority for the system of rites and ceremonies which had been instituted, for the very nature of a rite implies an authority behind it. Where Confucius is concerned a religious authority was as much beside the question as that of some external force; for both kinds of authority would have spelt destruction to that spirit of pure reverence which was the sole motive Confucius approved for the conduct of the superior man. He was far too sceptical to admit that the metaphysical world, which privately he revered, could exercise a psychological influence on human action, and his mind was much too independent for him to allow that personal decisions might be influenced by the external manifestations of crude force. He was therefore faced by the necessity of producing an authority sufficiently honourable to command esteem, and at the same time sufficiently distant to preclude all discussion or question of bias. Antiquity, with its saints and sages, for whom he felt a personal affection and esteem, represented to his mind this authority. For organized ritual implies an everlasting value conferred by the tradition of inherited culture, which is superior to all fortuitous change.

The scientific-historic element contained in the Confucian doctrines naturally helped to contribute to the spread of rationalism in his school. Investigation into the rites was an agreeable study, and owing to the multitude of external forms the spirit behind them was soon in danger of extinction. One side of his teaching did actually succumb to this danger, and degenerated into a spirit of petty formalism in which form threatened to submerge content. In addition, the bias toward the historical and legal elements imbued this school with a marked conservative flavour. And this was, at all events superficially, the main reason why his doctrines in particular were continually invoked and championed by the representatives of the existing order, so as to give moral support to the divine authority of the ruling classes.

It would nevertheless be wrong to emphasize this particular side of the development of the Lu school at the cost of its other tendencies. Mencius, for example, was an ardent advocate of manly pride in dealing with princes, and went so far as to justify revolution when it was based on moral right. History, too, showed that, apart from the politically tolerated Legists, upright men were always appearing in the School of the Literati who did not refrain, even at personal risk, from criticism of pernicious conditions.

Later on a number of discussions which took place in the Confucian school led to a further development in its ideas. The special question ventilated was whether morality was in conformity with nature. Mencius is the great champion of the theory of the inherent goodness of human nature.

It needs only nurturing and cultivating in order to turn naturally, without external influence, toward good, with the same inevitable tendency that makes water flow downhill. He therefore detests not only compulsory measures, but any utilitarian point of view where obedience to the moral law is concerned.

The slightly later Sün K'uang took a diametrically opposed view. In his eyes man has no natural aptitude for good. He can become righteous only by practising the rules of morality. Morality is not an outcome of the natural development of human nature, but a factitious creation of the saints and sages. Nor is it naturally achieved; it can be brought about only by continuous struggle against the lower instincts. To him, then, that which in emulation of Confucius he calls morality is not very different from that called law by others. It is no mere accident that Han Fei Tsï and Li Sï, two of the best-known exponents of the idea of the jurist state of Ts'in, belonged to his school. In appraising antiquity Sün K'uang also assumes an original standpoint, for he disputes the authority of the saints of dim antiquity and places that of modern sages above it. He values the idea of historic progress above that of the permanent worth of fixed ceremonies.

(2) *The Taoist School.* In addition to the Lu school, which in after days acquired the greatest influence, the Taoist school, especially toward the end of the period under discussion, gained widespread fame. Its chief authorities were Lao Tsï, Yang Chu, and Chuang Tsï. All three were more or less southerners, for which reason this school is rightly regarded as a southern antipodes to the Confucian school. As a school it is nothing like so narrow as that of Lu. We are at a considerable loss for the history of its leading personalities. A strange mixture of fact and fiction was current in comparatively early days, for actual facts are not nearly so highly prized in this school of thought as in the Lu school. Its main object is not the study of a fixed objective tradition, but the inward contemplation of cosmic conditions.

Lao Tsï, properly called Li Tan (Lao Tsï means ' the Old

Master'), was a native of a district which then already belonged to the state of Ch'u. He was an older contemporary of Confucius, and was employed as historiographer at the Court of the King of Chou. In later years he withdrew from public life, and died as a private individual, mourned by a circle of relatives and friends. A small collection of aphorisms, amounting to some five thousand words, subsequently known as the *Tao Tê King*, embodies the principles of his self-contained philosophy. How many of these aphorisms are to be ascribed to Lao Tsï himself, how many are earlier or later, can hardly be determined. In any case, the booklet was extensively quoted at a very early date, and Confucius once mentioned this doctrine as the teaching of the south.

Little reliable information exists regarding Lao Tsï's pupil Yang Chu and another Taoist, Lie Yü-k'ou (Lie Tsï), both of whom must have been more or less contemporary with Confucius. There is certainly a book bearing the name of Lie Yü-k'ou, but to-day it is almost unanimously assigned to a much later date. It is nevertheless based on sources from the period under review, some of which are not available elsewhere, and the doctrines of Yang Chu therein described tally remarkably well with those with which his great adversary, Mencius, upbraids him. Chuang Tsï, probably a slightly younger contemporary of Mencius, also came from the south. He has left a work in thirty-three chapters. These undoubtedly contain many later developments of his teaching. He himself may have been the author of the first seven books and of certain portions of the remainder.

While the doctrines of the Lu school may be classed as cultural, this southern school teaches a philosophy of nature. Its fundamental principle is Tao. This Tao (literally ' the Way ') does not signify, as with Confucius, the way of man, but the spontaneous, that which originates without agency in heaven and on earth. This spontaneity is the first and highest cosmic force. It is all-powerful and supremely good. It is not accidental, but purposeful ; for it embraces invisible and intangible forms—ideas which pass into all

PLATE 20

Bronze bell without clapper. Chou or Han dynasty. H. 310 mm.
(Eumorfopoulos Collection.)

living creatures and are manifested there. The cycle of life is in itself a revolution. Life is the issuing forth; death is the return. Life and death are but phases in the great cosmic life-cycle, which comprises all other entities, as well as man. All is transitional; nothing is eternal except the great principle which evolves all existing things. This transformation of the world of opposites, poles apart, is accomplished with irresistible force. This is right and good so long as it is untroubled by human interference. For in contradistinction to all other beings man enjoys, apart from immediate life, the capacity to name things. These names are the guests of reality. By their employment the empty images of eternally changing things are fixed and held fast, and thus a phantom world is created, the possibility of whose realization provokes dangerous cravings in man. But these cravings result in his entanglement in transitory things, and he is unhappy because he impedes the natural flow of spontaneous events. Therefore: back to nature! Cast off all knowledge and all desire. Let yourself be borne along on the great current of events! Do not live on illusions of the senses, but seek the Great Mother, who abides, eternal and unchanging, in the ever-moving stream.

In Chuang Tsï not only are these thoughts amplified into an actual system of meditation, but he seeks to render them scientifically fertile in order to remedy the one-sidedness of purely discursive intellectual knowledge by a view of life as a unity embracing all opposites.

The practical consequences of this philosophy were of various kinds. It delivered the individual from the woes of life. He let things take their course, and remained an objective onlooker. Resigned to the irresistible force of the workings of fate, he held aloof from the struggles of life. Society he abandoned to its own chaos, and made no attempt to check the wheel of fate by crazy endeavours to improve the world. It is this point which made Mencius such an irreconcilable opponent of Yang Chu. Yang Chu is in his eyes the anarchist who recognizes no authority beyond his own ego. Nor can it be denied that a certain quiescence, a lazy indifference, accompanied the practice of Taoism, especially in weaker natures.

These doctrines affected government too. No attempt must be made to improve or teach the people. Men's desires must not be awakened by knowledge; they must be kept in a state of contented apathy, with strong bones and feeble wills, full bellies and empty minds. State administration became something which functioned mysteriously, with the inexorability of natural laws. The ruler alone might fathom the mechanism of reward and punishment and the design behind its workings.

It is evident that here also lay concealed ideas of which a state with absolute monarchical powers, such as existed then in embryo, could well make use.

(3) *The School of Mo Ti.* Mo Ti, the founder of this school, may have been a younger contemporary of Confucius. Fifty-three books are attributed to him, most of which are of later date, but they nevertheless contain a complete exposition of his doctrines. Very little is known of his life. His school subsequently developed several lines of thought. On the one hand Hui Tsï, a contemporary of Chuang Tsï, represented a logical school which was chiefly concerned with the compatibility and incompatibility of attributes, and was in many ways reminiscent of the Greek Sophists. It also elaborated a system of logic quite worth studying in conjunction with the Indian and Greek systems. Sung Ping, on the other hand, developed Mo Ti's philanthropy in the direction of disarmament. General disarmament and condemnation of wars of aggression were the ideals which he upheld, and which at one time did play a part in the higher diplomacy.[1] The spirit of this school was very different from that of the other two. Sympathy was also its fundamental principle, but in contrast to the Lu school it took no account of the gradations in human affection imposed by relationship. Love for one's fellow-

---

[1] This naturally did not prevent wars from continuing their course until Ts'in had the whole of China under its thumb. It should be mentioned that in the discussions on these problems special stress was laid on the point that the justice of a war was more important than the absolute avoidance of wars in general.

men was to be universal, without respect of persons. The reason for this was that by this school love was regarded not as a natural instinct, but as a religious duty. Obedience to the will of God supplied the motive for universal love. This school was distinguished from Taoism, with its pantheistic tendencies, by its acceptance of a personal deity endowed with sensibility and will. From the standpoint of theism, the doctrine of a mute submission to fate was condemned. The world was governed, not by blind fate, but by the conscious will of God. From the same standpoint this school upheld the doctrine of the existence and activity of spiritual beings. Man was conceived as living on consciously after his death. For this reason the same importance could not be assigned to customs concerning burial and the dead as in Confucianism. The principle governing all these things was that of general utility—hence the commendation of thrift and the inimical attitude toward the arts (*e.g.*, the disapproval of music) which characterized this school.

The whole spirit of this school is one of religious asceticism. Its adherents sacrificed themselves for the world, relinquishing every comfort and every joy. The heads of the school, who succeeded one another in strict order, kept a tight hand over the whole community. As time went on a schism seems to have occurred between the orthodox branch and one with more liberal views. There is a rather sombre and very forceful austerity in this school. Nor did the courageous contempt of death displayed by its adherents, the loyalty and energy with which they devoted themselves to the service of humanity, fail to impress their contemporaries.

But humanity was to them, after all, nothing but a mechanical whole, not an organic growth. Everything in their doctrines is logical, rational, and extremely useful. But in this rational, positivist religion there was no room for the *imponderabilia* of the heart. No wonder, then, that the Confucianist Mencius regarded both Yang Chu, the " anarchist," and Mo Ti, the " communist," as stumbling-blocks. And when Confucianism had won the day, the teachings of Mo Ti were so totally discarded that up to quite recent times he has lived in popular memory merely as a detestable heretic. Certain of his doctrines which were publicly suppressed may possibly have managed to survive surreptitiously in the teachings of the secret sects which have always convulsed society in China from time to time. When Christianity came to China its adversaries did not fail to draw attention to its points of contact with the doctrines of Mo Ti. Modern times have, on the other hand, led to fresh study of the writings of this school, which has already produced very happy results.

(4) In addition to these three schools, all of which display well-marked differences, many others are enumerated, some of which, however, are more in the nature of definite specialist groups. Only one deserves individual mention, because it exercised a marked influence on the course of history and, although it absorbed elements from all three schools, enjoys independent significance. It is the *School of the Legists* (Fa-kia).

The original aim of this school was practical state administration. The following statesmen are noteworthy as initiators of its theories: Kuan Chung, the first politician in Ts'i to take account of the economic side of state rule, and Tsï Ch'an, of the Chêng state, who was rather older than Confucius, and who is said to have drawn up the first detailed legal code. But it was in the state of Ts'in that the real technique of state administration was first evolved. The men concerned were Shang Yang, Han Fei Tsï, and Li Sï. To this school belongs also Wu K'i, the well-known general, who took up his final abode in Ch'u, where he was killed.

The fundamental theory of these Legists was the Taoist principle of inaction. In this connexion the fact that Han Fei Tsï wrote the first commentary on Lao Tsï is not without interest. With these Legists, however, this 'inaction' acquired quite a special shade of meaning. They wished entirely to eliminate the human factor in the government of the state and the administration of the law. *Fiat justitia pereat mundus.* Thus they stand in direct opposition to Confucius and his school. The quite recent rescue of these theorists from oblivion is, on the other hand, by no means accidental. The idea of statute law as framed by them is absolutely modern. In addition, they appreciated the necessity for defining the meaning of the law, for much depended on the definition of the crimes and relevant penalties. Nor should any scope for arbitrary action be permitted. Finally, they emulated not only the perfected system of logic of Mo Ti's adherents, but their idea of equality before the law. Nothing contributed more powerfully to the abolition of the old system of rank than the fact that in administering the law no distinction was drawn between high and low. Even the highest official lived in continual dread, for he could never feel safe from the hand of the law.

The great advantage of this school of thought, which made it acceptable to the people, was the objectivity of its doctrines. This way of administering the law provided a great and universally attainable standard of action, to which all must conform. But the unscrupulous methods it recommended, the Machiavellian way in which the profit of the state was insisted upon as the end justifying all means, endowed its theories with a narrow harshness which finally rendered them intolerable. If these philosophers flattered themselves that by means of this extreme objectivity they could control arbitrary action on the part of a tyrannical ruler, statesmen such as Li Sï were to find out by experience that the sharp and faultless instrument they had created was equally effective when turned against themselves.

A comprehensive survey shows us how rich this period of political decline was in intellectual achievement. The effect of this mental activity was complete demolition of the old, unconscious, direct type of civilization. Everything became increasingly self-conscious. The collective element receded, the individual emerged. This emergence of individualism was so marked that alongside serious scholars we find frivolous Sophists rejoicing in their power to distort good and evil, and able to prove or refute anything by means of impudent rhetoric and dialectic. They were charlatans, of course, but even the most earnest sages worked, consciously or unconsciously, at discarding the old and preparing the new. Confucius himself, deemed such a conservative, is no exception to this rule. He also helped by his example to bear among the people the torch of knowledge, which until then had been zealously guarded by the high nobility, and thus placed it within the reach of all possessed of the necessary mental ability. Confucius's " noble man " is a purely ethical ideal, and no longer applies now to the noble by birth.

Since the natural organic basis for the structure of human society had given way, a new one had to be created. Imperialism, operating by sheer force, came on the scene next, and it was the state of Ts'in which applied it.

THE CHINESE MIDDLE AGES

CHAPTER V

THE UNIFICATION OF THE EMPIRE UNDER
THE TS'IN DYNASTY

WHILE the various states were rending one another in centuries of warfare, in the west was being built up, steadily and quite unnoticed, a new power which, like the Chou state in its day, was destined to make a new epoch in Chinese history. The territory in question was separated from the rest of China by a mountainous rampart. While the other states, therefore, were suffering unspeakably under the ravages of war, in the west comparative peace was being enjoyed at home. In addition, Ts'in had long been practising a steady and considered administrative policy, free from all idealism and aiming only at the intensive exploitation of the resources of its own wealthy area. This state had pressed into its service a succession of notable statesmen, all of whom worked consistently to one end.

In ancient China it was customary for the peasants, who were all bondsmen, to take turns in cultivating for their lords the pastures allotted to them.[1] In Ts'in, however, it was found more advantageous to abolish this institution based on the system of the "great family." It was reserved for the minister Wei Yang (also called Kung-sun Yang,

---

[1] The well-known *tsing-t'ien* method (well system) took its name from the ancient Chinese character for well (井). This symbol represents nine fields, in the central one of which lie the well and the dwellings. The eight outer fields were assigned to a group of eight families, with an annual change. The central plot surrounding the settlement had to be cultivated for the statutory lord. As this central field was rather smaller than the rest, owing to the houses on it, the revenues from it amounted to about one-tenth of the whole. The mathematically exact system described in the *Chou Li* was of course Utopian, and of later date. The idea of joint statute labour and of taking turns in cultivating the fields allotted to the peasants for their own use nevertheless formed the basis of the old agricultural system. As already mentioned above, however, the tithe contribution had long since been exceeded.

Shang Kün, or Shang Yang, *c.* 350 B.C.) to lay the foundations of the new system. The peasants were divided into
groups of five or ten families, responsible for each other,
hence bound to incessant mutual supervision. Families
having more than two male members had either to separate
or to pay double taxes. The number of fields, houses,
servants, and even garments was strictly controlled. Each
family had to live apart. The land was divided into districts
in charge of officials. Every man was liable to lifelong
military service. The law was enforced with inexorable
severity; there were no rewards, only punishments. The
military enjoyed preferential treatment, and all officials bore
arms. Success in war was richly rewarded, failure just as
severely punished.

Thus did the state organization of Ts'in become a faultlessly functioning machine. Clearly there was no longer
any room in this institution for a system of rank. A strong
central power had abolished it. For the rest, it is a noteworthy fact that of the men who assisted in the aggrandize-
ment of Ts'in, not one was able to carry on his work up to
his death. They were usually killed [1]—often in a very

---

[1] Wei Yang came from Wei. He was killed in 338 B.C., at the instance of
King Hui, and his body torn to pieces. Su Ts'in was a native of Lo-yang, in the
central territory. He had to fly from Ts'in, and was executed in Ts'i in 317 B.C.
Chang I, his great adversary in the struggle over the east-to-west and south-to-
north alliances conflict, had to leave the Ts'in state when King Wu succeeded to the
throne in 311 B.C. Wei Jan, whose military career had been particularly brilliant,
came from Ch'u. In 266 B.C. he was banished, with permission to take with him
his immense wealth, but he died of mortification shortly afterward, and his possessions were expropriated. Fan Tsü was a native of Wei. He sent his rival, the
famous general Po K'i, a sword wherewith to commit suicide, but finally he himself
had to make way for a cleverer successor.

Lü Pu-wei, the merchant, father of Ts'in Shï Huang Ti, came from either Han
or Wei. His life is characteristic of the period. He resided as a merchant in
Chao, where he came into touch with I-jên, one of the many illegitimate princes
of Ts'in, who was living as a hostage in Chao. He journeyed to Ts'in, and per-
suaded the principal wife of the crown prince of this state, who was childless, to
adopt his friend I-jên as heir. He then married a beautiful girl, with whom the
heir-apparent to the throne of Ts'in fell in love. She was already *enceinte* when
he handed her over to his friend. There followed in rapid succession the death of
I-jên's grandfather and father, and I-jên became King of Ts'in. His wife had
meanwhile given birth to a son, Ch'êng, afterward to become the Emperor Ts'in
Shï Huang Ti. Lü Pu-wei, the *impresario* of the young King, was appointed chief
minister, an honour which I-jên's son afterward enhanced by conferring on him

PLATE 21

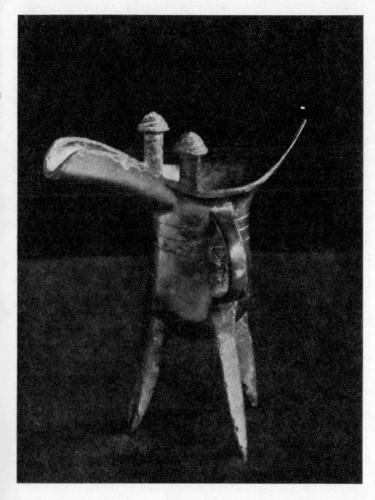

Beaker-shaped libation vessel of bronze (*tsun*), with three legs. Chou period.

horrible manner—if a new prince ascended the throne who as crown prince had conceived a grudge against his father's adviser.

The struggle between the alliances of federalists and of imperialists was a long one. There could be no doubts as to the ultimate issue. To a steel tool of extreme precision was opposed a corrupt mass of crumbling states torn by internecine strife. The action of their rulers, taking counsel of *dilettante* itinerant philosophers, was usually determined by the accident of personal Court intrigue, and while the Ts'in state was relentlessly devouring its way from west to east they still could not forget their petty feuds, and finally were all swallowed up by this Moloch.

Ts'in Shï Huang Ti adopted in dealing with the Chinese territories he subjugated a course similar to that he had formerly pursued when abolishing hereditary nobility in his native state; they were annexed and formed into provinces and districts. The feudal system was ended. The empire was divided after its conquest into thirty-six provinces, to which four more were added later. In this way was initiated the provincial system which has endured down to

the title of 'Second Father.' This was a recognized title of honour, but advantage was soon taken of the humour of the situation by the numerous adversaries of Ts'in Shï Huang Ti. Lü Pu-wei had literary as well as commercial aspirations. He assembled a band of scholars, who compiled for him, in emulation of Confucius, a work entitled *The Spring and Autumn of Lü Pu-wei*. This work is an invaluable source of information relating to the state of science and culture in that transition period. Even this talented organizer, however, who was probably the first man in history to make a kingly throne the speculative aim of a limited liability company, could not escape the fate of a minister of Ts'in. Accused of secret intrigue with his former wife, he was banished first to one place, then another. He decided to evade further consequences by poisoning himself.

The famous Li Sï, whose native state was Ch'u, first formed part of Lü Pu-wei's ministry, then succeeded him as Prime Minister. Han Fei Tsï, of the Han state, likewise had prospects of employment in the service of Ts'in, but he was suddenly thrown into prison, and poison was sent to him by his friend Li Sï. But the latter also died an unnatural death. Just before the downfall of the dynasty he was executed in a most horrible manner by the petty-minded successor of the great Ts'in Shï Huang Ti, who was under the sway of intriguers.

It is the irony of fate that this soulless state system, functioning with the deadly accuracy of a machine, should finally have gripped and destroyed its own creators. This system was cold and inhuman. It was necessarily successful, but the success continued to function mechanically when there was no longer any human impulse behind it.

this day, subject only to modifications in the size and method of division of the provinces. And the principle of continually transferring officials in order to preclude all possibility of personal relationship between the officers and their administrative areas is already to be found. Everything was sacrificed to the concentration of power in the central Government. So the union of Chinese states was established, and a complete revolution in former conditions effected, the chief visible signs of which were as follows :

(1) *Change in the Title of the Ruler.* The preceding historic dynasties had employed the designation *wang* (' king ') as the title of the chief ruler. In a religious connexion he was also called Son of Heaven (T'ien Tsï). The names ' august rulers' (Huang) or ' gods ' (Ti) given to the mythical rulers were not relevant here. The latter were worshipped in the capacity of superhuman beings and enlightened prototypes, and were shrouded in a twilight of what was practically religious worship. We have seen how the title of king was gradually usurped by other rulers, who thereby removed their territories from the general federation of states. This proceeding was not unlike that witnessed in the Holy Roman Empire. The rulers enhanced the halo of authority and ceremonial with which they surrounded their dignity. The barbarian rites introduced in Chao, for example, all tended in this direction. Nothing, however, could prejudice the ancient custom whereby every ruler had to submit, when he died, to the judgment of history. He acquired a temple name, and in this name was embodied the judgment on his character and his rule. Superficially most of these names ring magnificently, but to the initiated they bore very distinct shades of meaning. Duke " Ling " certainly implied a worthy prince, a divine being, but the licentious princes were similarly named. Designations such as Li (' the Terrible') or Yu (' the Gloomy') occurred rarely, but they were not rejected if they were considered appropriate to the characters of the deceased princes.

After the subjugation of the empire all this was changed. First, a title was devised for the ruler which was a combina-

tion of the mythical title Huang ('august') and Ti (*divus*)
—namely, Huang Ti. This corresponds precisely to the
Roman *Divus Augustus*; and if it is misleading to translate
the word *wang* by emperor or *imperator*, these names nevertheless exactly express the new title. The ruler was now
imperator. Similarly, new expressions were coined for Imperial decrees or edicts, and a special personal appellation,
Chên, which corresponds to the royal plural, was introduced
for the emperor. In addition, the former method of conferring a temple name was abolished, as it was disrespectful
for a son to sit in judgment on his father, or an officer on
his lord, after his death. In lieu of this, the future emperor
was simply to be known by the number of his place in the
Imperial line, " beginning with the First Emperor, even
down to the ten thousandth generation." The ruler himself assumed the title Ts'in Shï Huang Ti, 'the First
Emperor of Ts'in.'

It is true that this innovation, which also affords evidence
of the new spirit prevailing, was not lasting. The Ts'in
dynasty did not extend to ten thousand rulers, but came to
a deplorable end with the second Ts'in emperor.[1]

(2) *The Organization of Officials*. Out of the feudal
system had sprung a bureaucratic state, based on a separation of administrative functions, with an especially sharp
distinction between the civil and the military. Only in the
person of the emperor were both united. At the head of
the Government was a Prime Minister (*ch'êng siang*), concerned only with government—that is to say, with administrative matters. Quite independent of him, a general
(*t'ai wei*) had control over the army, and had no say in
internal administration or government. There were in
addition—again quite an independent body—the censors

---

[1] While the dynastic title remained Huang Ti, a modified temple name was
reintroduced later on. Under the Han dynasty rulers adopted the custom of
designating the period by specific names, which have been misinterpreted, especially
in European works, as the names of the individual rulers. Thus we read of the
Emperor K'ien-lung or Tao-kuang, but the former is merely the reign title
'Blessing of the Creative,' the latter the reign title 'Light of the Way,' which
names two rulers of the last dynasty had adopted. At first rulers used to change
these titles in the course of the reign, but as time went on it became the usual
practice to assign one title to each reign period.

(*yü shï*), whose sole duty it was to control the officials. Furthermore, as regards local officials in the provinces, the three offices of the Government, the supreme military command, and the inspectorate were strictly defined. Even the different districts boasted a civil and a military officer. For further safety all officials, right down to the district magistrates, were directly appointed by the emperor, so that this system of bureaucracy formed an excellent tool for an absolute, centralized monarchy.

(3) *A Consolidated State.* In the period of the Warring States all institutions and customs had shown an increasing tendency to develop independently. The agricultural unit of measure, the wagon gauge, laws, clothing, language, and even the writing [1] were all different in different parts of the empire.

After Ts'in had subjugated the rest of China everything was made uniform. The underlying notion was that military conquest would become effective only when the old customs and ceremonies were abolished and a new set of ideas formulated. Li Sï, the Prime Minister, was the chief exponent of this doctrine. Li Sï is usually represented in Chinese history as the evil genius who goaded on Ts'in Shï Huang Ti to the Herostratic endeavour to destroy the ancient civilization from top to bottom. The chief reason for this is that he had incurred the enmity of one wing of the Lu school—the very wing which afterward gained ascendancy—and therefore its successors laid the blame for all the mischief at his door. He was reproached more especially with the " Burning of the Books " and the murder of the *literati*. There is no doubt that the burning of the books was correctly imputed. The new Government measures were severely attacked by the Confucian opponents of Li Sï.

[1] The greatest divergences in language were in the southern states. Mencius calls the southerners "barbarians," tongue-twisters ; and at the time of the Wu kingdom political considerations necessitated the restriction of conquests to the Yangtse districts, for where the languages were analogous subjugated districts could be assimilated, but in the north such districts always remained alien. Although variations in script were not startling, there were nevertheless considerable differences, not only in the characters, but chiefly in the styles of writing. Karlgren the Swedish authority, has cleverly based his higher criticism on these linguistic variations in the old texts.

who invariably based their criticism on the sacred authority of the ancient writings. Li Sï therefore decided on a bold step, and ordered the expurgation from historical literature of all matter not dealing with the history of the Ts'in state. This involved a great part of Confucian literature—namely, the *Book of History*, the *Book of Poetry*, and the *Spring and Autumn Annals*. These works were not to be utterly destroyed, but to be preserved in the custody of the central Government. The copies in circulation among the people, however, were to be consigned to the flames. Yet another thing : any person desiring access to the works kept in the Imperial Library had to make application to authorized functionaries. The idea underlying this decree was no other than to counteract the movement introduced by Confucius for placing education in the hands of private teachers. For these private educational centres were homes of free-thought, from which criticism and judgment were always to be feared. It was no casual description applied to Confucius at a later date when he was given the name, based on a legend, of the ' throneless king ' who was to represent the descendants of the Chou dynasty. Two different worlds were in conflict here. The one possessed the power of State authority, an authority, moreover, having at its disposal all the contrivances of a faultlessly functioning machine. The other possessed intellectual power. The State desired to control education. Man's mentality was to be brought into harmony with externals. A strict system of censorship was introduced which did not content itself with combating open resistance, but sometimes even acted as an *agent provocateur*. This aroused the opposition of the other school of thought, and led to repeated conflict. The murdering of the *literati*, of which Ts'in Shï Huang Ti is also accused, has really no connexion with these matters. It was a question of a crowd of Court magicians who had made themselves unpopular. Ts'in Shï Huang Ti always had people of this sort around him, recruited mainly in the vicinity of Shantung, where sea and mountains meet. He was a highly superstitious man, and his mind was much occupied with the legends concerning the Isles of the

Blest, said to lie far out in the ocean.[1] But he did not allow these fantastic ideas to govern him entirely. When their exponents became a nuisance he never hesitated to have them destroyed. New ones could always be found.

It should not be forgotten that as a matter of fact the school of thought represented by the all-powerful Li Sï originated with Confucius. Li Sï was an actual pupil of Sün K'uang; but the doctrines of this school were not those of Mencius. A great deal of the uniformity in cultural institutions effected in the Ts'in period is nevertheless derived from Confucian thought. Confucius propounded the theory that cultural institutions might be created only by men who combined intellect with authority. Intellect was necessary to make the institutions sound, authority to ensure their uniform establishment. To Confucius the uniformity of cultural institutions was of supreme importance, for only on a foundation of uniformity could fixed moral observances be established.

This standardization was carried into every phase of life. A uniform system of weights and measures was most strictly enforced throughout the empire; implements were standardized; even wagons must have uniform gauges. Li Sï likewise introduced a new script. Although the system of the Greater Seal script had been generally accepted ever since its invention in 820 B.C. by the scribe Chou, different forms of script were evolved, as time went on, in the various states. Li Sï selected eight of these different systems and assigned them to the various classes of literature. This reform in writing was continued in the Han period, and is, in essentials, the basis of the Chinese script of to-day. This transformation of the script very greatly affected the whole of Chinese intellectual life, for when the old writings,

[1] These legends, which later on were incorporated into Taoist lore, bear quite distinct traces of Indian influence. The philosopher Tsou Yen (c. 336–280 B.C.) was a native of Ts'i. In contradistinction to the other philosophers, he evolved cosmic theories, of which that relating to the five elements is especially reminiscent of Indian cosmogony. The *Shan Hai King*, a fantastic geographical work, is frequently ascribed to him. As we shall show further on, these influences afterward became very widespread.

PLATE 22

Bronze mirror showing the Queen-Mother of the West and the King-Father of the East, together with celestial animals, inscription, and ornament. Han period. (R.Wilhelm Collection.)

the study of which had been prohibited by Tsʻin Shï Huang
Ti, came to light again, the script in which they were
written was no longer plainly decipherable. They had
to be transcribed in the new script, in the process of
which textual alterations crept in as a matter of course.
The break in the continuity of the Chinese script was thus
accentuated. The newly discovered works of antiquity
had to be transcribed and fresh explanations of them
furnished, for the old traditions were lost. There is, indeed, no disputing the fact that the Confucianism of Han
times represented something entirely different from the
original Confucianism. The Tsʻin period intervened with
dire effect.

(4) *The Great Wall.* Report credits Tsʻin Shï Huang Ti
with the building of the Great Wall in the north of China.
The expression " Chinese wall " has become a household
word signifying the artificial barring of the progress of
human civilization. Actually, very different issues were at
stake. Already in the period of the Warring States, when
wars had become chronic, the expedient was gradually being
employed of securing frontiers by means of a chain of
fortified posts. Walls resembling the Roman *limes* thus
came into existence. When Tsʻin had consolidated the
state, these walls were naturally abandoned as unnecessary.
On the other hand, as the border territories grew in strength
and their population in numbers, far more active endeavour
was made in China to keep out the barbarians. The old
tribal names, I, Ti, Jung, and Man, were originally applied
by the inhabitants of the ' Middle Kingdom ' to the border
territories. Tsʻin in the west, Chʻu in the south, Wu and
Yüe in the south-east, were regarded as barbarian states.
After they had little by little improved their conditions of
civilization, and these civilizations had been merged into
the Chinese, ancestors and progenitors were gradually
traced by means of whom kinship was established between
the inhabitants of these territories and the ancestors of the
Chinese. The lengthening of Chinese tradition in an
upward direction, which may be observed to an ever
increasing extent, was largely due to the way in which the

newly discovered progenitors were simply placed behind those that were already known and recognized. The designation ' barbarian ' was now applied to tribes farther beyond the frontiers. And, indeed, there were no more incursions of barbarian tribes in the south. But the northern and western steppes remained the centres from which, throughout the history of China, fresh invasions have periodically been made. Of the former states, those of Tsin in the north-west and Yen in the north-east were particularly exposed to these invasions. The comprehensive name for the northern tribes was Hu, for the western tribes Jung. Continuous warfare was necessary to hold them in check. In the course of this warfare the Chao state built in the north-west a fortified wall which formed the nucleus of the Great Wall of later days. The Yen state erected a similar *limes* in the east. The territories taken from the foreign tribes and situated within these walls were then annexed to the states in question.

At the time of the rise of Ts'in a people called the Hiung-nu [1] likewise gained ascendancy in the north, and after subjugating the other tribes finally occupied the entire northern frontier line of China, from Korea in the east to Kansu in the west. Ts'in Shï Huang Ti was well aware of this imminent danger. In the year 215 B.C. he dispatched the Commander-in-Chief Mêng T'ien northward with three hundred thousand men. The land lying within the great northern loop of the Yellow River was conquered, and advantage was taken of the existing wall fortifications to build a connected *limes* right along this northern frontier. This is the famous " wall ten thousand *li* in length." [2]

The real utility of this wall, as of the Roman *limes*, may well be questioned. It was doubtless a valuable bulwark which in times of strong government furnished support to

---

[1] They were already known in earlier days as the Hün-yü and under other names, and are usually identified with the Huns.

[2] The present remains in the north of China known as the Great Wall are of far later date. Owing to repeated conquests by the Huns the old wall gradually fell into decay without anyone troubling much about it. The project was not resumed until the T'ang period, and work on the wall was still going on in Ming times.

the frontier outposts in the north. But the pressure which drove men from the north toward the Chinese plain was too powerful to be resisted by mortal means, for it was the outcome of a politico-geographic situation. The comparatively primitive tribes of the bare, northerly highland steppes found in the well-cultivated and flourishing plains at the foot of their mountains a natural inducement to descend. This descent could sometimes be checked, but never permanently stopped.

During the struggles which took place after the downfall of the Ts'in dynasty we very soon see what a new menace the Hiung-nu constituted. Their chieftain Maotun was an adversary, on equal terms, of the Emperor Kao Ti, of the Han dynasty. Not only did the latter incur great risks in his attempt to drive back the Hiung-nu—the Chinese had to bribe this Khan's wife with gifts to influence her husband—but under the rule of his consort and successor, the Empress Lü, nothing remained but to give the Hun prince a royal princess as wife, in order to gain his friendship. Although later in the Han dynasty the Hiung-nu were repulsed for a time, such checks were never more than temporary.

When all is said and done, the Great Wall, this miracle of human will-power, erected with such blood and tears, is but the deplorable testimony of unceasing warfare. Like everything undertaken by Ts'in Shï Huang Ti, it is the monument of a colossal human will. This will achieved much, because it responded in many ways to the needs of the time. In this connexion may be mentioned his measures for the unification of China, which had long been ripe for an undertaking of this nature by reason of an internal exchange of culture. Other actions of his worked as a ferment, and influenced, but did not determine, events. Other plans, again—possibly those which lay nearest his heart, such as the establishment of his family as a permanent dynasty—came to a ludicrous end as soon as he had quitted the scene. And the curses of generations followed him. For though many of the individual acts for which he was blamed may have been unjustly imputed to him, yet in the unscrupulousness and cruelty which characterized him and which stained his path with blood lies the true cause of the hatred he excited. He does not rank among the creators of civilization, but among those demonic natures who are permitted to destroy old worlds in order to pave the way for those who come after.

CHAPTER VI

THE NATIONAL MONARCHY OF THE HAN
206 B.C.–A.D. 220

I. Form of Government and Administration

THE drastic procedure of the Tsʻin dynasty in matters of state administration necessarily aroused dissatisfaction, because the measures tending to unification formed but a part of the whole relentless mechanism of this form of government. Regional tendencies could not be suppressed at one blow. In addition, the cruelty of the new system had earned it a bad name. It is easy to understand, therefore, why the warfare which accompanied the sudden downfall of Tsʻin was fought under other flags. The theory of the day was that the world could not be the private property of one person. No wonder the romanticist Hiang Tsi, who in fighting for the kingdom of Chʻu he had consolidated displayed many fine ideals as well as harshness and cruelty, drew up a fresh programme of feudalism to win public opinion. We see here a resurrection of the federalist ideals. He organized an empire with an Imperial state (which was scarcely more than a phantasmagoria), a hegemonic state (over which he assumed control), and eighteen kingly states (which he distributed as fiefs).

The system was obsolete long before it had been tested thoroughly. But the idea of the distribution of power held certain attractions. The generosity with which King Wu of the Chou dynasty had allocated his fiefs was still regarded as an ideal pattern, and greatly influenced events in the immediate future. In the warfare that ensued victory fell, not to the romanticist Hiang Tsi, but to the crafty, tenacious, and unsentimental peasant Liu Pang, who first appeared as Duke of Pʻei, then, after the defeat of his rivals, as the first Han emperor. This man recognized the necessity for making concessions to public opinion, for he had a very keen practical sense. So he invested all his friends and partisans with territories without disturbing the plan on which the land was already divided and the officials organized. The two systems existed side by side. But he laid special emphasis on the necessity for maintaining reliable officials. The feudal states were really only an ornament. He kept a sharp eye on them, and on the slightest provocation handled them with iron severity. On one pretext or another each of his vassals in turn was deposed and extirpated. They nearly all learnt to expect it. The recovered territories were assigned to princes of the house of Han. In this way it was hoped to avoid the embarrassments arising out of the distribution of power and to secure perpetual supremacy for the house of Han. Vain endeavour! His own wife wielded the rulership with untiring energy as the Empress Lü, and with complete unscrupulousness wrought havoc among the Han princes. The system of a balance of power also proved a failure in other ways. For even the relatives soon became quarrelsome on questions of supremacy. Security seemed possible only by means of most rigid control. The feudal tenures finally became nothing but a formality. The princes invested with states remained in residence at the Court of the capital and enjoyed only the title of king. This title had long since been robbed of its ancient significance, and now meant nothing better than prince.

As the sphere of authority of the Han extended, a division of the empire into provinces was effected. At first, provinces (103) and feudal states (241) existed simultaneously, and were all subdivided into districts, which totalled 1314. The border territories were called *tao* (chief prefectures). Subsequently the whole empire was divided into thirteen provinces, subdivided into chief prefectures and districts. This was the beginning of the three-grade administrative system of China (province, prefecture, district).

Conditions on the land remained much the same as before, except that statute labour was lightened. Under the house of Ts'in it had entailed a very heavy burden, as work on the Great Wall and the Imperial palaces and mausoleums was continuous. But the relief did not last long. Various inventions and improvements connected with agriculture are mentioned in this period—for instance, the triennial rotatory system for crops.

Generally speaking, however, agricultural land soon assumed secondary importance, for the Han also speedily devoted themselves to urban civilization. As the Ts'in capital with its gorgeous palaces and libraries had gone up in flames during the struggles for supremacy—a catastrophe which contributed in far greater degree to the destruction of ancient literature than did the "Burning of the Books" under Ts'in Shï Huang Ti—the founder of the house of Han started to build a new capital at Ch'ang-an (quite close to the old capital, Hien-yang). The centralization of government accounted for the supreme importance acquired by this capital, as the official machinery for the entire empire had its mainspring there.

The extension of the monetary system was due to the spread of urban civilization and the rapid development of trade which characterized the Han period. We learn of the minting of various coins in the early days of this dynasty. Under the Ts'in dynasty gold had been the standard metal for larger amounts and an alloy of tin and copper for smaller ones. The basis of the currency was its actual metallic value. No State monopoly for minting existed while the currency remained a mere token of weight. Until quite recent times silver was dealt with like this. The minting firms marked the ingots they smelted and refined with a stamp that was a kind of guarantee for which the firm had to answer. A different situation arose when the Government, in view of the metal shortage, issued a forced currency. In the year 119 B.C. the Emperor Wu Ti had already experienced the necessity for having various coins of this nature minted. They were an alloy of silver and tin. The largest were circular, with a hole in the centre and a dragon as mint-mark, and weighed 8 *liang*, or ounces.[1] The medium-sized ones were square, were stamped with a horse, and weighed 6 ounces. The smallest were oval, bore a

[1] See H. Cordier, *Histoire générale de la Chine*, vol. i, p. 239.

tortoise as mark, and weighed 4 ounces. Naturally counterfeiters in great numbers took advantage of these conditions, inflation soon ensued, and the issue of these coins had to be stopped. Their place was taken by pieces of leather a foot long made from the skin of the white deer bred in the Imperial parks. These were in all likelihood the oldest forerunners of paper money. They bore a considerable fixed value. The expedient was employed of enjoining all the grandees who wished to appear at Court to obtain these squares, nobody being received in audience unless he presented ' currency ' of this kind.

Before entering into the economic consequences of the geographic expansion of the empire we must cast a glance at the intellectual side of Han civilization.

II. INTELLECTUAL CONDITIONS IN THE HAN PERIOD

(a) The Magicians

Owing to the intermingling of the various external influences, the mentality of the time had become far more primitive than it was at the end of the Chou period. The intellectual days of doubt and sophistry were succeeded by a time of wholesale belief in miracles. Weariness had come over the world. Attempts to set it in order by intellectual means had failed, and people now yearned for something beyond the senses and lent a ready ear to the words of magicians and sorcerers. The effects of this tendency were visible as early as the days of Ts'in Shï Huang Ti. In the Han dynasty they grew even more marked. World-weariness had reached its zenith. Some of the national odes of the Han period rank among the most melancholy in all literature. Ere this Yang Chu had laid stress on the vanity of earthly things ; but although his sentiment was that everything was futile, he found an escape in a liberty of mind that permitted him to assume toward his own actions and those of others the standpoint of an objective onlooker and to let things take their course unconcernedly.

This standpoint can of course be adopted only by individuals. No such lofty attitude can be assumed by entire

PLATE 23

Jade ring with two dragons and a phœnix. Used by the Empress in the
sacrifices to heaven. T'ang period. (R. Wilhelm Collection.)

communities.   Another fresh factor was the penetration of influences from the border states in the south, producing a remarkable revival in mythology.   The famous poem by K'ü Yüan, *Falling into Trouble*, opens up a new world.   The atmosphere is densely packed with spirits and gods—no longer just nameless forces, which even Confucianism recognized, but individual beings endowed with consciousness and will, who live and move behind the scenes.   It is difficult to estimate the extent of Indian influence in those early days.   Many things point to its existence, but detailed research is called for in this field.

These religious-mythological ideas were exploited by the ranks of the *fang shï* (magicians), who played an important part in Court life, since more than one emperor hoped to solve with their help the problems of transmuting gold and achieving immortality.   These magicians seized upon and interpreted in their own light the old natural religion of China.   They appropriated Taoism in the same way, for the metaphors and personifications of Chuang Tsï afforded numerous points of contact.   Needless to say, however, they completely transformed and mythologized Taoism. But the connexion proved lasting.   The Taoist philosophers, from Lao Tsï to Chuang Tsï, became the founders and sages of this popular religion, and the magic necromancy of the *fang shï* was amalgamated with their doctrines.   In this way was initiated a preliminary stage of the Taoist religion, which later on, by assuming Buddhist forms of organization, acquired the stability essential to a religious sect.   It is worthy of note that one of the paladins of the founder of the Han dynasty was subsequently honoured in Taoism as the progenitor of the 'Celestial Preceptors' (*T'ien Shï*), who formed a kind of Papal succession in Taoism.

(b) Confucianism

This magical form of religion discovered points of contact not only with Taoist philosophy, but with Confucianism as well.   One line of thought at least in Confucianism— that, for instance, which found expression in the *Doctrine of the Mean* (*Chung Yung*)—resembled the fundamental ideas of Lao Tsï. On the other hand, even Chuang Tsï is also connected with the Confucian school through his teacher T'ien Tsï Fang. The *Book of Changes* (*I King*), in which Confucianism and Taoism met on common ground, supplied yet another bond of union. It is true that Confucianism had developed other doctrines : the ritualistic, chiefly concerned with the elaboration of ceremonies; the historic, which will be discussed later ; and, finally, the politico-legal theories of Sün K'uang, which had points in common with the school of the Legists and with one branch of the neo-Moist school, among the representatives of which are Han Fei Tsï and Li Sï. The manner in which these various doctrines came into conflict is best illustrated by the fact that subsequently, on the occasion of the killing of the magicians by Ts'in Shï Huang Ti, the Confucianists championed their cause. A combination of the natural philosophy of Taoism and the historic principles of Confucianism is found in the Han period in a man like Tung Chung-shu, who interpreted the *Spring and Autumn Annals* of Confucius in accordance with the Taoist principles of duality (*yin* and *yang*). It was, indeed, this form of Confucianism which acquired prestige and influence in Han days.

At the beginning, however, the time was not yet ripe. The founder of the Han dynasty was entirely uncultured, and displayed toward all learning an outspoken contempt to which at times he gave most ludicrous expression. He was a thorough sceptic, and reckoned only with sober realities. To rites and ceremonies as such he was indifferent ; and only when the tone of his immediate circle became utterly unruly was he induced to have a Court ceremonial instituted by a second-rate Confucian scholar on the lines of that of the Ts'in dynasty. That distinctly pleased him. " Now at last I know how an emperor should be honoured," he is said to have exclaimed when the new ceremony was introduced. He did not, however, abolish the ban on Confucian writings. He once visited the tomb of Confucius, but only out of curiosity.

The triumph of Confucianism could not, however, be

permanently impeded. Various emperors might experience a personal inclination for the sorcery of the Court magicians, but Confucianism was, so to speak, the official philosophy of life. The change took place by degrees. First, the persecution edicts were abrogated; then, gradually, the Confucianists were raised to all kinds of important posts. Next, rewards were offered for the recovery of lost classical writings; and, finally, acquaintance with one of these writings was proclaimed the prerequisite condition for obtaining an official post. Thus the victory of the Confucian school was decisive. The time of conflict was over. Throughout Confucian scholars had stood their ground with courage and endurance. Henceforward, with occasional interludes, the scene is one of triumph for this school.

It is true that the doctrines now in the ascendant were no longer pure Confucianism. At the time of conflict with rival doctrines as many of them as appeared feasible had been assimilated. A considerable amount of good material had been borrowed from both Taoists and Legists. Alone the universality preached by Mo Ti could not be absorbed, for its principles stood in too striking antithesis to Confucianism. It was rooted out. Notwithstanding its ecclesiastical organization, this doctrine could not endure. Too strict and ascetic, after sharing the honours with Confucianism for a time in the Chinese states it finally fell a victim to its own excessive readiness to die. The reasons why the theistic doctrine of universal love failed in the East, while in the West it formed for centuries the basis of religious life, are worth consideration. These reasons were diverse. The activist theories of Mo Ti were better suited to what may be termed a 'younger' mentality. The Chinese were already too wise to cherish the naïve belief that the world could be bettered by universal love. Besides, the more a standpoint is insisted upon, the more surely will it create its own antithesis; and this applies equally to universal love. No less clearly is this shown in the history of Christianity than in the fate which befell Moism in China. Christianity, however, at least retained the semblance of authority, whereas the philosophy of Mo Ti perished. A possible explanation is that Christianity was not opposed by any philosophy endowed with the maturity, lucidity, and gentleness of Confucianism. But the main reason is probably that the direction assumed by Western development favoured individualism—the human soul in its purely spiritual aspect —whereas development in the East could not for many years to come free itself from the social basis of the family system. Confucianism, built up on the natural foundation of family life, was bound, therefore, to triumph here. The spiritual aspects awakened in the West by Christianity were brought to life in similar fashion in China by Mahayana Buddhism, due allowance being made, of course, for the different temperaments of the peoples concerned.

(c) The Triumph of Confucianism—The Canon

The consequences of the triumph of Confucianism are visible on the one hand in the setting up of a canon of sacred writings, on the other in the development of a highly conservative theory of government.

The Setting up of the Canon. The first step was the selection of the most ancient and reliable works : the *Book of Changes* (*I King*), the *Book of History* (*Shu King*), the *Book of Poetry* (*Shï King*), and the *Spring and Autumn Annals* (*Ch'un Ts'iu*). All these books were connected with the Confucian school, which elucidated and made use of them. The question is how far Confucius himself was concerned in their compilation. Modern Chinese scholars take a very sceptical view of the earlier attribution of much of this literature to Confucius and his disciples. Only the *Spring and Autumn Annals* are unanimously recognized as a recension of the political records of Lu by Confucius in person. It is no longer generally assumed that Confucius collected and edited the odes in the *Book of Poetry*. His chief activities in connexion with this work are now regarded as the recomposition or, in other words, the revision of the airs of the various odes.[1] The *Book of History* contains a number of forgeries and

[1] Liang K'i-ch'ao expressed this view in his lectures on ancient Chinese literature at the Ts'inghua University.

material of late date, extending even beyond Han times, which were probably delivered to the collecting authorities for the sake of the rewards offered. Confucius may quite well be assumed, however, to have employed this book as a source of instruction, for much of its content agrees with the views expressed, for instance, in the *Lun Yü*; and at quite an early date we find within the Confucian school a settled tradition of the scholastic use made of the work.[1] Doubts have likewise recently been expressed as to whether the *Book of Changes* owes anything to Confucius. But on this score tradition is far too well founded to admit of reasonable doubt. Besides these works, of which some were not lost after all and some came to light again in a more or less miraculous manner, other writings were discovered and canonized in the Han period. In Confucius's day the rites were in all probability taught mainly by practice and word of mouth. It is not very likely that a *king* (canon) existed ; or, if it did, which on the face of things is possible, it went astray later. During the Han period the traditional material was collected by the brothers Tai and issued in two different recensions. They are the *Record of Rites* (*Li Ki*), usually joined with the four works' noted above to form the Five *King*.[2] When later on the two other books concerning ceremonial usages, the *Chou Li* and the *I Li*, the spuriousness of which we have already discussed above, were added to these five, the canon of Seven *King* resulted. Three different versions of the *Ch'un Ts'iu* were circulated : those with commentaries by Kung-yang and Ku-liang respectively, and, finally, the revised *Tso Chuan*, which will be discussed later. Thus arose the collection of the Nine *King*. Finally came the addition of the *Book of Filial Piety* (*Hiao King*), the *Conversations* of Confucius (*Lun Yü*), the dictionary *Ér Ya*, and, last of all, the *Works of Mencius*. These were the thirteen classical works set up as a canon in the course of the Han dynasty. Subsequently

---

[1] *Cf.* the relevant passages in the *Lun Yü* and Mencius.

[2] To correspond to the six liberal arts (*liu i*) of the Confucian school, the Six *King* are sometimes spoken of, the sixth being music. No *Book of Music* exists, however. The records on music are found to-day in the *Li Ki*.

they were engraved on stone and given out as the standard works of the Confucian school. Not until the Sung period was a new selection made.

(d) The Conservatism of the State

Still more important than the literary establishment of Confucianism was the influence which this school of thought exercised on the form of government. The type of Chinese state organization created at this period was retained in essentials for thousands of years. It was amplified and improved, and was here and there adapted to altered circumstances and somewhat modified; but its fundamentals were preserved, regardless of changes of dynasty, right down to the time of the revolution through which China became a republic.

It was during the long reign of the Emperor Wu Ti (140–87 B.C.) that consolidation took place. This ruler was one of those personalities who left such a mark that later tradition celebrated them for centuries in legend and myth. An ardent visionary, he was deeply interested in the occult arts taught by the magicians. More than one of these cunning sorcerers succeeded in ensnaring the Emperor temporarily and in inducing him to undertake long journeys to the coast of the Eastern Sea [1] in order to visit the blessed genii. More than one of them was unmasked and then summarily put to death by the impetuous ruler. But he always came again under the spell of this magic, which in one instance disastrously affected the succession. The heir to the throne was set aside and perished, and a number of high officials were implicated, including a descendant of Confucius who had unearthed an ancient edition of the Classics. At last, when it was too late, the Emperor awoke from his infatuation.[2] He was impulsive

[1] The mountain Lao Shan in the former district of Kiao-chou is said to have acquired its name at this time. Previously it was called Ao Shan after *ao*, the sea-monster. This *ao* was changed to *lao*, ' tribulation,' by the people, who were sorely afflicted by statute labour and taxes imposed under the pretext of Imperial journeys (see the introduction to the *Topography of Lao Shan*).

[2] For details see p. 187 *et seq.*

by nature; while he respected the scholars and poets whom he attracted to his Court, in a fit of anger he would inflict the most barbarous punishments on innocent persons, such as the historian Sï-ma Tsʻien. Notwithstanding the passions that convulsed his private life, however, the development and consolidation of the state proceeded apace in the hands of able officials.

It was due to the efforts of men like Wei Kuan and Tung Chung-shu that Confucianism became the State religion.[1] Its adherents had already exalted Confucius almost to the rank of a god. He was worshipped as the 'throneless king,' and credited with utterances which were interpreted as a kind of Messianic prophecy on the Han period. Under the *ægis* of divinely appointed antiquity reforms were made palatable. How comprehensible that this tendency should have degenerated into a conservatism for which antiquity on its own merits provided an unimpeachable pattern! Such was the conception of nature that the immutability of God and of the universal principle (Tao) was held to be of primary importance. Thus all possibility of development in the universe was precluded. The ideal state was found in antiquity, whence it operated ceaselessly and unalterably through the ages. The requirements of modern times must of course find their justification in antiquity. The calendar of the Hia dynasty, in which the year started at the beginning of February, was adopted because it had been praised by Confucius. But justification was also found for a form of monarchy which inclined more and more toward absolutism, and used for its tool bureaucratic officialdom. Of course no amount of interpretative art could discover in the straightforward ancient writings a warrant for the innovations; hence the creation of accessory tradition.[2]

Thus arose a coherent cosmogony embodying equally

[1] *Cf.* O. Franke, *Studien zur Geschichte des konfuzianischen Dogmas* (Hamburg, 1920).

[2] Alongside the *King*, or canonical works (literally 'Warp'), were placed the *Wei*, or traditional works (literally 'Woof'). The authenticity of these traditional works was questioned at a fairly early date, but was accepted officially. The legend of Confucius's life was also established at that time, and has been handed down through the ensuing centuries almost untouched.

the magical ideas of the *fang shï* (Court magicians) and the echoes of the genuine Confucian doctrines. This cosmogony found general acceptance, and was systematically developed. It embraced the entire universe, heaven, earth, and all creation. A definitely co-ordinated system of sequences was created under which all knowledge and experience could be ranged. This system was founded on the dualism of nature represented by the light and the dark principles (*yin-yang*) and on the rotation of the five elements. Conformity to this system was regarded as proof of reality. This unadulterated logic steadily usurped the place of any independent efforts to examine the world of phenomena. Therewith were finally obliterated those potential beginnings of natural science and technical knowledge which were certainly coming into view toward the end of the Chou period. Tradition took their place.

Opposition was aroused only spasmodically. In the time of the Later Han appeared that sceptical eccentric Wang Ch'ung (A.D. 27–97), with his work the *Lun Hêng*,[1] in which he endeavoured to examine all accepted truths from the opposite point of view, and frequently found contradiction a more useful weapon than logical validity. He was followed by Chang Hêng (*c.* A.D. 150), who as mathematician and astronomer cast doubt on the literary tradition, reformed the calendar, and also, it appears, constructed some interesting seismological instruments. Opposition was continued in the T'ang dynasty by Liu Chï-ki (*c.* 713), and, finally, in the Ts'ing dynasty by Ts'ui Shu (1739–1816)[2] and kindred scholars. Not only were these opponents of stagnant tradition, however, isolated figures in their period, but their actual scepticism was aimed merely at the spurious pictures of Confucian days. They wished to clear the image of Confucius of the accretions of later times. Even they left untouched the words of the Master himself.

To describe the intellectual life of China at that time as completely stagnant would nevertheless be false. It was merely turning toward other spiritual spheres. And in this

---

[1] Translated into English by A. Forke (published in Hamburg).
[2] See the very important article by Hu Shï in *Kuo Hüe Ki K'an*, vol. ii.

PLATE 24

Faience vase with fauns' heads and flowers in relief. Pale green glaze. T'ang period.
(R. Wilhelm Collection.)

respect especially entirely fresh sources were opened up during the age of great travels to the West and the institution of relations with the foreign peoples round about. From without came the impulses—finally culminating in the penetration of Buddhism into China—which imbued her intellectual life with new vigour, just as Christianity had in its day affected that of Europe.

III. GEOGRAPHICAL EXPANSION IN THE HAN PERIOD

Ever since the early days of the Han dynasty the Hiung-nu had been dangerous enemies in the north-west. The Great Wall certainly supplied a possible means of defence, but the swift equestrian hordes of the Huns continually succeeded in detecting unguarded spots and wreaking great mischief. So long as China confined herself to the defensive and to driving back the invading brigands no improvement could take place. Only a drastic change of method could be effective. It was due to no passion for conquest that under Wu Ti China assumed the offensive; this course was essential in the interests of frontier security. Events took a course similar to that witnessed during the expansion of the Roman Empire. That the eccentric and energetic figure of the ruler lent a special distinction to this historically necessary action cannot be denied. For the movement of expansion swept not only northward, but equally to the far west, the east (Korea), the extreme south (Canton), the south-east (Fukien), and the south-west (Szechwan and Tibet). So it came about that under the Han dynasty China comprised for the first time within her frontiers the entire territory of those provinces which to-day we call China. The achievements of the Han period far exceeded in this respect even those of the Ts'in dynasty.

The effects of this extension of her geographical area on the civilization of China may well be imagined. The world suddenly widened out, for scientific voyages of discovery went hand in hand with military conquest. One would naturally be inclined to compare the effects produced on European culture by the discovery of America. But this does not furnish an exact parallel. There is a psychological difference between the results of expansion overland and across the boundless seas. A much better comparison could be found in the widening of the European horizon through the Crusades.

Let us try to visualize the conditions one after another.

(1) *The Huns.* The incursions of the Huns in the time of Wu Ti gave rise to the plan of not merely repulsing them, but gradually and systematically occupying the territory vacated by them and annexing it to the Chinese Empire. In this way the northern frontiers were considerably extended. There is no room here to trace in detail the victories and defeats of the Chinese armies; attention shall merely be drawn to the twofold success of the campaign as a whole. Contact with the Hiung-nu was not confined to warlike relations; little by little a system of barter had been instituted. The Chinese who occupied as colonists the territory annexed from the Huns found it necessary to adapt themselves to entirely new conditions. The soldiers too came into personal touch with the enemy. More than one Chinese general had fallen into the enemy's hands, joined their ranks, and even married a Hun princess. They had naturally disseminated Chinese customs and civilization to some extent among these nomads, chiefly to enable them to repulse the attacks of the Chinese. These deserters were desperate men. Even when a general had been captured by the enemy through no fault of his own the Emperor's wrath frequently vented itself on the general's family, which he extirpated root and branch. No wonder the sole survivor thereafter threw in his lot with the enemy! The foremost among the scholarly lyrics of the Han period tells the pathetic story of two friends, Li Ling and Su Wu. General Li Ling, cut off from his native land through an unavoidable reverse, bemoans his hard lot. Su Wu, taken prisoner by the Huns when acting as ambassador, remains loyal throughout the vicissitudes of captivity. Obliged to tend sheep for the nomads on their steppes, he clings to the token of his Imperial office until, after nineteen years' captivity, he succeeds in making his way home.

Enmity was not confined to encounters between the Chinese and the Huns. Reverses in the field and Chinese diplomacy had aroused dissension among the various tribes. At one time five chieftains (*shan yü*) were at war with one another. On the principle *divide et impera* China did not neglect the use of political treaties to deliver herself from the enemy. Political marriages had occasionally to play their part too. The stories, touching in their sadness, of the Princess Chao Kün, who was married to Hu Han-ye, a Hunnish Khan, and whose heart was divided between her old home and her children in the Hun country, and of the Princess Si Kün, exiled among the Wu-sun, have time and again been celebrated in lyrical and pictorial art.

At last the Huns were successfully subdued, their territory annexed to China. No longer could they venture to measure their strength against this aggrandized empire. Various scholars have traced a causal connexion between this repulse of the Hiung-nu and the westward movements of the North-west Asiatic peoples which were the indirect cause of migration, and thereby of the fall of the Roman Empire. Care should be taken to avoid premature conclusions on this point. On the other hand, an indirect connexion between this Chinese thrust, which convulsed whole territories, and the subsequent exodus to the West is quite conceivable. Detailed examination of the proceeding must be reserved, however, for a later occasion.

(2) *The Westerners.* During the early days of his struggles against the Hiung-nu, which met with little success, Wu Ti bethought himself of securing as allies the Yüe-chï (Getæ, Indo-Scythians), who had been driven away by the Hiung-nu and thirsted for revenge.

Chang K'ien, destined to become China's most famous explorer, complied with the Emperor's request to form alliances with these people. He had great difficulties to contend with at first. For over ten years he was kept prisoner by the Huns before he succeeded in escaping and making his way to the West. The Tarim basin and Pamir districts had been occupied, first by the Persians, then by Alexander. Bactria and Sogdiana were Seleucidian kingdoms. Even after the conquest of Bactria by the Getæ Sogdiana, with its capital Uriatubo, was still ruled by Greek kings. Chang K'ien penetrated into all these districts : the Tarim basin, Sogdiana, Samarkand, as far as the Getæ of Ferghana. He determined the routes to India through Kabul and Khotan, and also decided that another direct route to India must lie farther south.

He thus succeeded in opening up the road which was subsequently to provide direct means of communication with the eastern portions of the Roman Empire. The Chinese called that Western empire Ta Ts'in ;[1] to the Romans the Chinese were known as the Seres ('Silk People'). This trade-route, which for so long had been blocked by a mass of Turkic oasis states, now formed a connecting link between East and West.

Chang K'ien brought back to China the grape-vine,[2] the walnut, the jointed bamboo, and the hemp plant. A general also brought from those districts a golden picture (of Buddhist origin?). Here may be discerned those Western cultural influences which subsequently came to fruition in China. There is no doubt that Hellenistic art exerted an extensive influence over Buddhist plastic art, or that the Buddha type shows at all events many points in common with the Apollonian. It is highly probable that in Han times the outgrowths of this art had already reached China. Such influences should not, however, be over-estimated. In any case, East and West were bound together in those centuries by but a slender thread.

These western districts remained for centuries in the possession—the interrupted possession, it is true—of China. Not until the decline of Chinese power, in the course of the struggles succeeding the Han dynasty, did this gate to the Western world close again ; the nomad, and in his wake the all-engulfing desert sand, made an end of Chinese attempts at civilization in these areas.

The outposts of Chinese civilization and power in those

---

[1] Identified by Hess of Zürich with Ctesiphon, but this is disputed by others.

[2] *P'u-t'ao* in Chinese, which is probably a phonetic transcription of the Greek βότρυς.

territories of mixed races sank into the sand, leaving never a trace. But the desert sand preserved their ruins. The excavations conducted by Sir Aurel Stein, Paul Pelliot, Sven Hedin, Grünwedel, von Le Coq, and others have unearthed objects which afford direct insight into the life of those remote military colonies. As in Pompeii, so here also a long-buried civilization rose again out of the earth into the light of day.

From various objects, pictures, and manuscripts on paper, wood, and bamboo we gain an insight into the life and doings of those Chinese officials, who combined with the strict discipline of the Romans the serene calm of the Greeks. We get some idea of the precision and exactitude with which the wheels of administrative machinery revolved. We catch a glimpse of family life among those men on distant watch-stations, of their sad partings, their troubles, and the fate of their dear ones. We come across brief letters and notes containing invitations to a meal together, and find literary exercises and calligraphic efforts in the latest style alongside clumsy arithmetic by children of tender years.[1]

Alas! over all this animated life lurks fate, dark and threatening as a wall of storm clouds. The world was indeed made wider by these discoveries, but man was all the lonelier in that strange new world.

There are songs telling us of warriors in the field, of their thoughts and longings for home, whence the yearnings of their dear ones reach out to them. The following ode on some distant warriors expresses these sentiments:

> In the south, war;
> In the north, death.
> Lying stark and stiff on the open meadows,
> We shall be food for black ravens.
> Then bid them cease to pluck at the heroes
> Lying stiff and stark on the open meadows.
> But who else should get their rotting bones?

[1] Compare the lively description furnished by Conrady in his work *Die Chinesischen Handschriften und sonstigen Kleinfunde Sven Hedins in Lou Lan* (Stockholm, 1920). The disputed point—whether the place discovered is really Lou-lan, which Chinese scholars such as Lo Chên-yü doubt—does not signify here. In their bearing on the colonial life of those districts the finds are invaluable.

Sad is the murmur of the water,
Baneful the whisper in the reeds.
In glory we ride to battle on proud steeds,
But we fall, and neighing the horses wander riderless.

Apprehension was the distinctive feature of this extended world, above which the fateful shadow of destruction already hovered. All those settlements designed to protect the path through the desert toward the Far West and the goods travelling on it finally succumbed after a long and severe struggle to the irresistible encroachment of the desert sands. Such is the history of a dim possibility, revealed but to vanish again.

(3) *Korea.* In the east of the empire events took quite a different turn. Korea was occupied by an ancient dynasty which dated from the time when King Wu of Chou bestowed the district as a fief on the descendants of the Yin dynasty. Even if political bonds were often extremely loose, cultural relations had always existed between Korea and China. Under the Emperor Wu of the Han dynasty conflict had arisen with a part of the territory in which a usurper had set up a new kingdom in opposition to that of the Han. A combined attack from the south and the west resulted in the submission of Korea to Chinese suzerainty and its incorporation in the Chinese Empire.

(4) *The South.* Just as the empire was extended in the east and the north—to say nothing of the west—far beyond its previous frontiers, so penetration in the south was effected by various means during the Han dynasty. As far as Canton and beyond, the land was gradually brought under Chinese supremacy. Independent kingdoms temporarily in existence there had indeed already adopted Chinese civilization. Chinese culture represented at that time such a powerful moral force that no neighbouring peoples could withstand it. Political conquest followed, therefore, with no great trouble. Only in the mountainous districts of the present-day province of Fukien was pacification rendered difficult by the unfavourable character of the country. Hence the population was deported chiefly to the northern districts between the rivers Yangtse and Huai, leaving the

PLATE 25

Faience vase painted in brown on a grey ground. Sung period,
from a Ts'ï-chou kiln. H. 148 mm.
(Eumorfopoulos Collection.)

original territory almost unpopulated. But no new administrative centre was created. This is probably why the spoken language in the province of Fukien still differs so radically from that in the rest of China. In the south-west, too, China was extended as far as Talifu, and the way to Tibet discovered.

This expansion of the empire was brought about—like that of the Roman Empire—in the interests of frontier security. It would hardly have been wise to await the invasion of bellicose neighbours on the border and then make belated endeavours to expel them. The continuous warfare accompanying the expansion entailed a very heavy burden, of course, on the Chinese people. This time nevertheless remains a vital epoch in the history of Chinese civilization. It marks the staking out, as it were, of the area in which the soul of Chinese culture was subsequently to manifest itself. The assimilation of influences emanating from adjacent peoples was also of great historical import.

IV. INTERNAL DECAY AND ATTEMPTS AT REFORM

While China continued to expand, so that the reign of the Emperor Wu Ti has always been regarded as a kind of Golden Age in the history of Chinese civilization, traces of internal decay were already visible in the ruling house under this sovereign. There was at first little evidence of this in state administration. Government, as well as the conduct of war, was in the hands of able officials, and affairs followed a certain routine that had been evolved. Warfare against adjacent tribes automatically created appropriate methods. Heavy chariots of the old type, acting as a support to the intervening foot forces, no longer proved effective against the mobile equestrian forces of the Huns. The war-chariot vanished, therefore, giving place to light cavalry supported by heavy infantry, so that under the Han the military system was radically reorganized. One reason for the fact that, notwithstanding heavy losses, the country did not suffer so severely as might be expected was that numbers of criminals and other desperadoes were sent to the front as troops. If they perished it was no loss ; if they survived they were settled in the border districts, and formed a kind of cultural manure in those hazardous regions. As war paved the way for trade, money for financing the campaigns was always forthcoming. For all that, generals required to be peculiarly gifted to work with troops of such dangerous calibre ; and the many reverses suffered by the Chinese armies, in the struggles against the Hiung-nu, for instance, may be chiefly imputed to the unreliable nature of the troops. All the more comprehensible, therefore, is the nervousness apparent in King Wu's assumption that a captured general had perhaps not done his best. The wiping out of the entire family of a real or imaginary offender was a penalty not inflicted in isolated cases only.

The example furnished throughout the long reign of the Emperor Wu caused the entire Court life of the Han emperors to become more and more corrupt. An evil which steadily increased, until at last its pernicious influence permeated the whole of administrative life, was the power wielded by women and eunuchs. Even before Han times rulers had occasionally succumbed to such influences, but these cases were the exception. Not until the days of the Han emperors did these abuses become systematic.

Life in the Imperial palaces of the Han, with its splendour and luxury, has acquired an almost mythical halo. The charm of female beauty was a force that brought about very real political consequences. Not only did a lovely Court dame who succeeded in bewitching the ruler's heart become all-influential and overshadow every rival—sometimes even the Empress herself—but it frequently occurred to the family of the favoured one that they also might bask in the rays of Imperial patronage ; and if there were ambitious men among the brothers or other relatives of the favourite, they disdained no means to acquire the influence necessary to place their family in power. In this way arose whole dynasties of ministers and field-marshals, who maintained their authority in the empire for generations, until they were overthrown by some hostile party, which then supplanted them.

Apart from the families of the Court ladies, the circles formed by the Emperor's favoured youths and eunuchs comprised all manner of unscrupulous and ambitious elements. Although in such cases the risk of the creation of 'dynasties' was far less, since the influence of these people was usually confined to their own persons, on the other hand the unscrupulous and low character of the rabble which kept the princes ensnared rendered this influence more pernicious. The relatives of favourite concubines usually came of high-class, well-educated families who, when in power, at all events boasted a certain tradition among their stock-in-trade. And finally, to make confusion worse confounded, there was the host of sorcerers and magicians that battened on the superstitions of Court circles.

A catastrophe induced by intrigues of this nature which occurred while the Emperor Wu was still on the throne is well worthy of note as an illustration of the general trend of events. The Empress Wei, who was in the Emperor's good graces, had succeeded in having her son Kü declared heir to the throne. Intrigue was aroused by this step among various officials and palace eunuchs, who took advantage of the Emperor's proneness to superstition to make away with the heir. At the palace the magicians, as already noted, were pursuing their mischievous practices, and were employed by the occupants of the harem. They could make wooden and paper images and animate them with magic spells, so that these figures exercised a maleficent influence on the persons against whom they were directed. The Emperor was aware of these activities, but did not oppose them. One day, however, during his customary mid-day siesta, he dreamt that a troop of these wooden goblins, armed with sticks, was trying to beat him. Terror-stricken, he awoke, feeling bruised and ill. A certain Kiang Ch'ung, one of the Crown Prince's most bitter enemies, declared that the illness was induced by an evil spell, and that its causes must be strictly investigated. The Emperor granted him complete authority, which Kiang Ch'ung immediately used to scatter destruction among his enemies in the noble families of the capital: Their houses were searched, the floors torn up. Where magic was suspected the inmates were taken prisoner and tortured until they confessed and informed against others about whom they were questioned. Terrible bloodshed resulted in the capital, and the victims of this inquisition are said to have numbered tens of thousands.

Having wrought havoc among his adversaries in the capital, Kiang Ch'ung announced that the trail led into the palace itself. Here the eunuch Su Wên was helpful. The apartments of the Empress Wei and of her son Kü, heir to the throne, were soon reached. The rumour was spread that under the flooring of these apartments there had actually been found wooden images employed for black magic. In his indignation the heir-apparent killed Kiang Ch'ung with his own hand. But Su Wên, the eunuch, escaped. The Emperor was at the time in his summer palace at Kan-ts'üan. Thither the eunuch fled with the news that the heir had risen in revolt and had designs upon the Emperor's life. The latter, wild with rage, gave orders to nip the rebellion in the bud. The Crown Prince perished, the Empress Wei was driven to commit suicide, and the entire family, with all its dependents, was executed in most barbarous fashion.

This scandalous proceeding aroused such general indignation that the Emperor, who had in the meantime recovered from his indisposition and realized his mistake, mourned his son with tears, had the family of Kiang Ch'ung extirpated, and the eunuch Su Wên burnt alive. He made solemn acknowledgment of his error, and vowed amendment for the future.

Now the Emperor Wu, who occupied the throne for so long, was a man of marked individuality. If such things could happen at his Court, how easily can one imagine the consequences of similar intrigues under princes of weaker personality! The Court histories of Han times are one unbroken *chronique scandaleuse* of happenings of this nature.

It would be superfluous to enter into the details of these scandals within the harem walls but for the fact that they affected the whole of the nation's economic life. If the increasing tendency of Han culture to centre in the capitals was a menace to agriculture because the needs and requirements of the peasants escaped the attention of the ruler, party struggles made matters far worse. Large landed estates were formed, and the peasants crushed into a still viler state of bondage. According as additional funds were required to carry on the struggle for supremacy, the more must the bondmen be squeezed, as if they were not already sufficiently oppressed by the burdens of war. For since the abolition of the old feudal military system, when the ruler's chariot, around which the light-armed forces congregated, was the centre of manœuvres, the higher ranks no longer needed to take the field in person. Military service and its attendant burdens were thrown more and more on that section of the population which lacked the power to evade them.

It is easy to realize how the progressive disorganization of society must inevitably prove a menace to the ruling family. The day was once more at hand when, the grip of the ruling house having relaxed, amid much internal strife and confusion a new dynasty was to fight its way to the helm. By a remarkable combination of circumstances, however, the course of events was diverted into another channel. During the last few decades of the era under review relatives of the Empress Wang had risen to power. Especially prominent among them was Wang Mang, who had steadily gained ascendancy under the Emperors Ai and P'ing. He had a talent for attracting followers, and his partiality for antiquity in particular made him popular with a wing of the Confucian school which included such well-known men as Liu Hin, the collector and book-compiler, and Yang Hiung, the philosopher. Half against his will he permitted himself to be thrust into the foreground by his persistent admirers, as has been the case with similar characters down to quite recent times. Ultimately he was responsible for the poisoning of the Emperor P'ing, and placed on the throne a little child, in whose name he administered the affairs of the Empire—as a second Duke of Chou, so it was said— until he judged the time ripe to step from the dignity of Imperial regent to that of emperor proper and to found the

Sin (or ' New ') dynasty. He took advantage of the fact, ever becoming more obvious, that the state of things under the Han government had become indefensible, and was careful to draw up all his regulations in sharp contrast to those of the Han dynasty. Everything was to be reformed and made new; nothing should remain as it was. But the singular part of his policy was that the needs of the time were not the objects of his study, but that in all things he deemed it essential to revert to the pattern of highest antiquity, so as to enforce his reforms under cover of its authority. In this he miscalculated. The times when antiquity commanded any authority on its own merits were long since past. Outside a narrow circle of unworthy scholars the formalities introduced by his antiquated methods merely rendered his reforms troublesome and unpopular.

The actual reforms present an astonishing medley of quite advanced ideas for radical economic improvement and antiquated external forms. We are concerned here with the first attempt to establish a new order of society on a socialist basis after the old order, under which excessive demands were made on private property, had failed. The attempt, however, was bound to remain Utopian, for it was modelled solely on the State and family communism of ancient times, which could not, of course, be instantaneously adapted to State machinery so complicated as that of the Han. Social and economic reforms can be effected only by natural development from a stage already attained, not by arbitrary reversion to a more primitive economic stage.

Wang Mang's reforms covered five different issues :

(1) *Reform of the Official System.* This reform really amounted to the restitution of archaic titles and dignities. The Minister of Agriculture was entitled Hi Ho (the names of the two families of officials under the ruler Yao in the *Book of History*). There was also a Minister of Forests (Yü), a Minister of Works (Kung Kung), and so on—all of them names with an almost mythological ring.

(2) *Agricultural Reform.* The land policy of the nobility had created a wide disparity in the size of land tenures, and the question of restricting the extent of private estates

PLATE 26

Porcelain dish with blue and red underglaze painting. K'ang-hi period.
(R. Wilhelm Collection.)

had long since been mooted. But these reforms had been thwarted by opposition from the landed nobility. Wang Mang now proceeded to confiscate all land under the head of ' royal land,' and all agricultural labourers were termed vassals. Neither they nor the estates could thenceforth be sold. If a family consisted of less than eight members, and their land exceeded the amount determined by the well system, the surplus portion was farmed out to relatives and neighbours. All those who formerly owned no land and were now allotted some willingly conformed to the new system. Anyone daring to protest against this new and sacred regulation was prosecuted.

(3) *The Economic System.* On the advice of Liu Hin a number of departments were created to assume public control over the necessaries of life—namely, the production and sale of salt, wine, iron, wood, the water-supply, the currency, copper-smelting. These monopolies were upheld under pain of death.

(4) *The Currency.* Bronze coins, the first specimens of which weighed half an ounce, had been cast as early as the Ts'in dynasty. Under the Emperor Wu of the Han dynasty appeared a coin of very convenient weight, the five-*shu* piece. Wang Mang started by introducing a number of different exchange media.[1] When such variety proved unpractical, he had a coin of small denomination minted, as well as a larger, knife-shaped coin, worth fifty units. But even these standards were subsequently revised.

(5) *The System of Tenures.* Endeavours were made, on the model of the newly discovered *Chou Ritual,* to effect a fresh division of the empire under which the various officials would receive new titles reminiscent of the old feudal ones. In this way were restored the ten thousand states supposed to have existed in antiquity.

On reflection, the whole undertaking presents in its main features an attempt to realize Utopia. The ruler was not

[1] Gold, bronze, copper, tortoiseshell, and cowrie shells were used as currency. Bronze, gold, silver, tortoiseshell, cowries, and cloth were valid as exchange media. There were six tokens of cash currency, one of gold, two of silver, four of tortoise-shell, five of cowries, ten of cloth—twenty-eight varieties in all.

without vanity. He prided himself on his *rôle* as public benefactor and on his deviation from the path of his predecessors. For one thing, he sought to remedy the serious abuses created by the fief system of the high nobility, which threatened to undermine the entire social order. He also bethought himself of assuming Government control over sources of supply to prevent private exploitation. By reason of the extraordinary garb in which they were robed, however, these social ideas, though excellent in themselves, did not materialize. They were decked out in such antique guise. At one stroke were to be achieved those Utopias of a Golden Age descriptions of which abounded in literature.

For this the ruler lacked the cool discretion that advances patiently, step by step. Perfection was to be attained at one bound. His ideas followed hot on one another, each being instantly proclaimed as an edict. And so what in the morning was an order had become a prohibition by the evening. Names and titles changed in kaleidoscopic fashion. In the end it all came back to the old order of things. For, to make matters clear, it was frequently necessary to append the superseded names, which thus held their own against all new modes. The rush and agitation of the reforms prevented the machinery of State from running smoothly. Ultimately none knew what was right, and general uncertainty prevailed in consequence.

Certain results were nevertheless achieved. With the disintegration of the large landed estates a peasant class was again built up. But they were a surfeited body; after their needs had been satisfied all further interest on their part in the existence of a socialist Government was dead. Profiting by the general state of uncertainty, the unsatisfied elements banded together in brigand hordes throughout the country. The people had not yet lost all memory of the Han dynasty. Contemplating now the complete failure of the machinery of State, they forgot the abuses of former days and longed only for the old system. Liu Siu, a youthful leader of one of these bands, who traced his descent from the Emperor King of the house of Han, came forward, and under cover of the general tumult collected an ever larger following.

Wang Mang, who opposed him with troops, was defeated. The capital was besieged, plundered, and burnt, and Wang Mang perished in flight. His head, exhibited in the market-place, was stoned by the rabble until it fell to the ground. Such was the end of the first attempt at social reform in the Chinese Empire.

Liu Siu ascended the throne as the Emperor Kuang Wu, and gradually subdued the rebels. The capital was transferred to the east, to the former site of Lo-yang, for which reason the new dynasty was called the Eastern Han. But the reign of Wang Mang, A.D. 9–25, was treated as an interregnum and struck off the annals.

V. THE LATER OR EASTERN HAN DYNASTY
(A.D. 25–220)

The reign of the Emperor Kuang Wu is a bright spot in the history of Chinese civilization. The ruler had grown up among the people. He was a Confucian scholar, and was surrounded by men of similar ways of thought. The new rites for the public worship of God were arranged on a very different system, therefore, from that governing the official ceremonies pitched together in semi-casual fashion by the founder of the first Han dynasty, the peasant Liu Pang. The sacrificial rites established by Kuang Wu reveal a considered ceremonial quite plainly influenced by Taoist ideas. The later antagonism between Taoism and Confucianism does not date back to these times, in which, since the days of Tung Chung-shu and others, a connexion existed between the natural philosophy of Taoism and the moral tenets of Confucianism. The noteworthy side to Kuang Wu's rule is the full consciousness with which he applied morality to the service of his policy. In his reign were coined the catchwords of "the ancient loyalty between servant and prince," "the revival of the ruling house," which throughout Chinese history have proved so inspiring. Not only were relations between himself and his lieutenants most satisfactory—an attitude comparing very favourably with the behaviour of the founder of the Former Han dynasty

193

—but education was encouraged in every possible way. The schools were centres not merely for the cultivation of sciences, but also for the advancement and fostering of morality and the inculcation of definite ideals. The ruler enjoyed great popularity, and did not forget the life he had lived among the people, for whose complaints and grievances he retained a ready ear.

A wonderful expedient for endearing his policy to the people was the reverence he showed to scholars and loyal officials of the former dynasty. The honour he paid them gradually created its effect even on the public mind. He knew how to make his intentions clear in comprehensible symbolic language. By these means civilization was placed on a moral basis which provided men of like sympathies for centuries ahead with a firm foundation that greatly facilitated their work, since they could invoke these proceedings as legitimate acts. Here lies one of the differences between the Former and the Later Han dynasties.

Court history soon resumed the old channels. Eunuchs and favourites, with their families, once more acquired dominion. Greed and corruption ultimately reached the throne; it was toward the end of the Han dynasty that the practice of selling official posts, now quite an accepted thing in China, first came into vogue on a large scale.

Public opinion in the form of Confucianism now raised a loud voice, however, against this state of affairs. Even in the darkest days there had been upright men who did not refrain from proclaiming their incorruptible judgments, and who created a public conscience that proved a distinct force. Not even the worst types of men could afford, once they were in power, to continue giving free reign to their vices; they had to walk warily, and to preserve at least an external semblance of propriety. These guardians of the public conscience, the ' pure critics ' (*ts'ing-i*), as they were called, thus enjoyed considerable prestige throughout this period. To give an example of the manner in which this public opinion worked: One Huang Yün had found favour in the eyes of an influential man, Yüan Kuei, who desired him as a son-in-law. But Huang Yün was already married, and was therefore obliged to repudiate his legal wife on insufficient grounds. He thereby forfeited his reputation as a man of honour for the rest of his life.

These guardians of the general conscience were not merely concerned with exerting pressure on public opinion; they also possessed the personal courage to uphold their convictions at all times, or to suffer for them if necessary. In the capital itself was growing up a strong party of these *literati*; they influenced Government morality, and even powerful men feared their censure.

Only the eunuchs dared to take up arms against them, for while the power of this party was still unbroken its enmity spelt danger even to the Emperor's prime favourites. The first collision occurred in the year A.D. 166. The eunuchs accused the heads of the party of scheming with scholars of the Academy to form a ministerial party whose aim was to discredit the Emperor's rule. The weak Emperor Huan, then on the throne, was greatly enraged, and issued an edict ordering the arrest of the adherents of the party. One of the Censors remonstrated strongly, which only augmented the Emperor's wrath. He incarcerated all those who had been arrested, and offered rewards for the capture of the remainder. Not until the intervention of the Empress's father, T'u Wu, who as field-marshal occupied a position of authority, were they permitted to return home, when they still remained under strict observation. Public opinion, however, unanimously championed these martyrs to a just cause. Honourable designations were found for them, their steadfastness in suffering became the subject of open discussion, and the indignities they had undergone served but to heighten their power.

In the year 169, in the reign of the Emperor Ling, a still more violent outbreak occurred. The eunuchs were now fighting for their lives; driven into a corner, they abandoned all restraint. The trouble started with the accusation and death of over a hundred *literati* and the banishment of their families to the frontiers. T'u Wu himself was one of the victims. Seizing the opportunity, the eunuchs wrought fearful havoc among their adversaries. They secured the person of the Emperor and made short work of any who incurred their displeasure. Of a further seven to eight hundred persons some were thrown into prison, others executed. Not until the year 184, when the rebellion of the Yellow Turbans broke out, were the survivors released for fear lest the anger aroused by these persecutions should add fresh fuel to the revolution. But the downfall of the dynasty could no longer be averted. Once more an accumulation of causes was hastening the end. The peasant masses congregated around individual leaders who knew how to attract them with promises of social reforms and expectation of magic aid. The house of Han, which had fallen foul of its own best forces, came to an inglorious end at the hands of ambitious mercenaries, who, having usurped supremacy, bore the defenceless Emperor along on all their raids and retreats.

VI. The Rise of Religious Communities in the Later Han Period

No religious communities existed in China in the days of antiquity. The ancient cult was associated with the family and the State. Apart from temple attendants, no specific priesthood developed, for the heads of states and families were likewise their priests. Moism might possibly have engendered a religious institution, for of all the indigenous Chinese schools of philosophy it displayed the greatest tendency to develop into a kind of priestly hierarchy. Moism, however, disappeared during the struggles of the Warring States without leaving a trace of this sort behind. The nearest approach to an organized Church might have been found among the magicians (*fang shï*). They exerted no small influence even on political matters, and under Ts'in Shï Huang Ti and Han Wu Ti played a really important part. Wang Mang believed to the last in the possibility of divine aid against the advancing troops of the Han. On the other side, Kuang Wu, the founder of the Later Han dynasty, was also induced to come forward by various

196

prophecies on the part of a Taoist soothsayer.[1] Even the Confucianism of Tung Chung-shu, the reformer of Confucian doctrines under the Han dynasty, was greatly influenced by the ideas of the magicians. This is shown in his treatment of the *Book of Changes* and the *Spring and Autumn Annals* of Confucius, where he interprets the Confucian doctrines with the help of the *yin-yang* principle of duality and that of the five elements. A number of other Confucianists followed in the same tracks. The inference may be drawn that by the Han period the empire had attained a degree of civilization at which, just as in the Roman Empire, the lack of a universal religion was felt, and that all these were but preliminary stages, comparable to the antecedents of Christianity in the Roman Empire.

Viewed from this standpoint, the place occupied by Buddhism in China corresponded to that of Christianity in Europe. Both were alien religions, both underwent decided changes in their new homes, and imbibed certain influences from competing religions. Buddhism was officially introduced into China in the reign of the Emperor Ming Ti, who in A.D. 61–67 had sent a mission into India—to procure, so legend runs, the god whose golden image had been revealed to him in a dream. Lo-yang was made its headquarters. There is, however, distinct evidence that Buddhist images and teachings had already reached the Chinese people before this date by way of Central Asia, where Buddhism had long been practised. After the destruction of the I-kü, and the institution of neighbourly and commercial relations between Ts'in and the western territories, continual mention is made of golden images—those, for instance, derived from Hellenist-Buddhist sculpture, which were set up in the Imperial palaces; for the art of representing the human form in sculpture first came to China in the wake of Buddhism, and, like the ancient Christian art, displays distinct Hellenistic origins. The first sutras mentioned in China date from

[1] Not without an ironical side is the story of Liu Hin, Court librarian to Wang Mang, who, having received oracular evidence that Liu Siu was to inherit the empire, changed his name to Liu Siu so that the plum might be his. He had no luck. Fate produced the real Liu Siu, no less a man than the future Emperor Kuang Wu.

the time of Ai Ti, at the beginning of the Christian era. Then in the reign of Ming Ti arrived the aforesaid mission from India, bearing sutras and images of Buddha on a white horse. Lodgment was accorded to it in a *sï* (this word originally denoted a residence for Court eunuchs, but was subsequently employed as a general term for official quarters), where the Indians who had accompanied it remained, and translated a number of Buddhist texts into Chinese. After their death the place was consecrated as a Buddhist monastery, " the White Horse," and from this time the term *sï* gradually acquired the meaning of a Buddhist monastery.

One cannot say of Buddhism, it is true, any more than of Christianity during the first few centuries, that it immediately became an authorized religion. For political or other reasons alien religious establishments have always been tolerated at the Chinese Imperial Court, though the exercise of the religions in question might not be permitted in China.[1]

Again, the campaigns conducted by the generals Ma Yüan and Pan Ch'ao in the western regions, which led to their reunion with China after an interval of sixty-five years, must clearly have contributed in a high degree to Chinese acquaintance with Buddhist teachings.

One of the Emperor's brothers applied himself zealously to the study of Buddhism, but owing to his political untrustworthiness he was banished and degraded in rank. He committed suicide. The extent of this scandal, which involved over a thousand persons, naturally did not help to favour the spread of Buddhism in China. Among the masses, however, in whom the yearning for religion and salvation was becoming ever more insistent, the Mahayana form of Buddhism, which in cultural type corresponds to the Early Catholic Church, became increasingly popular. Its adherents, however, might occupy only lay positions in the community. The Chinese were still prohibited from shaving their heads and entering a monastery. Nearly all

[1] The various lama temples in Peking, no less than its Russian and Catholic Churches, are modern examples of alien religious establishments that are officially tolerated.

PLATE 27

Painting on silk of a woman with attendants under a tree.
T'ang period.

the priest-monks of that time belonged to the western Hu tribes, so that the Buddhism of those days still wore an entirely alien aspect. Not until the reign of the Emperor Wên of the Wei dynasty were the Chinese permitted to take the vows and enter a monastery.

Apart from direct influences of this nature, Buddhism also exerted very vital indirect influences on China in that it stimulated Taoism to become a religious system. The magicians of Ts'in and Han times borrowed various elements of the incoming Buddhism, and on the pattern of this religion established a religious system of their own. Borrowing from the monastic disciplinary rules of Buddhism in particular became more and more extensive. The Taoist monastic system is entirely built up on the Buddhist model. Some of these developments are, of course, only of later date. It was chiefly in the T'ang period, when special veneration was shown to Lao Tsï—he was regarded as the progenitor of the ruling house—that Taoism gained a fairly firm foothold on the path prepared by Buddhism.

The magicians of the Han period gradually divided into two distinct schools. One strove to attain immortality by meditating on the mysteries of the philosopher's stone (the School of Meditation). The other sought to heal sickness and banish evil spirits with amulets and charms, and was known as the School of Amulet Magic. This latter school was, from its inception, not very unlike a religious church organization. After the advent of Buddhism Lao Tsï was elevated more and more to the level of a divinity in rivalry with Buddha. He was worshipped under the designation of T'ai Shang Lao Kün (' the Great and Ancient Ruler on High '). In the same way that Taoist legends had previously represented Confucianism as being influenced by Lao Tsï, so in time myths arose in which Lao Tsï, after his withdrawal from the world, was made to visit the Hu tribes, there to propagate his doctrines and prepare the ground for Buddhism in those parts. Thus did Taoism develop into a religious community. Its founder was one Chang Taoling, a descendant of the Chang Liang who in his day was so helpful to the founder of the Han dynasty. After long wanderings through the empire, his chief place of sojourn being in Szechwan, which is still to-day the home of religious movements, he compiled a work, announced that he had attained Tao, and took up his abode on the Lung Hu Shan (' Dragon and Tiger Mountain '), in the present province of Kiangsi. He entitled himself 'the Celestial Preceptor' (*T'ien Shï*), and composed charms to expel sickness and evil spirits. After his death the power to conjure spirits devolved upon his descendants, who carried on the work of their ancestor on the Dragon and Tiger Mountain and inherited the title of *T'ien Shï*. These hereditary Celestial Preceptors are frequently called the Popes of Taoism, an entirely unjustifiable designation, since the bearers of this title have never wielded more than a purely moral dominion over the Taoist community in China. They were never upheld by a hierarchy, as were the Popes of the Church of Rome.

Toward the end of the Han dynasty there arose a number of Taoist agitators, such as the Yellow Turbans, the so-called Rice-thieves, and others, who furnished the first illustration of that connexion between religious secret sects and political upheavals which was subsequently to become a characteristic phenomenon in China. Right down to the nineteenth century times of unrest and revolution have produced new religious sects, and *vice versa*. The persecutions of these sects recorded in Chinese history are chiefly connected with their political activities; for on the whole Chinese Governments have displayed considerable tolerance in purely religious questions so long as no actual political issues resulted from such religious beliefs. Apart, however, from the frequently changing sects, which supplied to many a cultural and political movement a background that should not be overlooked, there evolved from the notion of these hereditary Celestial Preceptors of Taoism something in the nature of a Taoist Church. Establishing itself ever more securely, in the course of centuries it was always borrowing fresh elements from Buddhism, until it developed into a national religion of equal potency and running on parallel lines with the rival creed. And thus it lives on in the history of China.

CHAPTER VII

THE DARK AGES: PERIODS OF POLITICAL DIVISION
220–588

I. THE DOWNFALL OF THE HAN DYNASTY—THE THREE KINGDOMS

COMPARISON may quite aptly be instituted between the period of the Han dynasty and that of the Roman Empire in Europe. It is not merely invited by the fact that they were contemporary. Just as the legacy of Greek civilization, distributed over the extended arena of European history, fused with the religious and philosophic elements penetrating from the East—the new-born Christian Church being the vessel in which this fusion took place—so it was during the Han period that the cultural inheritance of China was first collected and sifted. China resembles the Rome of later antiquity in yet another respect—namely, in the spread of religious influences from Near and Central Asia—the same influences in part that reached the West—and their growth in a common nursery with Buddhism, then becoming a world religion. Contact was established between the fringes of these two civilizations. It seems that a mission sent by Marcus Aurelius actually found its way into China.[1] In any case, the connecting links forged in the Former Han period still existed in the days of the Later Han. Conversely, the cultural inventions of China were steadily spreading over and stimulating ever larger areas in the West. Brush-writing had been invented by Mêng T'ien as early as 215 B.C., in the dynasty of the Former Han. In A.D. 105 came the invention of paper by Ts'ai Lun. In A.D. 175 the Confucian texts were inscribed on stone tablets, and thus standardized for the first time. From these tablets rubbings

---

[1] A Syrian merchant headed a mission purporting to come from King An-tun of Ta Ts'in, which arrived from the West in A.D. 166.

on paper were made, a process which became very popular after the invention of ink in A.D. 400, and which gradually led to the employment of wood blocks for printing. In the succeeding period came the printing of books.[1]

All these inventions found their way to the West. It is quite easy to trace the route from East to West.followed in the course of centuries by paper and book-printing.

As regards political conditions, the Eastern Han dynasty ended in a welter of senseless struggles for supremacy. Of the two great evils experienced at the Court of the Han rulers, one was the presence of the Empress's relatives. They had several times—last under Wang Mang—brought the dynasty to the verge of destruction.

The Charybdis to this Scylla was the eunuch pest, responsible for such mischief as the destruction of the *literati* in the years 166–169. The dynasty came to an end in the midst of a war to the knife between these two parties. One of the Empress's relatives planned to destroy the eunuchs, and conspired to this end with a general. Before they could act, however, the eunuchs trapped and killed him. But revenge was at hand. The general, seeing his own safety threatened, brought up his troops and slaughtered two thousand eunuchs at one fell swoop. Another general, the fat and brutal Tung Cho, took advantage of the disorder literally to steal the Emperor. Having sacked and fired the capital, Lo-yang, without sparing the tombs of the emperors or the nobility, he collected a following of several thousand persons and carried the Emperor off to the west, with the intention of transferring the capital to Ch'ang-an. This day marked the end of Han civilization. What with looting and burning, innumerable priceless memorials of art and literature were lost. Tung Cho was chased by other troops, and his exodus rapidly assumed the character of a panic flight. Jealousy and squabbles broke out in his own army. He was murdered and his corpse exposed to the worst indignities.

Having gained distinction in these struggles by his well-

[1] The first experiments in printing are found in Buddhist monasteries as early as the seventh century. The oldest extant example of printing comes from Japan, where it was executed in A.D. 770 by command of a Buddhist empress.

disciplined troops and the breadth of his political views, one Ts'ao Ts'ao succeeded in acquiring control over the last Han emperor, thus providing his family with the opportunity to ascend the throne. Ts'ao Ts'ao plays a remarkable *rôle* in the history of Chinese civilization. A man of intellect—there exist quite a number of poems and literary essays from his pen—he was nevertheless accused of treachery and unscrupulousness, and is regarded as the type of a talented traitor. This was the reason why the dynasty founded by his family was never officially recognized. For judged by the extent of its dominion, this dynasty, which assumed the name of Wei, was undoubtedly the continuation of the Han dynasty. It never succeeded, however, in bringing the south under its sway. The naval engagement at the Red Wall on the Yangtse in A.D. 208, in which its whole fleet was destroyed, established the division of the regions north and south of this river which was to occur so often in subsequent Chinese history. The house of Wei maintained supremacy in the north. The south was divided between the dynasty of Wu, on the Lower Yangtse, and that of the Minor Han, in the west of the empire. This is the epoch of the Three Kingdoms, whose conflicts marked the heroic age of China. The heroes of this period, Liu Pei, the scion of the house of Han, his loyal general Kuan Yü, worshipped later as the God of War, and the master of craft, Chu-ko Liang, together with their great antagonist, the treacherous Ts'ao Ts'ao, became popular figures of romance, and are still to be seen on the stage at the present day.

On the whole this was a time of bloodshed and misery, as well as marked deterioration in the general standard of living. One reason for this was the severance of the foreign trade connexions formed during the Han period, upon which the State had come to depend. To the consequent disorganization of economic life were added warfare and famine. Even the gradual reunion of the empire and the establishment of the Tsin dynasty, for which a general of the house of Wei was responsible, brought no general restoration of order. The surest sign of the ravages of the preceding years is the fact that the national census taken in the year

280, after the consolidation of the empire under the Tsin dynasty, showed a total of only 13,863,000 persons, or one-half the population of A.D. 200.

In addition to all this, the Turkic Hu tribes, who claimed descent from the Han dynasty, and assumed its family name of Liu, were steadily gaining ascendancy in the north. In 311 and 316 respectively the capitals Lo-yang and Ch'ang-an were pillaged. Kingdoms were established in the north by various foreign tribes. The Tsin dynasty had to retreat south, and the empire was again divided. This epoch is described in Chinese histories as "the harassing of the Middle Kingdom by the five Hu." Actually there were not five, but only three tribes—namely, a Turkic, an East Mongolian, and a Tibetan tribe. The mightiest among the kingdoms to arise in Northern China was that of the Toba Tatars. Its seat of government was originally at Yün-kang, later at Lo-yang. In the history of art it achieved fame chiefly through its Buddhist sculptures in the cave-temples at Yün-kang and Lung-mên. It was in these times, too, that Buddhism was declared an authorized religion, first by a foreign, and then by the native dynasties.

This is the period of Chinese migration, corresponding in many respects to the Dark Ages in European history before the Carolingian renaissance. In both places—in China as in the Roman Empire—there was a rapid dwindling of the hitherto cultured classes of society. Barbarian tribes, of new and undegenerated blood, streamed in vast numbers into the land and mingled with the remnants of the old population to produce fresh races. Simultaneously was adopted a universal religion, penetrating from without. It is peculiar to both these universal religions—to Buddhism here as to Christianity elsewhere—that they dissolved the old cultural-psychological ties and at the same time helped to deliver the world from the oppressive spirit of fatalism. The life of man lost its stark reality, and was propelled instead into a wider and therefore consoling metaphysical state of redemption. The striking part about the spread of these two universal religions over new territory is their divergence from their original tendencies. Christianity,

PLATE 28

Bridge over a stream. Painting ascribed to Fan Hua-yüan.
Sung period (?). 145×72 cm. (Oppenheim Collection.)

the eschatology of which was originally confined to the present life, and which foresaw the end of the world, followed by the establishment of the Kingdom of God upon earth, became transcendental. The Kingdom of God withdrew into heaven, where the souls of the faithful might take refuge from all earthly ills. Its ultimate descent to earth became more and more problematic, expression of such a hope increasingly confined to spasmodic outbursts on the part of the people. Even so did the aspect of Buddhism change. Out of the denial of the doctrine that life is the source of all suffering grew the mild religion of the Pure Land, rejoicing in the hope of rebirth in the blessed Western Paradise, in the presence of which hope the importance attached to Nirvana steadily diminished.

Between the twilight of the gods in the East and the West, however, an essential distinction must be drawn. Civilization clearly did not reach so low an ebb in China as in Europe, and recovery was therefore far more rapid. By about the year 600 a renaissance may be observed in China which to some extent combined the gradual processes of renovation to be seen in the Carolingian, Ottonian, Hohenstaufen, and the Greco-Italian renaissance after the fall of Constantinople.

For this there were various causes. In Europe the population in the actual centre of culture declined markedly both in vitality and numbers. While Italy and Greece were being laid waste by barbarian inroads, new empires were growing up, mainly in the colonial border districts of Germany. The old civilization, however, was never very deeply rooted here. The consequence was a very marked lowering and coarsening of social conditions. It should not be forgotten that illiteracy was · so general that even the rulers had to limit their signatures to a cross. All the remnants of the ancient civilization had taken refuge behind monastery walls, and the Church of Rome represented the culture of Rome, which impressed the younger races as something foreign and unsympathetic. An irreparable breach in the fabric of civilization resulted. Civilizations are highly perishable products. Let one or two generations neglect the cultivation of their intellects and culture will be irretrievably wiped out. Thus on European soil—under the stimulating influence, indeed, of Roman civilization—something entirely new had to arise. This event, if erroneously regarded as a renaissance or rebirth, must be classed as an altogether hybrid product. In the history of civilization no such thing exists as rebirth, only new birth, cradled perhaps in the arms of the ancient civilization, or else revelation of the elements of a civilization which, though they may have been obscured for a time, are nevertheless present.

We find the old elements of civilization in China severely damaged, but not in ruins. The thread of continuity is not broken. There are many reasons to account for this. The outlying border territories—which in Europe formed the chief arena of new history—did not isolate themselves from the sources of civilization. On the contrary, the barbarian kingdoms establishing themselves on Chinese soil displayed a marked tendency to preserve Chinese civilization as a desirable thing. The Toba Tatars, for instance, made the adoption of Chinese customs and language compulsory, and Chinese culture was also promoted by other Turkic rulers. The south, too, where Chinese civilization, although not indigenous, had nevertheless been deeply rooted for hundreds of years, continued to flourish as a permanent storehouse of living tradition. Through the courage of its adherents Confucianism had proved a public moral force to which all who strove for power must bow, if not in deed, at least in word. Thus was Chinese civilization endowed with a dignity which was more effective than a decaying military power.

Moreover, although China, through the agency of Buddhism, was penetrated by and adopted a number of Indian, Hellenistic, and, if the Amida cult be included, Persian cultural influences, Buddhism was not the guardian of the ancient civilization, but at most represented an equivalent stage of civilization. It is true that out of religious conviction more and more of the eminent intellects turned toward Buddhism, but it would be far more correct to say that Buddhism rather than Chinese civilization gained in prestige thereby.

The Chinese aristocracy, which was recruiting fresh strength at that time, imparted such distinction to the Chinese name that it became an intellectual force before which even the power of foreign rulers paled. The distinctive character of Chinese literature is probably one reason why Chinese tradition has proved more enduring than the Roman. The alphabetical script employed in Europe reproduces only the pronunciation of the language. When this pronunciation alters and the spoken language becomes incomprehensible the whole literature loses its meaning. So it comes about that those contributions to literature belonging to early linguistic stages are consigned to the realms of antiquity, where they moulder and cease to count as a live factor in civilization. The Chinese script, on the other hand, has remained in principle ideographic. It is probable that the pronunciation was handed down through committing traditional material to memory. But the fact that this pronunciation changed—

Fig. 14. Development of the Chinese Characters

The right-hand column shows the form of the seal characters, the adjoining one that of a later date, the centre column the characters as still written. The next column on the left shows the cursive script, which is a somewhat abbreviated form of the correct script, and the last column on the left the so-called grass character, much abbreviated.

after the penetration into China of foreign tribes radical alterations in this respect are, indeed, continually to be found—by no means rendered the script unintelligible. For centuries, on the contrary, it has led an existence practically independent of the spoken language, and provided a living record of the progress of civilization. This is the main reason why nothing once acquired by Chinese culture ever disappears entirely, and why its traditions have survived all changes in race and language. In Germany, for instance, Gothic

207

material has now practically vanished from current literature, which comprises the products of a couple of centuries
at most. In China, Confucius and Mencius still survive in
the consciousness of civilization. The employment of ideo-
graphs in Chinese script, so frequently described as weari-
some and prejudicial to progress, has thus had a good
deal to do with the persistence of Chinese civilization and
the balance maintained throughout Chinese history. The
steady development of mathematics in Europe, with such
remarkable effects on the whole of modern science, may
possibly be ascribed to similar causes. Mathematical
signs are independent of pronunciation, just as Chinese
characters are. It is easy to understand, therefore, why
it was precisely Leibniz the mathematician who saw
in Chinese script the best universal medium for scientific
thought.

It should not be forgotten, however, that the continuity
maintained, despite changes in race, in China's economic
system contributed in great degree to continuity in her
culture.

II. The Development of Religious Thought during the Periods of Dismemberment

We have observed the steady absorption into Confucianism, during the Han period, of certain magical ideas,
and have seen how its dogmas became in consequence ever
more ponderous. The influence of Tung Chung-shu [1] was
particularly strong in this direction. In the Later Han
dynasty, as already noted, came Wang Ch'ung, who with
his rational, even rationalistic, doctrines opposed Confucian dogma. He sought justification for his criticism to
some extent in the naturalistic principles of Taoism. In the
Taoism of these times we find, apart from the doctrines of the
magicians which ensnared public opinion, a very noteworthy
scientific school of thought, which worshipped nature on the
one hand—it regarded the 'Way of Heaven' as the impersonal
law of nature operating unaided—and on the other empha-

[1] See O. Franke, *Studien zur Geschichte des konfuzianischen Dogmas.*

sized the freedom of mankind, a view which opposed the
theory of absolute State control.   This school even indulged
in anarchist theories, a great feature being the categorical
denial of the use of ceremonial in promoting civilization.
The philosophers of the latter part of the Han dynasty and
the early days of the Three Kingdoms inclined more and
more toward this free, critical mode of thought, but not without paying for their free-thinking and the boldness of their
criticism either directly or indirectly with their lives.   The
Taoist texts of Chuang Tsï and Lao Tsï were reissued, with
new commentaries in which additional emphasis is laid on
the scientific standpoint of naturalism.   When, for instance,
heaven is explained as " a comprehensive term for heaven,
earth, and all creation " it is evident that any anthropomorphic
conception of God is finally cast aside.   The pioneer in this
new philosophical mode of interpreting the old works was
Wang Pi.   Although he died in the Wei period, at the early
age of twenty-four, he initiated in his commentaries on the
Book of Changes and Lao Tsï an entirely original line of
thought.   This book of divination, the explanation of which
was formerly so overloaded with antiquarian detail on
oracular procedure and all manner of symbolic matter that
its meaning was entirely obscured by the technique of the
soothsayer, he converted into a book of wisdom, affording
a firm foothold to the thinker in all its images and symbolic
expressions.   In the writings of Lao Tsï, too, he traced a
quite consistent aim, and reduced his sayings from a loose
compendium of mystic reflections to a body of free philosophical aphorisms.   In those days, when dynasties resorted
to meaningless invocation of the moralists of old to conceal
the fact that they habitually usurped the throne from their
predecessors, Confucianism gradually came to be recognized as the official religion of the civilized world.   But
because it lent itself to the concealing of true facts and the
masking of events under fine names and forms it became
an ever hollower sham.   The old Confucianism, breathing
uprightness and true manliness, had resolved itself into an
opportunist, drawing-room philosophy, hiding unpleasant
realities under such expressions as " culture by means of

ceremonial." These Court philosophers were, of course, always ready to place all manner of stumbling-blocks in the way of the free-thinkers—not by meeting their ideas with more profound ideas of their own, but by resorting to State interference to silence their antagonists.

On the other hand, the days of the Wei dynasty witnessed the development of a school of free-thought whose exponents set forth their bold and presumptuous ideas in conjunction with those of Lao Tsï and Chuang Tsï. They extolled vacuity, turned their attention from politics to metaphysics, and drowned the sorrows of life in wine. To this school belong the Seven Sages of the Bamboo Grove, an intimate circle of philosophers and poets who kept aloof from the toils of society. Yüan Tsï was their chief. He ignored all ceremonial, and was accused at Court by one of his enemies of actually tasting flesh at his mother's funeral. The usurping family of Sï-ma, the founders of the Tsin dynasty, nevertheless sought the moral support of this man, who was feared on account of his mental superiority. They desired to connect themselves with him by marriage. The harassed poet had no option but to get so drunk for ten days in succession that business with him was beside the question. This coterie was known as the Ts'ing T'an, or School of Pure Speech. They would not sully their conversation by mention of worldly matters, but oscillated between humorous sallies and devotion to nature. It is possible that a great part of the texts which pass to-day as the work of Chuang Tsï, Lie Tsï, and even Lao Tsï originated in these circles, but it would be going too far to assign their entire writings to this period.

Between the upholders of a pragmatism decked out in Confucian phrases and the exponents of free-thought a life-and-death struggle naturally ensued. As the pragmatists held the instruments of power they had recourse to them, and either executed or banished their opponents. But the spirit cannot be vanquished by sword and knife. These free-thinkers left their mark on literature. The poet T'ao Yüan-ming, with his *Home Again* and *The Peach-blossom Fountain*, contributed in far greater degree to the fame of the latter part of the Tsin period than did the numerous—the far too numerous—gentlemen of the Court with their sharp tongues and dangerous weapons. Thus did freedom abandon the stagnating ranks of Confucianism for those of the Taoist anchorites, and the naturalistic views of these thinkers with their unsophisticated freedom pave the way for the Nihilism and yearning for deliverance of the Buddhist religion. Thus was the seed of critical thought, sown in the past by Wang Ch'ung, absorbed by the universal religion of Buddhism, where it sank like a stone in the sea. Taoism, on the other hand, was soon to be diverted into the quest for the philosopher's stone and the preparation of the elixir of life. In the Sung period, however, Buddhism was to provide a fresh impulse to a reformed Confucianism with pietistic tendencies, which picked up and continued to weave the thread where Wang Pi had dropped it.

III. The Results of the New Aristocracy

Our historical survey would be incomplete without reference to a factor arising from the penetration of the young barbarian tribes into the domain of Chinese civilization—namely, the rise of a new aristocratic spirit.

We have seen how the old social grades of Chou times disappeared as a result of economic development during the centuries following Confucius, and how the sole remaining distinction after the time of Ts'in Shï Huang Ti was that of ruler and subject. During the Wei and Tsin dynasties, however, historical conditions once more favoured the growth of a new aristocracy. A system had been evolved for procuring a suitable class of officials. Able and upright men were to be selected throughout the country and recommended for posts in the central Government. They were distributed into nine grades, the immediate purpose of which was to constitute an official aristocracy. But the method according to which the process of selection was conducted favoured the acquisition of influence and power by the great families, who had profited by the turmoil and unrest in the land to gain possession of large estates. The heads of these families resided in the towns, where they could influence Government affairs. They enjoyed the additional advantage of being able to withdraw to their estates whenever circumstances seemed to make this desirable. Gradually, therefore, power was removed from the hands of the central Government and passed entirely into those of the landed aristocracy. All the higher posts were occupied by the nobility. A man of the people might be as able and upright as he pleased—he could never rise above the lower grades. The poorer families now sought a new means to secure official berths. They entered the service of the influential aristocratic families in an administrative capacity. Ostensibly they were placing themselves as 'pupils' under 'masters,' but in reality they were secretaries and agents to the nobility. This state of affairs soon created a wide breach between aristocracy and *bourgeoisie*, for society too became more and more exclusive. Even among the aristocracy themselves there were different stages of rank which were sharply distinguished, such as 'ancient families,' 'families of the second class,' 'latter-day families,' 'ennobled families.' The distinction maintained between nobility and *bourgeoisie* was still sharper. Even in regard to marriage, conventions became so rigid that marriage between the two classes was stigmatized as shameful. This did not prevent the *bourgeoisie*, of course, from aping as closely as possible the manners and customs of the aristocratic class. Every man aimed at appearing better than he was. The *parvenu* who succeeded in associating with the old families had achieved his aim in life.

This tendency to exclusiveness was naturally accentuated by the intermingling of races that was taking place so freely, especially in the north, where foreign tribes were pouring into China. The noble families now guarded their blue blood more jealously than ever. The changing dynasties were regarded with cold contempt, for although they wielded a certain measure of power, what were they but upstarts? In the south, where the ruling families were of Chinese descent, the aristocracy displayed less reserve. True, the families Liu of P'êng-ch'êng, Siao of Lan-ling,

PLATE 29

Mountain scene, with a sage crossing a bridge. Painting ascribed to Hü
Tao-ning. Fourteenth century. 148×90 cm. (Oppenheim Collection.)

and Ch'ên of Wu-hing could not boast of entirely unmixed blood, but once they were on the throne this was winked at, and it was not even thought ignominious to form ties of kinship with them. Occasionally, therefore, we find a scion of the Wang or Sie families from the high aristocracy marrying a princess, or one of their daughters occupying the Imperial throne, no great heed being paid in exclusive circles to these irregularities. Things were very different in the north. There racial distinctions had to be reckoned with. Of the twenty-five empresses of the Wei dynasty only eleven were of Chinese descent, and not one of these came of ancient lineage. These conditions persisted right down to the T'ang period. The seven greatest aristocratic families did not dare, it is true, openly to defy the Emperor's edict against further intermarriage; but they continued to intermarry their daughters surreptitiously; none of them formed matrimonial ties outside their own narrow circle.

There was, of course, an ironical side to the situation. There were surnames of the same sound among the aristocracy and the *bourgeoisie*, and the latter gradually contrived to worm their way into the pedigrees of the great families or parcel them out among themselves. In time, then, all Chinese families became aristocratic: they were the sons of Han. Thus the insistence on noble blood developed into a more or less harmless sport.

In reality such phenomena are invariably the outward signs of corresponding economic conditions. In this instance they were induced by the system of large landed estates. China was cut off from international traffic, and therefore experienced a reactionary period. The peasant risings that brought the old empire to an end at the close of the Han dynasty had thrust the country back into a state of mere plodding existence. But during this period of seclusion vigour was renewed. The foreign tribes were gradually assimilated. In Buddhism a religion was found that united the whole of that vast domain of civilization. Not only did emperors become monks, but public life was so strongly influenced by Buddhism that at that time

China may practically be said to have been Buddhist in the same sense that Europe was Christian.

Thus the tendency toward unity reasserted itself. One after another the lesser dynasties collapsed. Without any violent conflicts the empire passed into the hands of the house of Sui and again formed a united whole.

CHAPTER VIII

THE ERA OF CULTURAL PROSPERITY

THE DYNASTIES OF SUI (589–618) AND T'ANG (618–907)

I. GENERAL CONDITIONS

THE rise of the Sui dynasty was swift, as if some inward spring had been released. We find no individual man of note accomplishing the task. The first emperor was weak and hesitating, the second an eccentric and capricious spendthrift. They are merely a bridge to essential historical developments. The consolidation of the empire that ensued was a natural consequence of existing tendencies. Because Yang, the head of the house of Sui, was not the right man for the work, his house was speedily supplanted by the T'ang family. The Sui period was nevertheless a time of active development. The Great Wall in the north was extended; the digging of the future Imperial Canal was begun; war was waged against Korea; in the west and south palaces were built and fleets launched. Legal and financial reforms were elaborated, only to be rejected in favour of other schemes. In order to alter existing methods of appointing officials so as to abolish the supremacy of the aristocracy a new examination system was instituted. All these things point to fresh strides on the path of civilization. When finally the house of T'ang usurped the place of the ill-starred ruler of the Sui dynasty there were present all the prerequisites for an unparalleled cultural revival. It not only preceded in point of time that of the empire of Charles the Great and of the Arabian caliphate, but achieved a far higher level than either of these Western renaissances.

The restoration of the capital to Ch'ang-an in the west was a significant factor in the early days of this revival, for therewith was renewed the problem of a projected world empire. We are faced here, indeed, with one of those remarkable phenomena, occurring from time to time, the recognition of which makes history far easier to grasp than when it is divided according to dates and rulers. To wit, a process began in the Later Han period that took some five hundred years to mature.[1] This process was nothing less than the reconstitution of the Chinese race. The western and northern Hiung-nu tribes (commonly called the Huns), originally the enemies of Chinese civilization, had in various

Fig. 15. The Founder of the T'ang Dynasty

ways been gradually absorbed into it. This was effected in part by the inter-marriage of their princes with the Chinese ruling house, in part by colonization in areas under Chinese influence, and for the rest by the conquest of Chinese territory and consequent adoption of its nationality. A case in point is that of the Toba dynasty, whose rulers imposed Chinese manners and customs on the people in place of their national language and dress. This process sometimes destroyed the external unity of the Chinese race, and even threatened to undermine it fundamentally. It was now complete, and the T'ang period witnessed the accomplishment of what had been in preparation since Han times, half a millennium before. The day of Imperial unity was once more at hand. Fresh expansion started in the west. Along with Buddhism, the religion connected with these movements, waves of Hellenistic influence from the West swept into China. This Hellenistic influence was now

[1] The Chinese philosopher Mencius regards half a millennium as the normal period of incubation in such cases. *Cf.* the attempt at the end of his work to evolve a philosophy of civilization, which Sï-ma Ts'ien, the historian of the Han period, continues, probably on more correct lines, with reference to his own theories and attitude toward Confucianism.

absorbed. No wonder, then, that in the T'ang period China produced a free and noble classic art unrivalled anywhere outside the sphere of these geo-political conditions.

It is true that the conditions of the time were abetted by the emergence of a personality fitted to make this renaissance one of the most brilliant ever experienced in the course of human history. Li Shï-min, son of the Duke of T'ai-yüan, was this personality. Following his counsel, his father rose against the throne, and, after the assassination of the Emperor Yang, of the house of Sui, made himself head of the empire. His father subsequently resigned the throne to him, and he successfully defended it against the intrigues of his brothers. Under the reign title Chêng-kuan he created an administrative system extending over the whole empire. He was not merely Emperor of China, but Great Khan of the adjacent tribes. These tribes were no more the enemies of former days, the Hiung-nu, the Sien-pi, the Yüe-chï, the K'iang, and so on, for they had long before been absorbed into Chinese civilization.

When reflecting how much longer it took in the West for the Roman Empire to celebrate its renaissance under the Franks and Saxons, we must remember that conditions in China were more propitious than in Europe. The Yangtse formed a boundary beyond which these tribes never penetrated very far. And in the north, moreover, as we have seen, the foreign tribes had been merged into Chinese civilization. Among other evidences of this is the fact that the literature of the Sui period included a number of text-books of the Sien-pi, nearly all of which had disappeared by the middle of the T'ang period. There was no longer any demand for them.

Of the ninety-eight Prime Ministers in power in the course of the three hundred years of the T'ang dynasty no fewer than eleven were of foreign descent. There was alien blood even in the ruling house, commencing with T'ang T'ai Tsung (Li Shï-min). It is this fact that accounts for the fundamental difference between T'ang culture and that of former days.

The foreign tribes to be reckoned with now are : in the west, chiefly the Turcomans (T'u-küe), the Tibetans (T'u-fan), and the Uighurs (Hui-ho); in the north, the ancestors of the Mongols and Manchus, the Koreans, and the Japanese; in the south, the present-day tribes of Yünnan and Annam.

Foreign intercourse was now resumed. The old points of contact in the west existing in Han times were, however, not always easy to recover. In some places the inhabitants had changed and the language was different.[1] Through the translation of Buddhist texts considerable knowledge had been acquired of the phonetic rendering of foreign sounds. If the endeavour in Han times had been to find the closest Chinese equivalent to the foreign words, the present aim was exact reproduction of the native pronunciation. Similarly Germans used to speak of Mailand and Venedig in lieu of Milano and Venezia. This intercourse was accompanied by far-reaching effects on religion and culture. Hüan Tsang and I Tsing journeyed to India in order to bring back the Buddhist Scriptures; ambassadors and visitors came to China from foreign lands; as Marcus Aurelius in former days, so Haroun al-Raschid now sent envoys to China. Traffic was not resumed overland alone. Active exchange trade took place by sea, and Chinese ships could be seen as far from home as the Persian Gulf. Even to-day Japan is not the only place where the T'ang period is regarded as the high-water mark of Chinese civilization. In the Pacific Ocean the Chinese are still called "the people of T'ang."

II. The Examination System and the Literary Renaissance

The level attained by T'ang civilization is not surprising; it was due to a general concentration of intellectual forces. The art and literature of the T'ang period attained one of those rare zeniths in the history of classic culture. In

---

[1] During T'ang times the southern pass across the Pamirs remained steadily blocked by the Tibetans (T'u-fan), notwithstanding a victorious Chinese campaign. The power of the Tibetans attained its zenith in the eighth century, when they actually occupied Ch'ang-an, and it was destroyed only by the Uighurs.

poetry we find Li T'ai-po, Tu Fu, and Po Kü-i, accompanied by a corresponding number of calligraphic experts, whose names are unknown in Europe simply because this art is not yet appreciated here. In painting we have such names as Yen Li-pên, Li Sï-hün, Wang Wei (who was also a poet), and Wu Tao-tsï. The music of the Emperor Ming Huang, not unjustly described as universal music, was famous, and in plastic art the name of Yang Hui-chï is prominent. And these, be it noted, are only the stars, behind which are ranged some hundreds and thousands of other names.

The T'ang period may also claim credit for perfecting the examination system for the appointment of officials. We have already observed the power acquired by the aristocracy through the system of local selection of able and upright men—a power to which even the emperor had occasionally to bow. As soon, therefore, as the Sui dynasty realized that it held the empire in its hand it naturally began to devise means to shatter this power and to make personal ability the passport to officialdom. So the examination system was devised. The Sui dynasty was too short-lived for this reform to be carried through. But in the T'ang period the public service was actually renovated in this way. The tests originally comprised various sciences, such as mathematics, history, jurisprudence, and calligraphy. Soon, however, preference was given to the qualification for the *tsin shï* examination, which was based on a knowledge of the Classics. The classical works most highly esteemed during the T'ang period were the *Li Ki* (*Record of Rites*) and the *Tso Chuan* (*Tso's Commentary*).

Public examinations, however, were only one of various roads to office and distinction in T'ang times. The emperor was still enabled, by virtue of reliable recommendations or his own choice, to appoint exceptionally brilliant men, frequently to very high office. But this procedure became more and more rare, and was not held in anything like the same public esteem as advancement by the successive stages of examination. For the candidate had to undergo not a single test, but a whole number before he reached the top of the ladder and was himself qualified to act as examiner.

Highly remarkable is the manner in which, in time, this system effectively shattered the power of the hereditary nobility and substituted in their place a kind of intellectual aristocracy. It must be confessed that this system ultimately forfeited a great part of its value, that the examination standard became more and more stereotyped, and that on this account the whole of official Chinese education has tended, especially during the last few centuries, toward superficiality and formalism; for examination requirements invariably govern, to a very great extent, the studies and work of those who anticipate entering for them. Nor must the fact be overlooked that even these tests did not entirely destroy the power of the hereditary aristocracy: the same old families still wielded dominion. They had very different means at their disposal for giving their children suitable education than had the uncultured country-folk, whose offspring were probably prepared for examination by some unsuccessful candidate. Quite apart from this, in the acquisition of general knowledge as well as of cultural refinement the value of tradition and personal connexions cannot be disregarded. The examination system nevertheless remained in force, and even became a kind of idol hypnotizing the intellectual life of whole generations by fixing their gaze on the glorious goal—an official post—and the path to this goal—the State examination. Notwithstanding the retention of their great traditional power by the distinguished families, who certainly enjoyed great moral prestige throughout the country, there is no doubt that new blood was continually being imported, and that little by little the bureaucratic system was pervaded by a democratic element that always reconciled the masses to the system as a whole. Could not every man make his way into the circle of the mighty, provided he possessed the necessary industry and talent? Therefore the *élite* were regarded with admiration, perhaps also with envy. But they were tolerated, and the ordinary man continued to cherish hopes of a place at the table of the gods, either for himself or his relations. Regarded objectively, this focusing of interest on examinations—which may aptly be described as a passion shared

PLATE 30

Painting on silk of Taoist magicians preparing the elixir of life.
(R. Wilhelm Collection.)

by Germans and Chinese alike—was of course prejudicial to cultural progress. From a subjective standpoint, however, it provided the ruling authorities with a wonderful means of diverting the gaze of the intellectuals in particular from possible Government abuses, and gradually converting them into active exponents of the system by the slow fulfilment of their hopes.

In every branch of art the T'ang period was a time of exceptional brilliance. This brilliance was not maintained for long, it is true. The illustrious reign of T'ai Tsung was followed all too soon by the cruelty of the Empress Wu. Like the Han Empress Lü before her, she plotted to thrust the house of T'ang from the throne in favour of her own family. In short, she was one of those female rulers with fine brains and masculine energy who have cropped up in China from time to time, and by reason of their exceptional position have done more harm than good. The arts all attained to full glory at the Court of the Muses of Ming Huang (Hüan Tsung, 713–755), as famous for the names of Li T'ai-po and Tu Fu as for that of the fair and dangerous Yang Kuei-fei, whose beauty and criminal passion for the Turkic general An Lu-shan brought disaster on both the empire and herself. The dynasty never quite recovered from the havoc wrought in the capital during these disorders. The latter part of the T'ang period is a time of political decay.

Nevertheless, just as in Greece the political decline of Athens after the brief period of prosperity under Pericles did not stem the progress of art, so it was in China. And even as in Athens the era of decline saw the production of great prose-writing, so again was it in China. The poetry of the T'ang period represents a final stage, the prose of that time a budding stage, of development. In the poetry, which found expression in the form of intensely compressed, short lyrics, a method of presentation was created in which rhythm and the development of the theme went hand in hand. This form is comparable to that of the classical sonata in music. There also is established a final harmony between content and form. It was only natural, therefore, that T'ang poetry should frequently employ and adapt old material, especially that of the Han period. This re-embodied material, then, resembled a precious stone whose full brilliance was now displayed by new cutting. By very reason of its classical nature, however, this form was ill-suited to express fresh, individual experiences. Po Kü-i, the most subjective poet of the later T'ang period, frequently makes use, therefore, of more untrammelled forms.

T'ang prose, on the other hand, as we have already said, represented a new beginning. At the first glance it seems extraordinary, because the movement leading in this direction assumed the form of a renaissance, a revival of antiquity. We must not be misled by this, however. Every vital renaissance is something more than a revival. So it was in the T'ang period. The more ancient Chinese prose is remarkable for its highly concise, semi-rhythmical style, in which parallelism is used for the development of the thought. During the time of the Six Dynasties, ever since the days of the "Seven Scholars of the Kien-an period," literature had been growing more superficial and verbose, and in the Sui and early part of the T'ang period appreciation was confined to the stylistic tricks of the prose essay. The cultivation of this artificial style still continued, chiefly as a Court accomplishment. But, at the same time, a new movement was set on foot at the beginning of the T'ang period, under the banner of the ' old ' style, which strove to promote a freer and more natural method of prose composition. This movement culminated in Han Yü, an exponent of Confucianism and a zealous opponent of what he called Taoist and Buddhist superstitions, but also something of an eccentric in his taste for the antique. He was an honest and sincere representative of the old literary style.[1]

[1] To be sure, a part of his campaign against the magicians he conducted by magic means. A well-known story tells how he was banished from an official post to the wild tribes in the extreme south. He at once started to civilize the people and to spread Confucian teaching. A menace to the neighbourhood in the form of a crocodile was making enormous havoc among men and beasts, but none dared to attack it. A proclamation by Han Yü—a model of the new prose style—in which he bids the monster quit the vicinity, is still extant. As a parting gift he sacrificed a pig to the crocodile, and, lo and behold, the creature, so the story goes, obeyed his command and vanished.

The style originated by Han Yü and adopted by his disciples has survived down to the present day, though the artificial style continued to flourish alongside it. The cultural value of this movement cannot be appraised without studying it in conjunction with developments in the sphere of poetry. Mention has already been made of the fact that the Court poetry of the T'ang period displayed the highest perfection of form imaginable. For all that, its effects are not forced. The entirely natural facility with which the poets express themselves within the strict limits imposed is an admirable feature of their art. We must not forget, however, that in the T'ang period, apart from Court verse, popular poetry arose, and that a poet like Po Kü-i was in constant touch with the masses. He is said to have read all his verses aloud to an old woman of the people, and not to have rested until they ran so as to be intelligible to her. We must assume Chinese colloquial speech to have altered fundamentally since Han times owing to the assimilation of many foreign tribes. This whole literary movement, then, implies an effort to break through traditional forms and regain contact with the spoken language. We find similar endeavours made in Chu Hi's circle during the Sung period, again in the drama of the Mongol dynasty, and in the novel of Ming and Ts'ing times. It is represented to-day in the active movement which has been started to regain touch with the spoken language (*pai hua*), and which has achieved fame as a literary revolution.

III. THE DEVELOPMENT OF FOREIGN RELIGIONS ON CHINESE SOIL

Just as the widespread traffic of T'ang times caused Chinese influences (paper, the compass, and so on) to find their way west, so a great number of religious movements penetrated into China from without. The easy tolerance prevalent in religious matters during the T'ang period induced great activity in religious life. No particular religion was exclusively adopted by the Chinese, but the co-existence of all systems was permitted, and first one, then another, was favoured, either from personal inclination or for political reasons.

(1) Islam had connexions with China at a fairly early date. Mohammed knew China, and commercial traffic between the Chinese and the Arabs seems to have existed as far back as the first half of the fifth century. In T'ang times Chinese ships from Canton called at ports as far up the Persian Gulf as Basra. Arabia was known to the Chinese as Ta Shï, a name derived from a Persian transcription of the name. As early as the first half of the seventh century Islam was introduced into China by emissaries, and a mosque erected in the province of Canton. At a later date Islam came in from the north with the Uighurs.[1] Judaism seems likewise to have reached China from the West, though it was also represented in coastal towns; it maintained itself longest at Kaifeng, where traces of it were still to be found in the nineteenth century.

Islam continued to take root in China until the reign of Wu Tsung (841–846), a superstitious Taoist who in prosecuting the other religions suppressed Islam too. Islam also suffered in the terrible ravages wrought throughout the empire by the rebel Huang Ch'ao in 876. In the destruction of Canton, at that time an international port of first-class importance, a hundred and twenty thousand Mohammedans, Jews, Christians, and Zoroastrians perished. That date marks a revolution in the whole of China's intellectual life: the days of prosperity were over. True, the insurrection was quelled. But as the fall of the dynasty soon followed, exact statistics of the devastation inflicted on China by this catastrophe are not available. Historians agree, however, that this rebellion was even more terrible than that of the Turkic general An Lu-shan, which is estimated to have cost the lives of thirty-six million people.

(2) Christianity found its way into China during the

[1] Hui-hui, the designation under which Islam is known to the Chinese, comes from their name for the Uighurs (Hui-ho, or Hui-hu). The cult of Islam, which is very widespread in China (especially in the west and south), is still confined in the main to persons of foreign nationality. Although the Mohammedans have adopted Chinese surnames, their foreign lineage is still evident. A common name among them, for instance, is 'Ma,' which is an abbreviation of Mohammed.

T'ang period in the form of Nestorianism.[1] Persian monasteries were set up in various important towns.

Several emperors, among others the famous Ming Huang, displayed a deep interest in this religion. Even after Persia was overrun by the Arabs China remained well disposed toward this alien religion. The monasteries were now no longer called Po Si Si (Persian monasteries), but Ta Ts'in Si (Roman, or, to be more exact, Syrian monasteries). On the stone monument erected in 781 in the old capital of Ch'ang-an (the modern Sianfu) is inscribed a detailed account of the work of the Nestorians in contemporary China. Certain peculiarities fostered by the Taoist sect Kin Tan Kiao ('Religion of the Elixir of Life') make it seem not improbable that Taoism, a very melting-pot for all manner of alien religious systems, imbibed certain Nestorian influences. Under the afore-mentioned Emperor Wu Tsung the Nestorian monasteries were likewise suppressed. The monument was buried, and was not exhumed until the Ming period. So Christianity gradually disappeared from China.

(3) Zoroastrianism, the dualistic Persian religion of fire-worshippers, also penetrated into China. When the spread of Islam in Central Asia was followed by the persecution of other religions, the adherents of Zoroaster took refuge in China, where they went unmolested. Apparently no Chinese adopted this religion; its priests, at all events, were all foreigners. But a regular system of official sacrifices was instituted in order to link these people to the country by the bond of religion, just as was the case with the Mongolian lama temples erected in Peking in much later times. Whether permanent vestiges of Zoroastrianism are traceable in the Buddhist Amida cult is a question deserving closer study.

(4) China was the recipient, not only of the orthodox Persian fire-worship, but of the great heretical religion of Manichæism. This remarkable universal religion, fated to be condemned as sectarian wherever it appeared, was

---

[1] King Kiao in Chinese. In the reign of T'ai Tsung the monk O-lo-pên came to China, was lodged by the Emperor in the Imperial Palace at the capital, and entrusted with the translation of the Holy Scriptures.

225

essentially alien to the Chinese character. The enforced celibacy and abstinence from medicines, for which latter healing by prayer was substituted, and naked burial in particular, were things that scandalized the Chinese. So we find even the tolerant Ming Huang prohibiting the practice of this religion by any but foreign races. But the Uighurs had adopted Manichæism as a popular religion, and China was frequently dependent upon them for help; therefore a certain tolerance was displayed. Manichæan monasteries were set up, and even honoured with Imperial tablets. Quite a string of places are named in which these monasteries might be built. Together with the Syrian and Zoroastrian, they represent the three foreign Churches. But this religion also was finally banned by the Emperor Wu Tsung. Only among the Uighurs did it survive until the Sung period.

(5) The prosperity of all these religions was more or less dependent upon Imperial favour. Apart, perhaps, from Mohammedanism, not one of them struck firm or independent roots in China. In this respect they could not compete with the old religions.

Even before T'ang times Taoism had been a great force, especially under some of the northern dynasties. It came noticeably to the fore during the T'ang period, because the surname of Lao Tsï, the founder of Taoism, was Li. Now the surname of the house of T'ang was likewise Li. As the names of Lao Tsï's descendants could be traced right down to Han times, the house of T'ang declared its descent from Lao Tsï, and worshipped him in the official temples under the name of T'ai Shang Hüan Yüan Huang Ti (' Supreme, Wonderful—Primordial Lord and God '). The Emperor Wu Tsung in particular, in his exclusive worship of Taoism, which so long, at all events, as he was in power took the form of intolerance toward other religions, was one of the most ardent supporters of this cult.

(6) In spite of all persecutions,[1] however, Buddhism

---

[1] The chief persecutions mentioned in Buddhist records are those of the three Wu—namely, the persecutions under the Emperors Tao Wu Ti of the Later Wei dynasty, Wu of the Northern Chou dynasty, and Wu of the T'ang dynasty.

PLATE 31

Woodcut, showing a woman with attendant praying in a Buddhist temple.
Ming period. (R.Wilhelm Collection.)

remained the true religion of China. So greatly had it developed that its doctrines were now being amplified by original Chinese thought.

Buddhism also had spread chiefly in the territory of the northern dynasties. But in the south too it attracted all the most notable scholars. In the latter part of the Liang dynasty the Emperor Wu became a signally devout follower of this religion, to which he was converted in the year 517, at last actually becoming a Buddhist monk. It was during his rule that Bodhidharma, the Indian monk (popularly called Ta-mo in Chinese), came to China from India and disseminated the doctrine of meditation.[1]

Bodhidharma's wanderings led him across the Yangtse to Lo-yang, where he paved the way for unity between the northern and southern schools of Buddhism. Then in the T‘ang period were undertaken the famous pilgrimages to India of Hüan Tsang and I Ching. Conversely, China was visited by the great Buddhist Amogha (Pu K‘ung) the Tantrist, and others. Now began the time of the great translations from the Sanskrit whereby Buddhism was adapted to the mentality of the Chinese people. It is true that by now Buddhism had lost its uniformity. Its ranks comprised a medley of different sects, at loggerheads with one another. But spiritual life at this time was full of animation. The T‘ien-t‘ai school and the Amida cult (the doctrine of the Pure Land) had the best following. And the workings of Buddhism exercised a decisive influence on the intellectual life of China, not excluding Confucianism itself, as the Sung period subsequently showed.

IV. Decline and End of the Middle Historical Period

Mention has been made above of the various grave catastrophes experienced in the T‘ang period which decimated

---

[1] Ch‘an, or, in Japanese, Zen. Possibly the chief reason for the spread of this doctrine is that, like the Tantric school, which was gaining ground, and in which a special feature was the burning of paper at burials, it embodied a number of pre-Buddhist as well as genuine Buddhist elements.

the population and dealt the death-blow to cultural prosperity. General conditions were in part responsible, of course, for these events. The rising under the Turkic leader An Lu-shan apparently occurred when the empire was at the zenith of its prosperity, and it seems almost incredible that he should have been able to reduce the country to a state of such thorough chaos and that even the capital succumbed to his onslaught. But, looking a little deeper, we discover a variety of causes which not only rendered such things possible, but which finally threw the empire into a fresh period of disorder.

The high degree of prosperity existing in the early part of the T'ang dynasty was chiefly the work of a single man, the former Crown Prince Li Shï-min, an extraordinarily brilliant personality. But personal qualities alone can ensure no permanence to a foundation, and study of the ruling family soon reveals the same picture as under previous dynasties. Feminine dominion, an attempted revolution by the ambitious Empress Wu, Court intrigues, and schemes of crafty eunuchs make up the Court history of the T'ang as they did that of the Han dynasty.

Of more importance, however, were those centrifugal forces whose workings were not slow to disintegrate the empire, and ultimately brought about its downfall. In the pacification of the country the military commanders stationed at important centres, especially in the border territories, were entrusted with the supervision of several districts, so that apart from military authority they acquired increasing administrative control. Although these posts were not hereditary, we have here a phenomenon analogous to the development of the sovereign power of the margraves in the Holy Roman Empire. These very powerful military leaders exercised within their own areas an authority which was almost independent of the central Government, and after An Lu-shan's rebellion had shown how easily it could be overthrown from such a coign of vantage these despots became more and more arrogant. Regular strongholds were formed. Things reached such a pitch that if one of these generals died the son of the deceased would assume command over his father's troops and refuse to recognize the successor sent by the central Government; or the troops would select their own leader, and force the Government to accord belated sanction to their choice. If this system of satrapy, for which China's regional tendencies have at all times afforded favourable soil, contributed largely to the loosening of the Imperial tie, the division of the central authorities into two distinct camps was no less detrimental. Very natural, therefore, was the state of exhaustion resultant on the efforts required to stamp out the rebellion of Huang Ch'ao. The end was most pathetic. Among the commanders victorious against Huang Ch'ao were two antagonists: one Chu Wên, a former gang-leader of the defeated rebel, who had submitted to the Emperor, and Li K'o-yung, a Turkic general. Li K'o-yung asked permission to be revenged on Chu Wên. Upon the Emperor's refusal he sacked the capital. The Emperor perished in flight, and was succeeded in 889 by his brother. While open warfare was in progress between the two rivals, the eunuchs seized the young Emperor and ruled in his name. Chu Wên released him, and exterminated the eunuchs. Finally he murdered the Emperor and set up a minor in his place. He then had all the Imperial princes strangled at a banquet and all the remaining supporters of the house of T'ang murdered in one night. Then he placed himself on the throne and founded the Later Liang dynasty.

This was the signal for a fresh dismemberment of the empire, for it was clear that the other generals would not submit. Now begins a period of chaos that lasted over fifty years. Later historians have endeavoured to reduce this chaos to some kind of order, but this is no more possible than with events in China to-day. The belligerent leaders occupied smaller or larger areas, as the case might be. Each refused to recognize the other. There no longer existed any authority, however impotent. Therefore the name " the Later Five Dynasties " given to this period in Chinese histories is misleading. The only justification for describing these as successive dynasties is that each family in turn deposed its predecessor, and that most of them established their capital at Kaifeng. There were in addition, however, a whole string of sovereign states, among which the province of Szechwan in particular played a certain cultural *rôle*.

The ancient splendour of China is now enshrouded in nocturnal gloom. Incessant struggles for supremacy laid waste the land. This warfare, although lacking decisive military issue, devastated the country and impoverished the people. The propertied classes were subjected to perpetual raids and pillaging,   became poorer and poorer. Still more difficult was it . r the indigent peasants to exist. They joined the brigand hordes which were everywhere harrying and burning the country, or sought their daily bread in Government or military employ. It was the ambition of every ruler to found a great and mighty dynasty. A number of them who had no sons adopted unrelated children merely in order to have heirs. This accounts for the existence of ruling families of different name within the same dynasty. Shï King-tʻang, the head of the Later Tsin dynasty, probably went furthest in this respect. In order to seize the throne he sought help of the Tungusic Kitan, and when this move was successful not only ceded sixteen northern districts to this foreign tribe, but had the effrontery to adopt the chief of the barbarian horde as his father.[1]

In such circumstances it may be well understood that the serious Confucian spirit which still flourished in Han times now became a vanishing quantity. Gifted *literati* wrote memorials in which they recommended themselves for vacant posts, and the history of those days could show a counterpart of Talleyrand. This was Fêng Tao, the " ever gay old man," who served seven ruling families in succession,

[1] By this cession of Chinese territory the Kitan, a tribe of Eastern Tatars, came into power. They established in the north a dynasty of their own, from 937 onward called the Liao. Its original capital at Liao-yang was transferred later to Peking. Kitai, or Cathay, the European name for China in olden times, is derived from the word Kitan. The Liao were subsequently driven out by a sister tribe, the Ju-chên (Djurdjen). In Kashgaria they founded the kingdom of Karakitai, while the Ju-chên later called themselves Kin and conquered the whole of Northern China, only to be swept away by the Mongols. The Manchus, founders of the latest Chinese dynasty, were related to the Kin.

and in the midst of revolution always knew how to steer his bark successfully among the rocks. The amazing thing is that he composed a laudatory poem on himself as the " ever gay old man," and enumerates with great satisfaction the various honours and dignities he acquired in the course of his lively career.

It is difficult, however, to depict the entire life of any period by means of such generalities. While everything seems, on the one hand, to be in a state of decay, on the other intellectual life is progressing. And so even these dark times left a legacy that was to herald new life, not only for China, but for all mankind : the invention of printing.

Quite successful attempts at printing had already been made, for some time past, in Szechwan, chiefly in Buddhist quarters. Book-printing, however, was first made known to the world at large through the efforts of Fêng Tao, that " ever gay old man " of whom we have just been speaking. The event occurred in connexion with a new edition of the Classics.

In order to ensure a reliable text of the classical Confucian books they had been inscribed on stone as early as the Han period, and again, for the last time, during the T'ang dynasty. From these stone tablets impressions were taken on paper by means of inked squeezes, the characters showing white on a black ground. Fêng Tao now recommended the use of wood blocks in place of stone slabs, and the rulers of the Later Chou dynasty gave instructions to this effect in 932 ; by 953 the whole of the Nine Classics had been printed.

The spread of block-printing dates from this time. The fruits of this invention reached maturity in the Sung dynasty, when printed books came into vogue, in which art notable achievements were recorded within the lifetime of the dynasty. Owing to the ease with which printed books could be circulated education was rendered largely accessible to the masses. It is thanks to the possibilities created by this invention that Confucianism has become a possession of the whole Chinese nation. In the Sung period, too,

Pi Shêng invented printing with movable type. As a result of commercial intercourse these inventions found their way west, like the earlier inventions of paper and the compass. They were taken over by Gutenberg and the other European printers, and inaugurated a new era in the history of mankind.

MODERN HISTORY

CHAPTER IX

THE ERA OF SELF-COMMUNION
THE SUNG DYNASTY (960–1279)

I. REORGANIZATION OF THE STATE AND RELATIONS WITH BORDER TRIBES

THE Sung period represents in Chinese history an end and a beginning. On the one hand, existing cultural material was examined as a whole and deductions drawn. In the political sphere stock was taken of Chinese possessions, and revealed a marked decline in comparison with T'ang times. The bridge to the West had been broken down. In the north new danger was imminent in the shape of various East Mongolian tribes, known as the Kitan (Liao), the Ju-chên, and the Kin, who penetrated one after another into the northern plains of China and there started to form the nucleus of a new state. The remaining territory, however, was brought under one government. In the intellectual sphere similar conditions prevailed. Here also the legacy from the past was surveyed. In art as well as in science the work of collecting began. The era of great catalogues and encyclopædias is now ushered in. In philosophy and religion much the same happened. Buddhism was now naturalized on Chinese soil; doubtless because this religion was driven from its native land, intercourse with India ceased, and the spiritual acquisitions of Buddhist thought benefited Confucianism. These are retrospective points.

On the other hand, the times called urgently for reform. A final solution had to be found for the agrarian problem, and this task was performed only after long party warfare, in the course of which a change of front took place. In the intellectual domain, too, new forces were emerging. Art was getting into closer touch with nature. In place of sculpture,

233

painting came to the fore. And in literature fresh seeds were sown, destined to develop into new literary forms, the drama and novel of later days. Similarly, the world of ideas was stimulated by Neo-Confucianism, which, although it was accompanied on the one hand by the danger of spiritual routine and stagnation, on the other proved an incentive to further progress in thought in the shape of the renaissance and reforms of the Ming and Ts'ing periods.

The founder of the Sung dynasty came straight from the camp to the throne. With some reluctance he permitted his

Fig. 16. The Founder of the Sung Dynasty

officers to throw the yellow robe round his shoulders, and, if only in self-defence, was then obliged to carry through the fight for the throne. An honest and straightforward man, he was noted rather for his practical common sense than for brilliant intellectual gifts. He is said to have been a sincere Confucianist, supplying just the element of order needed as a nucleus round which a new monarchy might crystallize. Without much ado the wreckage of the different states passed into his hands, and unity was re-established. He knew his own mind. As in the case of the founder of the Han dynasty, he had risen to power through the co-operation of a number of lieutenants. The cunning peasant of Han made a poor return to his paladins, by destroying them one after another and then gathering the reins of power into his own hand. Chao K'uang-yin, the father of the Sung dynasty, went more honourably to work. When the main task had been accomplished, he called his trusty followers together and quite frankly proposed that they should retire from their military posts. Upon their unanimous agreement he amply compensated them with lucrative berths. He took this opportunity to dispense with those dangerous institutions the frontier governors. In fact, he succeeded in combining within the central Government, not only the supreme military command, but the control of finance. This arrangement was clearly of great importance for the centralization of the Government. Subsequently, however, at the time when Yo Fei was defending the empire against enemies in the north, it became evident that in consequence of this arrangement generals in the field could be greatly impeded through intrigues at the capital. Furthermore, as the capital in the neighbourhood of the modern Kaifeng had been abandoned, frontier defence directed from the existing capital proved far more arduous. In former days, as we have seen, so long as the pendulum of barbarian incursions and Chinese expansion swung between west and east, it was always a time of expansion when the capital was in the west, nearer to the frontier, while its transfer eastward invariably implied a decline in power. The pendulum was now swinging in a new direction. Centuries of climatic change, in the course of which the western areas became desert, while the north-eastern districts of modern Manchuria gained in importance, must be regarded as the main cause of this shift in direction. From now onward, at all events, inroads are made by barbarians from the north, and the place of the former western and eastern capitals is taken by a southern capital (Nanking) and a northern capital (Peking). However, the logical conclusion—the transfer of the capital to the north—was not reached until the Yung-lo reign period in the Ming dynasty. For the time being the northern tribes were decidedly on the offensive.

When the dynasty had established itself firmly numerous attempts were certainly made by the central Government— some under the leadership of the Emperor himself—to subdue the northern tribes, or at all events recover the annexed territories. But in vain. After a number of serious reverses these attempts had to be abandoned. Nothing remained but to suffer the presence, in the neighbourhood of the northern frontier, of a foreign kingdom, which, it is true, was steadily assimilating Chinese civilization.

At first the northern kingdom was occupied by the Kitan, a branch of the ancient Sien-pi. In the east this kingdom extended to the sea, in the west to the Altai range, in the north to the mouth of the Amur, and in the south as far as the Great Wall, so that the northern part of Chihli, including Peking, fell within its boundaries. This kingdom was given the name of Liao. Its capital was situated at Liao-yang, on the Liao-tung peninsula, afterward at Peking. This kingdom likewise claimed the Imperial title for its ruler. Every attack on the part of the Sung was repulsed with great loss. All the remaining northern tribes—Tatars, Ju-chên, and Koreans—joined forces with the Kitan, and demanded of the Sung the cession of districts to the south of the Great Wall which they had temporarily occupied in earlier times. The Sung dynasty could not bring itself to cede territory, but agreed to a yearly payment of 100,000 ounces of silver and 200,000 pieces of silk. In the treaty concluded between them the Liao Emperor recognized the Sung Emperor as his elder brother, and the latter acknowledged the Empress-Dowager of Liao as his aunt. In 1042 the payments were increased. But the chief thing was that peace was restored and China had saved her face, for no territory had been ceded.

To these embarrassments was added another in the northwest, where the Si-hia had established a kingdom midway between the Liao and the Sung, and, having obtained securities from both these powers, had finally set themselves up as an empire. Their sole link with China consisted in the fact that their ruling house had borrowed the name of Chao from the Sung, and that they received an annual grant for the maintenance of auxiliary forces. This grant was of course only another form of the tribute paid to the Liao. In reality the Si-hia did as they pleased.

II. THE REFORMS OF WANG AN-SHĬ

These annual and not inconsiderable payments proved, as may well be imagined, a heavy drain on the Chinese exchequer. Finally the burden became intolerable, and the

PLATE 32

Woodcut, showing a female dancer performing at a feast.   Ming period.
(R.Wilhelm Collection.)

problem arose how the empire could be sufficiently strengthened by internal reforms to free it from such an ignominious position. This was the reason why the renowned Wang An-shï took the helm with his plans for agrarian reform.

Wang An-shï, who was in power from 1069 to 1076, was a statesman of immense energy. His methods and unscrupulous manner of enforcing them are reminiscent of the West. All his ideas were reasonable in themselves. That he could not maintain his power was due to his reckless and drastic methods of reform, in the carrying out of which he did not shrink from making enemies on all sides. Thus he excited a controversy between reformers and conservatives that endured for several decades and in which the two parties practically changed places in the end. He nevertheless established certain principles that have supplied taxation authorities with a criterion for all time in dealing with the agrarian system.

His aim was twofold : the reform of the financial and the military systems. For these two projected reforms everything else had to make way. Here is an outline of his main schemes :

(1) *Finance.* The State system of finance had been taken over by the predecessors of the Sung in a hopeless state of chaos, and the Sung cannot be said to have improved it. Wang An-shï now appointed an official commission whose duty it was to draw up a uniform budget of revenue and expenditure. Under no circumstances might this budget be exceeded. An annual saving of some 40 per cent. resulted.

Then he attempted to extend his financial scheme into other fields. His " green sprout " loan achieved most fame. At the time of the spring sowing the intendants of circuit, taking each case on its merits, were to make loans to the peasants, to be employed as capital for the efficient cultivation of their land. After the autumn harvesting these loans had to be repaid with interest. The means of repayment were raised by resorting to the pasturage set apart for communal purposes. In this way the farmers were enabled to incur the outlay necessary to increase the yield of their land.

A second step was the abolition of statute labour. A yearly sum was paid into a redemption fund. A regular system of employment on public works was then instituted, and the workers remunerated out of this fund. In this way was abolished that uncertain factor statute labour—which included military service—and the farmer could count on a regular supply of labour. These measures met with violent opposition from the enemies of Wang An-shï on the pretext that the peasant had no ready cash, and would be obliged, in order to repay his debt, to fell his valuable timber and dispose of his farm-stock. Their advantages nevertheless proved so great that they still form part of the agricultural system in China.

A further and most fundamental measure was the institution of a regular land-survey system. After careful re-measurement the capacity of each individual allotment was assessed and the tax on it fixed accordingly. The aim of this scheme was to supply an accurate basis for the incidence of land taxation.[1]

Another measure, instituted in 1074, required property owners to furnish a declaration of their possessions. The inventory had to include everything, right down to pigs and poultry. Only daily food necessities and table utensils were left untaxed. A check on the veracity of the declarations was provided in a clause bestowing upon any person who detected a false statement one-third of the amount subject to a penalty.

A system of common responsibility for families residing in the same district (*pao kia fa*) was also introduced, and is still customary in China.

[1] As a result of this poll-tax—for at bottom it was nothing else—vital statistics showed a marked decline. The population decreased from 29,092,185 in 1066 to 23,807,165 in 1075, and cultivated land by nearly 50 per cent. These figures do not necessarily represent the real decrease. It was to the advantage of the people to make their households appear as small as possible, to avoid this *per capita* tax. When we find, however, that after the abolition of the tax in 1727 the population had risen to 102,750,000 in 1753, as against 25,284,818 in 1724, it is evident that not only was statistical trickery at work, but that the poll-tax acted as a strong deterrent to any excessive growth of population.

Trade was likewise supervised and officially controlled. All stocks were valued, and subjected to an annual duty of 20 per cent. on the security of buildings and goods. Goods not redeemed after a certain date were liable to a further penalty of 2 per cent. In order to ensure the adjustment of supply and demand, and to eliminate local speculation as far as possible, a systematic classification of articles of commerce was undertaken.

(2) *Military Measures.* Warfare against the border tribes had caused the troops to multiply beyond all bounds, so that they were a general burden.[1] Here also Wang An-shï went energetically to work. All troops not actually employed on frontier defence he enrolled as a territorial force, and all those not needed for this purpose he sent home. He thereby effected a very drastic reduction in the army. He then ensured the maintenance of internal order by the creation of a system of militia closely corresponding to the system of local responsibility described above. Ten families represented a unit of defence (*pao*), fifty a superior unit, and ten superior units a head unit. In charge of each of these organizations was a headman. All families with two men had to supply one for the militia. Every five days a militiaman had to present himself for defence service, to maintain public security. Furthermore, the headmen received instruction in the art of defence, which they in turn had to impart to the militia. The necessary mounts were supplied by the Government and their upkeep entrusted to individual families in return for a rebate in their taxes. These families were then responsible for the care and maintenance of the horses. Inspections were held once a year. Regular musters were also held, to ensure that all weapons were kept in good condition.

Since the aim of these reforms was to supply the State with a military backbone, it is only fair to admit that they were attended by some degree of success against various adjacent tribes. The agrarian reforms, too, seem to have effected an actual reduction in the cost of living. Wang

---

[1] In the reign of T'ai Tsu (960–977) the troops numbered 378,000 ; in that of Ying Tsung (1064–68) they had increased to 1,162,000 !

An-shï himself once said that while the reforms were in force corn was as cheap as water.

No conspicuous success was achieved, however, and it is most surprising that we should find so many of the most eminent brains and personalities of that time in the ranks of Wang An-shï's most bitter opponents. How is this? Regarded from a European standpoint, all Wang An-shï's reforms sound rational, almost modern, in principle. The energy with which he grappled with an obsolete system would certainly have earned him in Europe the name of a great man. His conception of a state was that of a perfectly functioning machine. And seeing that, by means of sweeping reforms, he created the conditions needful for the perfect functioning of State machinery, he would undoubtedly have met with some success in European circles, where numbers of sympathetic helpers would have flocked to his side.

Not so in China. There he was regarded as an innovator, and that clinched the matter. Even when he stood at the height of his power a number of his most eminent contemporaries came forward and fearlessly censured his policy without regard to the dangerous consequences they might draw on their own heads. The antagonism was one not merely of methods and aims, but of temperament. Wang An-shï, himself one of the *literati*, hated the hollow stylistic exercises in vogue at the literary examinations. He introduced a new kind of examination essay that permitted greater independence and freedom of form, and was to be distinguished by originality of thought rather than polished style. The ethical basis of the *Spring and Autumn Annals* of Confucius was especially distasteful to him, so he eliminated the book from the syllabus. Thus literary differences were added to those existing in a practical sense, and although the *literati* themselves were split into three camps they soon joined forces against the innovator. On their side we find the names of the historian Sï-ma Kuang, who wrote the first universal history of China, the man of letters Ou-yang Siu, the poet and philosopher Su Tung-p'o (Su Shï), and later on the heads of the Sing-li school.[1]

[1] The philosophic school of 'rationalists.' See below.

PLATE 33

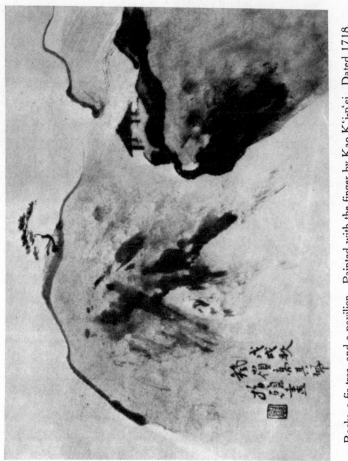

Rocks, a fir-tree, and a pavilion. Painted with the finger by Kao K'i-p'ei. Dated 1718.
(R. Wilhelm Collection.)

Whereas in Europe it would be quite possible to imagine such reforms crowned with success, it was otherwise in the China of that date. The reformer himself was energetic and full of zeal for the public welfare, but among those entrusted with the execution of the work were men who employed the power in their hands to oppress and exploit the people. Furthermore, although the political results that were to justify the new methods were not entirely lacking—a few advantages were gained on the northern frontier, and the aborigines (the Man) of the south and west subjugated—they were not so striking as had been anticipated. Times were too disturbed for such sweeping reforms to bear much fruit. Before they could take full effect the Emperor Shên Tsung, Wang An-shï's protector, died, and the work of reform came to a complete standstill. Its opponents were by no means united among themselves. There was a Lo party, headed by the Neo-Confucianist Ch'êng I, a Shu (Szechwan) party, led by Su Shï, and a So party, of which Liu An-shï was one of the moving spirits. But although at war with one another chiefly on literary issues, they were united enough in their antagonism to Wang An-shï. The Empress-Dowager, who was acting as regent for her young son, eagerly took advantage of the popularity of Wang's adversaries to make propaganda in favour of her rule. Their influence was used on the side of the throne.

Subsequently opinion veered round, and Wang An-shï's partisans seized the helm. But the programme of reform had become a mere party shibboleth. Power was turned to account to expel opponents ruthlessly from every post. A stone monument was even erected, upon which their names were to figure to their everlasting shame. So the fight continued. The old party naturally gained in influence and prestige from persecution. The new party used its power for its own advantage. This was the beginning of a time of confusion.

On the heels of the Tungusic Liao, another Tungusic tribe, the Ju-chên (Djurdjen), had gained ascendancy under its leader Akuta, who founded a new dynasty called the Kin. Treaties were now concluded with this tribe and heavy subsidies paid. Further weakened by rebellion at home, China sank into a state of increasing impotence. The remnants of the Liao, pursued by the Kin, turned west, and founded in Kashgaria the kingdom of Karakitai, which maintained itself until 1199.

The Kin, however, provoked by the Chinese, poured into China, seized the capital, and carried off the Court into captivity. The Sung dynasty had to withdraw south of the Yangtse, but even there found no peace. True, they had the courageous general Yo Fei, who inflicted considerable damage on the Kin. He, however, fell a victim to the intrigues of his rival Ts'in Kuei, who, released from captivity by the Kin, was upholding their cause at the Imperial Court. *Rôles* were now reversed. Ts'in Kuei belonged to the party of innovators. But whereas formerly this party had been in favour of vigorous action against foreign aggressors, while the conservatives advocated negotiation and temporizing, Yo Fei was now the knight *sans peur et sans reproche*. He has impressed his name for all time on the memory of the Chinese people, while Ts'in Kuei, the innovator, was held to be the advocate of a slothful peace.

Fate could no longer be held in check. What the Kin could not accomplish was completed by the Mongols, who had risen in the rear of the Kin, and with whom the Sung in blind folly had joined hands, only to find themselves the object of attack after the Kin had been destroyed. In the year 1279, when the last naval engagement had terminated in victory for the Mongols, a faithful minister of the house of Sung drowned himself in the sea near Canton with the little nine-year-old Emperor upon his back.

III. Art and Culture during the Sung Period

If the Sung dynasty won scanty laurels in the political field, it made up for this by the important place it took in the history of Chinese culture. This was a time of peaceful meditation and inward assimilation. Under the Emperor Hui Tsung (1101–25), the last of the Sung rulers who reigned north of the Yangtse (his successor was abducted by the barbarian Kin, and the Court had to retreat to the south), systematic study was made of the bronzes in the Imperial collection which had survived from antiquity and the results published in the form of a large illustrated catalogue, a magnificent specimen of wood-engraving. The great encyclopædia of Ma Tuan-lin, arranged under categories and comprising the whole field of contemporary knowledge, appeared in the Sung period. State academies of painting were opened, to foster fixed traditions in art and thus provide posterity with the means of studying the technical accomplishments of old masters. Not until our own times have the eyes of Europe been opened to Sung achievements in the domain of ceramic art. In various furnaces placed under the supervision of State officials porcelain was produced that has remained the delight of all connoisseurs. The art of book-printing also deserves mention, for although, as we previously pointed out, it originated at an earlier date, it reached the height of perfection in the Sung period. It was then that those works were created which have furnished a pattern for all time as regards printing technique, lay-out, and an harmonious and artistic appearance.

The Sung period cannot be called decadent. A new consciousness of the external world was born. Landscape became an integral part of the human mentality. Through landscape man approached nature in a new way. Art was enriched by poetry, and the forms adopted by the latter were free in comparison with the severe style of the T'ang lyrics, and permitted an outpouring of personal emotion. It is not correct to call Sung art naturalistic, as is frequently done. For nature is not the reproduction of objective phenomena, but an expression of inner experience. This period of culture may far more aptly be termed romantic, in contrast with the classicism of T'ang. Not that the personal element was lacking in those times, but it was fettered by the objective classical forms then obtaining, and just because it did not find expression, but only gleamed in places through the artistic framework, it imparted to the pure work that inner tension inherent in the true classic which preserves it from frigidity. In the Sung period sentiment reigned supreme, though not in such degree as to destroy form; but it expressed itself freely, was appropriating new realms. Not only nature in landscape, but the content of the storehouse of the past was now inwardly digested and mastered. The production in the Sung period of Sï-ma Kuang's first universal history of China, going back to the mythical period, is not purely fortuitous. The attitude toward antiquity of such a period is necessarily subjective. The relics of antiquity may be collected with loving devotion, but the new feeling for life gives them a different form. Thus Sung scholars assumed a superior attitude toward traditional material. They turned it inside out in their interpretations. None dealt more arbitrarily with ancient records than the devout Chu Hi, who took the texts of the *Great Learning* and the *Doctrine of the Mean* out of their traditional setting, by means of textual alterations and additions converted them into two independent works, and then presented them to the world, together with the Confucian *Conversations* and the *Works of Mencius (Mêng Tsï)*, as the Four Books which henceforward dominated the intellectual life of China.

The painting of the Sung period is also a new art. To trace symptoms of degeneracy here, as has been attempted, is pure affectation. Sung art can no more be called decadent as compared with T'ang art than can the Gothic style in comparison with the Romanesque. It is no mere accident that among the graphic arts painting now comes to the fore while sculpture takes second place. The Sung were no strangers to sculpture. But theirs is no longer the severe, monumental type of art; it is now animated by a pictorial and personal spirit. We find sculptured portraits, landscapes used as accessories to the figure, Kuan-yin seated on a rock, a tree-stump looming up. Sculpture is, of course, a medium as ill-suited to express landscape as painting is well adapted to the purpose. Sung painting was perhaps the first in the world to enter this new field. It shows the truest feeling for nature. Ever since the T'ang dynasty two schools had been struggling for mastery. They go by the names of the northern and the southern schools. The northern set greater value on modelling of form, correctness of outline, and movement of line. It is the more conservative school, concerned chiefly with draughtsmanship and faithful reproduction of the object represented, yet by no means true to the accidents and irregularities of nature, only to essentials. Perspective is to this school no mathematical exercise in imaginary lines of vision, but serves to arrange things within the limits of the picture so that their essence or spirit may be freely expressed. The southern school is far more radical. In order to express things as a whole it ignores detail. It does not picture individual objects, but a complete experience, all the details in which are but tones in a symphony. It was but natural, therefore, that art of this nature should resort to black-and-white technique, and produce wash-work in which subjects are expressed in mysterious whirls of black and white. The picture is no longer produced by the mere application of paint. The empty spaces are just as important elements of the whole as those touched with the brush. Together they compose the impassioned, almost visionary expression of inner experience. " It is the non-existent in things which makes them serviceable," said Lao Tsï once. This corresponds with the opinion of the artist who said that the parts requiring most thought were those not to be touched with the brush. How natural that many of these marvels should have been the work of monks belonging to the Buddhist School of Meditation ! For equally in meditation is to be found that grasp of life as a whole which distinguished these artists.

The best guide to the understanding of these phenomena is a study of religious developments in the Sung period and the consequent formation of the so-called Neo-Confucian school. Buddhism had made a complete spiritual conquest of China. Not only is Chinese sculpture, and in a certain sense Chinese painting too, inconceivable without the influence of Buddhism—Greek influences reached China through the agency of Buddhism in the same way that they were spread through Europe by Christianity—but intellectual life as a whole was steeped in it. So much so, indeed, that

Chinese Buddhism, besides forming a distinct province in Indian Buddhism, was an active factor in perfecting the creed. It would be no more possible, therefore, to ignore China in writing a history of Buddhist doctrine than to pass over German theological developments in compiling a history of Christianity. But the time came at last for the assimilation of what was, after all, an alien influence. It was possible only by amalgamation with Confucianism and Taoism. This intellectual achievement stands to the credit of Neo-Confucianism.

Its accomplishment, however, necessitated an organization that would supply the required degree of personal intimacy between teachers and pupils, like that existing of old between Confucius and his disciples. The official system of schooling and examinations, in which subjects and methods were governed by political considerations, was not suitable. Remember the energetic attacks made on this system by the financial reformer Wang An-shï, when he actually eliminated from the curriculum the vital Confucian work, the *Spring and Autumn Annals*.

The required intimacy was provided by the study circles (*shu yüan*). They had arisen in opposition to the official system of examinations, which was becoming more and more frigid and formal, and was useful only as the gateway to an official career. Their aim was intimacy, warmth of feeling, sincere conviction ; education was to be promoted for the sake of its ennobling effect on character, not as a mere stepping-stone to a political career. Thus Ku Hung-ming's comparison of Neo-Confucianism with the Pietist movement in European Protestantism is to some extent justifiable.

These study circles grew up round distinguished scholars of moral and literary repute. They were by no means situated in the centres of political administration—for State schools existed there—but were for the most part hidden away in wooded valleys or along the shores of rivers, in some idyllic spot. There the master dwelt with his disciples, and knowledge and education were imparted by direct personal tuition. The pupils evidently took down in writing the words of the teacher, for a number of works still exist in which glimpses of the spiritual life of these communities may be caught. That the Buddhist monastic idea played some part here is undoubted. But it was in keeping with an ancient Confucian ideal. Did not Confucius in his old age gather round him a school of this nature?

Then came the invention of printing. So long as the teachings of the sages had to be committed to memory by pupils whom the masters instructed from the old manuscripts kept in public libraries, schools were perforce tied to places with such institutions. But during the Sung period, when great zeal was displayed in the collection of old manuscripts, the spread of printed books had augmented steadily ever since the Nine Classics had been cut in wood and printed on paper at the instance of Fêng Tao. The printed book, which gradually assumed its present form, took the place of the laboriously written, and therefore costly and rare manuscript roll. Not only did great printing works spring up, with trade in the printing and sale of books, but private persons had their favourite works printed out of pure interest. Thus the study circles could readily be supplied with the libraries so essential to their activities. These circles now provided a noteworthy means of personal contact between followers of the Confucian school. A living tradition came into being and was carried on. No Church was this, but a community of mutually sympathetic souls in which doctrinal differences, even antagonisms, could exist without destroying its *esprit de corps*.

In order to understand the spiritual atmosphere prevailing in these schools we must take a brief survey of the various sources on which they based their teaching.

One of these sources is the Taoist doctrine (Tao Hüe) of abstraction. Its originators, Lao Tsï and Chuang Tsï, derived their principles from Nature herself. They sought the automatic laws of nature manifested in life. These natural laws, this cosmic conception, of Lao Tsï were surrounded by a halo of mysticism, and the fundamental idea worshipped in this ' Mysterious Mother of All Things ' was really something impersonal. The theory of an immanent, rational, but impersonal law of nature—for so may the Tao of Lao Tsï perhaps be best defined—was a quite untrammelled theory, sharply opposed to superstition or any sort of narrow clericalism.

It is one of the ironies of history that just this independent, almost cynically naturalistic philosophy should have supplied the foundation for an organized cult of an extremely superstitious character. The transition was brought about by the magicians (*fang shï*) of the Han period when they employed the works of Lao Tsï and Chuang Tsï as textbooks for their magic. There is a psychical condition in which magic and natural science come very close together. Astrology and alchemy have played a similar part in Europe. Of course it was the magical element in Taoism which made it popular. The reason why it caught the fancy of the people and the Court was that it held the secret of the philosopher's stone (*kin tan*), which confers immortality, was acquainted with all manner of charms and spells, and knew how to make gold and find the entrance into Fairyland. More than one emperor followed this religion—several died from indulgence in the elixir of life. As late as the Sung dynasty the Emperor Chên Tsung (998–1022) became an ardent devotee of Taoism after receiving a heaven-sent book containing all the secrets of the universe. This Taoism was quite compatible with worship of Confucius. The same Emperor, on one of his pilgrimages to the sacred mountain T'ai Shan, stopped to visit the tomb of Confucius, and utilized the occasion to ennoble the sage of antiquity as king. In a general way it should not be forgotten that besides the Taoism of the magicians and the Taoism of the monks (who, after they had drained Buddhism dry and appropriated its doctrines, conducted a strenuous campaign against the Buddhists in which first one side, then the other, was victorious), yet another Taoism, that of hermit sages, lurked along seashores or in mountain vales. In the solitude of nature this Taoism stood aloof from the life and activity of mankind, reverted beyond the times darkened by superstition to the spiritual freedom of Lao Tsï and Chuang Tsï, and explored the mysteries of the universe in the *Book of Changes* (*I King*).

The *Book of Changes* is the great link between Taoism and Confucianism. In it are expressed all mutations of the phenomena observed in connexion with the laws of nature and suited to serve as the basis of a naturalistic philosophy. The *Book of Changes* supplied the foundation for the Neo-Confucianism which was taking shape in Sung times. All manner of Taoist ideas, however, had already become bound up with this book, and were also taken over. Thus Shao Yung, one of the spiritual fathers of Neo-Confucianism, read into the *Book of Changes* the doctrine of a 'former heaven' (*sien t'ien*), which is derived from Taoist sources— possibly also showing signs of foreign (Persian ?) influences —and which throughout the metaphysical ideal world assumes an emanation of the world of reality from the transcendental First Principle. The other originator of Neo-Confucianism, Chou Tun-i, introduced into his commentary on the *Book of Changes* the famous *t'ai-ki-t'u* (diagram of the Supreme Ultimate, which also figures in Gothic art in the fish-bladder design). This conception of a dualistic primordial monad was originally used in connexion with the secret devices for prolonging human life, and was of course interpolated into the *Book of Changes* only as an afterthought. It seems likewise to have been of other than Chinese origin.

To these influences were added others from the Buddhist School of Meditation (Ch'an Hüe, the Zen school of Japan), in which the attainment of wisdom was dependent upon stillness and mental concentration. The three moving spirits of the new Confucianism, the two brothers Ch'êng Hao and Ch'êng I and Chang Tsai, whom posterity regarded as the transmitters of Confucianism pure and simple, were in reality strongly influenced by both Taoism and Buddhism. Their metaphysic shows this quite clearly. It assumed two basic principles : spirit (*li*) and matter (*k'i*). In their teaching matter corresponds exactly to the Taoist Nothingness and to the Buddhist Void. When this matter (literally, breath, air, force) becomes concentrated, the objects of sense are produced ; when it expands again, it falls back into the great void. Events in this sphere are regulated by the impersonal but nevertheless rational law of the spirit (*li* = order, reason), and through the coexistence of spirit and matter arise all the various combinations of being.

This doctrine was most comprehensively stated and systematized by the universal scholar Chu Hi, who flourished in the Southern Sung period (1130–1200). Of outstanding interest in his teaching is the application of the dualistic principle in the ethico-psychological field. The old Confucianism was divided into two schools, which violently attacked each other's views; the one asserted that the nature of man was evil, the other—which finally triumphed —insisted that man, since his nature was determined by a decree of heaven, must be essentially good. Chu Hi assumes the existence of two principles. The real, spiritual, essential nature of man (*sing*) is naturally good. But in order that man may come into being as an individual, this nature (*sing*) must be clothed with matter (*k'i*). This matter varies in quality, being denser or more rarefied, richer or poorer, as the case may be, which accounts for the distinction between men: wise men and fools, good men and bad. Matter (*k'i*) manifests itself in instincts and desires. Man's ethical task consists in combating and suppressing that which is derived from matter and is consequently impure—that is to say, instincts and desires. This explains the specific asceticism of the Neo-Confucian school, and exemplifies the way in which every dualistic theory postulates this attitude in the domain of ethics.

For the rest, the philosophy of this school is a most exalted one. As a spirit or rational being, man is one with the fundamental principles of heaven and earth. On the other hand, he must look upon every one, even the poorest and most destitute, as a brother dependent upon his help.

Two lines of thought were visible even in the initial stages of this school. One was concerned with moral education, the basis of which was serious-mindedness and reverence, the other with the cultivation of science, with perfection of knowledge as the goal. The means employed by the school of morality were meditation and composure, while the scientific school aimed at a comprehensive knowledge of the world. The subjective school was strongly influenced by Taoism and Buddhism; the objective school, although its doctrines were founded on the *Great Learning (Ta Hüe)*, may nevertheless be regarded in the main as the outcome of the philosophy of Ch'êng I.

These two schools of thought developed later into independent systems. The contemplative school grouped itself chiefly round Lu Kiu-yüan (1139–92), also known as Siang Shan. This school produced the famous philosopher Wang Yang-ming (1472–1528), whose intuitive philosophy in its marked aversion from all controversial discussion was fundamentally opposed to Neo-Confucianism, which in his day had long been predominant, until he forced it into the background. The scientific school, which was devoted to research, systematic study of the works of antiquity, and their rational elucidation, gathered round Chu Hi. A wonderfully prolific worker, Chu Hi actually re-created the whole of the classical literature of China. He wrote commentaries on the *Book of Changes (I King)*, the *Book of Poetry (Shï King)*, the Confucian *Conversations (Lun Yü)*, the *Works of Mencius (Mêng Tsï)*, the *Great Learning (Ta Hüe)*, and the *Doctrine of the Mean (Chung Yung)*. These commentaries subsequently determined the interpretation of the ancient texts, and it was not until the renaissance movement in the Ts'ing period (1644 to date) that the historical sense of those old records was again approached with any degree of philological conscientiousness. Before Chu Hi's theories gained the day, however, they had to suffer many attacks. For the very emphasis placed by Neo-Confucianism upon naturalness rendered its bias conservative rather than progressive, and the ideas of expediency or utilitarianism were alien to it. From the ethico-psychological standpoint, moreover, it laid exclusive stress on the value of education, and disliked violent changes. These above all were the reasons why the entire Neo-Confucian school was resolutely opposed to the radical reformer Wang An-shï. But as Wang An-shï's party often had the upper hand, the Neo-Confucian school frequently found itself proscribed. Chu Hi died during one of these periods of persecution, and it was not until nine years after his death that the wind veered round and he was honoured with the posthumous title of Wên Kung ('Duke of Culture') and his tablet placed in the Confucian temple, whither he was followed by the other heads of the school.

What ranges this school in the centre of interest is the fact that it brings into uniform focus, so to speak, the whole course of Chinese civilization. Here we find united all the spiritual and cultural influences that acted on China. Hence proceeds the understanding of what is beautiful and attractive in Sung art. This school is the ripe fruit of thousands of years of development, and with it the old China comes to an end. Its place is taken by a new product, still in the making.

CHAPTER X

THE GROWTH OF A NEW CHINA

THE DYNASTIES OF YÜAN (1280–1368), MING (1368–1644),
AND TS'ING (1644–1911)

WITH the arrival of the Mongols new storm-waves broke over China. At first wherever these fierce, unbridled hordes penetrated savage destruction ensued. Under the Great Khan Temudjin (Jenghiz Khan) great piles of enemies' heads marked their tracks. In the west they spread to the confines of Eastern Europe, in the east to the Yellow Sea, thus creating the greatest empire ever known. The savage period of this race lasted a comparatively short time; in China especially they rapidly assimilated Chinese manners and customs. Their early proclamations were worded in a barely comprehensible gibberish. But Chinese were soon employed in their service, and organized the administration on their behalf. Kublai Khan was already the model of a sage Confucian ruler! The assimilation of these sons of the desert was, indeed, all too rapid. For less than a century were they able to maintain their sway, and when they were overthrown their mentality had already been submerged in the higher civilization of China.

The period of their supremacy, however, was one of unexampled expansion. It was then that China really became known to the world, no longer as a far-off, legendary land, but through the descriptions of travellers who had seen it with their own eyes.

Giovanni di Monte Corvino, sent to Peking (Khan Baligh) in 1289 by Pope Nicholas IV, was the first real Catholic missionary in China, although the country had previously been visited by occasional Papal envoys and other travellers. Marco Polo, the Venetian, who made a journey to the East with his father and uncle, reached China in 1275, and was

253

most hospitably received by Kublai; he ranked for years, in fact, among the special retainers of the Great Khan, and went on important missions for him.

The accounts of these travellers show to what a high stage of civilization China had then attained, far above that of Europe. The Chinese inventions of paper, book-printing, the compass, and gunpowder were at that time finding their way westward, and were slowly filtering through to Europe, where they inaugurated a new era. It may be mentioned, incidentally, that China was also acquainted with paper money and inflation (already experienced, as a matter of fact, at an earlier date). China was at this time the centre of a traffic that spread its web over the whole of the known world. Not only had the Mongolian hordes conquered vast foreign territories, and thus broken down the barriers that had hitherto separated China from the West, but in addition travellers came from all the great Western lands to the Court of the Great Khan, were all well received, and were full of the splendour and hospitality they had found there.

As regards population, the slaughters perpetrated by the first Mongol invaders, which marked the climax of a long sequence of wars, were accompanied by a rapid decline in the number of inhabitants, resulting in larger holdings of land per head of the population. Generally speaking, the most important land regulations of Wang An-shï had been retained in the form to which they had been reduced in the course of the Sung dynasty. Education likewise continued on the lines laid down by the Sung. The Yüan dynasty was the decadent descendant of the Sung dynasty. Only in two realms was anything new and independent created—namely, in those of the drama and the novel. From the border territories a new type of musical instrument, the stringed instrument played with a bow, had been brought into China, and revolutionized Chinese music. A new class of song or air (k'ü) was then introduced, and rapidly became popular.

The Mongol rulers are said even to have included the composition of airs among examination tests, and it is quite likely that such things formed the subject of competitions at Court. The rhythm and tonality of these airs corresponded to the alteration of the Chinese language that took place under the influence of the northern dialects. The Northern Chinese dialect, which was just beginning to assume definite shape, and afterward came into use all over China as the official language, is quite different from the older spoken Chinese. Not only did one of the tone-groups disappear, but all the final consonants except *n* and *ng* dropped out, and a sound midway between *r* and *l* was gradually formed.

These airs became the chief musical element of the theatre. As early as Kin times songs had been given with lute accompaniment, and gradually developed into connected plays with incidental music. Little by little the orchestra was supplemented by wooden wind-instruments. Pantomimic performers in costume took the stage, while a singer chanted the words. Gradually the stage play developed, in which the actors sang and also spoke in recitative. Thus originated the 'mixed plays' (*tsa hi*), besides which 'historical pieces' (*chuan k'i*) were also given in the Yüan period. At first dramas consisted of four acts, but these were increased to forty or fifty in the historical pieces. This branch of art reached a high degree of perfection under the Mongol dynasty. The hundred selected plays of this period have remained the classic examples of dramatic literature. A number of them have been translated into European languages. It is true that from a literary point of view drama did not occupy as high a place in China as it did in Greece. Playwrights did not rank as poets in the classical sense. They often remained in the obscurity of the people at large, and official scholars never recognized their art as a legitimate class of literature. The theatre has nevertheless exercised a great influence in China among high and low. Stage plays are witnessed by all classes of society, and it is mainly through them that the memory of ancient heroes is kept green.

The era of expansion under Mongol rule was succeeded by another era of contraction under the Ming dynasty. This dynasty was founded by a former monk who had assumed the leadership of vagrant bands in the endeavour to expel the foreigners from the country. Coming from the south, he advanced to the Yangtse and established his capital at Nanking, then called Kin-ling. This is a very distinct case of a southerly swing of the pendulum, counteracting the northerly swing that brought the Mongols into the land. It was soon evident that the dynasty would be unable to maintain itself unless it transferred its capital toward the northern frontier. So the third Ming ruler, whose reign period is known as Yung-lo, removed to Peking, where he set up his capital. At the same time, the Great Wall in the north was carefully repaired and extended ; notwithstanding which serious and protracted fighting took place along the northern frontier.

The Ming dynasty was at the outset distinguished by the cruelty and bloodshed that must accompany the establishment of an absolute monarchy. On the slightest suspicion whole families were slaughtered. Executions frequently ran into tens of thousands. The people had flocked to the standard of the Ming because they were sweeping away the hated foreign dominion, but it was soon realized that the oppression of absolutism had become immeasurably worse. A glance at the gigantic edifices of the early Ming period, such as the Great Wall, the walls and palaces of Peking, and the tombs of the Ming emperors laid out across whole valleys, gives some idea of what the people must have suffered under the stress of these labours.

The Court mistrusted the officials appointed by the ordinary system of examinations, and attempts were made to invest members of the family with important territories. As a matter of fact, Ch'êng Tsu (Yung-lo) took advantage of a viceregal position of this nature to usurp the throne. From that time a very watchful eye was kept on the attitude of the enfeoffed princes.

As the places of the regular officials were taken by favourites and eunuchs, it is scarcely surprising that the dynasty soon began to show signs of enfeeblement. Events occurred such as the raising of the eunuch Wei Chung-hien to equal rank with Confucius. He built himself a magnificent mausoleum at the mountain monastery of Pi-yün Sï, near Peking, but the tomb remained empty, for he came to

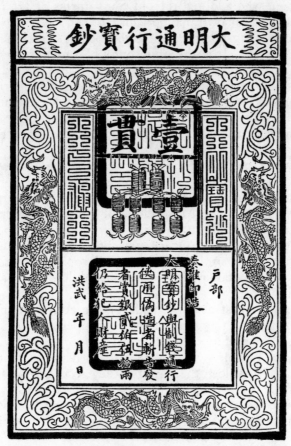

Fig. 17. Chinese Paper Money from the Beginning of the Ming Dynasty

an ignominious end at the hands of the executioners, and thus forfeited an honourable burial.

Effeminacy and superficial brilliance characterize the whole of this courtly Ming culture. How fine and delicate is the porcelain manufactured in this very period, with its thin shell and musical ring and decoration in underglaze blue or overglaze enamels ! [1] It then attained that perfection which has made Chinese porcelain so famous. And how decadent is the work of painters like T'ang Yin and K'iu Shï-chou, who adopted the old Sung forms of art in order to indulge their own mannerisms !

Wang Yang-ming's philosophy belongs likewise to the Ming period. It is the philosophy of a genius—which he was. But as not all men are geniuses, it degenerated among his less gifted disciples into a purely superficial brilliance. The new type of public examination, into which the eight-legged essay—corresponding to the German *Chrie*—was now introduced, had much the same effect, and a complete ossification of the system resulted.

Toward the end of the Ming dynasty the Jesuit fathers arrived in China, and met with an excellent reception at the Imperial Court. They even succeeded in converting to Christianity the last Ming emperor and his mother. Not only did the Jesuits introduce Western science into China, but they aroused in Europe such interest in China and her wisdom that the study of Chinese philosophy was rated high enough to be taken up by serious philosophers such as Leibniz.

Mention must also be made of the active colonial expansion toward the south-eastern archipelago. There the Chinese came into conflict from the very start with the European colonists who were also arriving at that time. Politically they lost the day, for they received no support at all from the Ming Government, who had liquidated all Chinese colonial possessions, even in the west, and went so far as to regard the mere fact of emigration as a punishable offence.

In literature a word must be said about the novel and the romance, the beginnings of which, it is true, go much farther back, but which were now being developed on systematic lines. These literary productions, written for the most part in a language corresponding to the colloquial speech of daily life, were not officially recognized, but they

---

[1] The enamel colours were possibly borrowed from *cloisonné*, which came to China from Persia.

were read and generally admired by every educated Chinese. Besides the historical novel, such as the *History of the Three Kingdoms* or the *Story of the Hundred and Eight Sworn*

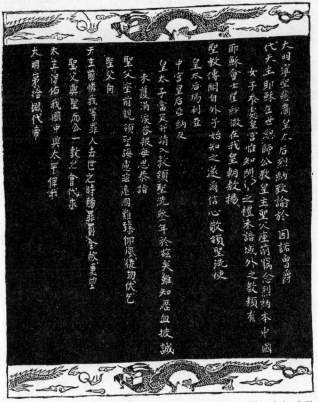

Fig. 18. Letter from the Dowager Empress Yung Li, of the Ming Dynasty, to the Pope at Rome
Like the last Ming emperor, this empress became a Christian.

Brothers of Mount Liang (Shui Hu), there was the novel of manners, which developed noticeably in the ensuing period and produced such works as *The Pilgrimage to the West*, *The Dream of the Red Chamber (Hung Lou Mêng)*, and *The Secret History of the Literati (Ju Lin Wai Shï)*.

All this, however, did not prevent the downfall of the Ming dynasty, amid a chaos of fierce insurrections. Its heritage fell once more to a house from the barbaric north, the Manchus, who claimed descent from the Kin. The Manchu period (Ta Ts'ing dynasty) was again a time of expansion. China then attained her greatest dimensions: Mongolia, Manchuria, Korea, and later on Turkestan, Tibet, Annam, and Cochin-China made up the outer ring of Chinese possessions. K'ang-hi and K'ien-lung were emperors who governed in the true Chinese spirit, and figure among the best rulers that China has ever known.

Intellectual life was by no means dead. In the fields of philological and original historical research in particular remarkable results were achieved. But we have now reached the limits of our theme. Henceforward Europe is to appear upon the scene, setting movements on foot which are radically different from any that have gone before and whose ultimate issue is still undecided. The history of Chinese civilization has now become part of that of humanity as a whole, in the evolution of which we are all concerned.

CHRONOLOGICAL TABLE

Prehistoric and Legendary

Fu Hi. Invention of nets and traps for hunting and fishing. Breeding of the six domestic animals. The eight diagrams.

Shên Nung. Invention of the plough. Markets. The five kinds of grain. The use of herbs for medicinal purposes.

Huang Ti. Invention of wheeled vehicles and ships, of clappers for night-watchmen, mortars, bows and arrows, houses, burial rites. Establishment of the sexagenary cycle, writing, the twelve-tone scale. Division of the land into provinces. The well system. Sericulture.

Yao. Astronomical determination of times and seasons. Wars against the Miao. Introduction of the five punishments.

Shun. Organization of the administrative system. The music of Shao.

Yü. The regulation of the waters. The nine bronze tripods with the nine provinces.

Beginning of the Period Authenticated to some Extent by Finds

B C.

c. 2200–1766. Hia dynasty. Cessation of elective sovereignty. Beginning of hereditary dynasties. The calendar of the Hia. Earliest ceramic finds.

c. 1766–1150. Shang dynasty. Earliest finds of oracular bones (inscribed) and bronzes. The oldest portions of the *Book of Poetry* and the *Book of History*. King Wên, while in prison, interprets the sixty-four diagrams of the *Book of Changes*.

Beginning of the Historical Period

c. 1150–249. Chou dynasty. The era of patriarchalism and feudalism.
c. 1150–722. Western Chou dynasty.
    c. 1150. King Wu.
    c. 1115. Duke Tan (Chou Kung) as regent. The time of classical literature. The earliest popular songs of the *Shï King*, the *I King*, parts of the *Shu King*.
      776. The first dated eclipse of the sun. The beginning of exact chronology.
      770. Transfer of the capital to Lo-yang.

CHRONOLOGICAL TABLE

The Three Kingdoms—The Heroic Age

A.D.

220–264. Wei dynasty.
221–264. Minor Han dynasty.
229–280. Wu dynasty.

The Tsin Period

265–316. Western Tsin dynasty.
317–420. Eastern Tsin dynasty. The first mention of tea.
375. Incursion of the Huns into Europe.

The Division between North and South

North

386–535. Northern Wei dynasty (house of Toba).
534–543. Eastern Wei dynasty.
535–557. Western Wei dynasty.
550–589. Northern Ts'i dynasty.
557–589. Northern Chou dynasty.

South

420–479. Earlier Sung dynasty.
479–502. Ts'i dynasty.
502–557. Liang dynasty.
557–589. Ch'ên dynasty. Powerful influence of Buddhism on Chinese sculpture in the north. First mention of the compass. The painter Ku K'ai-chï.
446. Persecution of Buddhism in Wei.
527. Arrival of Bodhidharma in Canton.

The Reunification of the Empire

589–618. Sui dynasty. Unification of the empire. Construction of the Imperial Canal.
618–907. T'ang dynasty. Second renaissance. Beginning of book-printing. Earliest porcelain. Use of gunpowder in fireworks. Trade with Arabia and Persia. Silkworm eggs and paper find their way to the West. Manichæism. Parseeism. Islam. Jews. Nestorians. Buddhism flourishing. The age of great poetry and painting.
733. Division of the empire into fifteen *tao* (provinces).
781. Erection of the Nestorian tablet at Sianfu.
845. Persecution of Buddhism. Destruction of the monasteries.

The Five Dynasties

907–923. Later Liang dynasty.
923–936. Later T'ang dynasty.
936–946. Later Tsin dynasty.

263

A.D.
947–950. Later Han dynasty.
951–959. Later Chou dynasty.
953. Printing of the Nine Classics.

THE SUNG PERIOD

960–1127. Northern Sung dynasty.
1127–1279. Southern Sung dynasty. The flourishing of pictorial art. Neo-Confucianism. The age of philosophy and historical research. Invention of movable type. Employment of gunpowder for military purposes. Porcelain. Knowledge of paper and the compass reaches Europe.
984. Organized search for old writings.
997. Division of the empire into fifteen *lu* (provinces).
1036. Ban on political discussions.
1055. Raising of Confucius's descendants to the rank of duke.
1068. Wang An-Shǐ appointed counsellor.
1072. Promulgation of Wang An-Shǐ's reforms.
1086. Abolition of the reforms in taxation.
1094. Reintroduction of the reforms.
1130–1200. Chu Hi.
1183. Ban on Taoist teaching.
1202. Prohibition of unofficial historiography.
1206. Jenghiz Khan becomes the Great Khan of the Mongols.
1215. Occupation of Peking by the Mongols.
1227. Death of Jenghiz Khan.
1271. Marco Polo starts on his journey to the East.

In the north are the following barbarian dynasties :
907–1125. Liao (Kitan) dynasty.
1125–1268. Western Liao dynasty.
1125–1234. Kin (Ju-chên, Tatar) dynasty.

MODERN HISTORY

1280–1368. Yüan (Mongol) dynasty. The period of greatest expansion. Age of the drama and the novel. Introduction of sericulture into Europe.
1281. The burning of Taoist books.
1368–1644. Ming dynasty. National reaction. Segregation from the outside world. Flourishing of ceramic art and *cloisonné*.
1380. Creation of the six ministries.
1412. Restoration of the Imperial Canal.
1421. Transfer of the capital from Nanking to Peking.
1472–1528. Wang Yang-ming.
1517. First Portuguese ships at Canton.
1530. Canonization of Confucius as Chǐ Shêng Hien Shǐ.
1557. Occupation of Macao by the Portuguese.
1575. First Japanese ships at Canton.

A.D.

1592–98. Occupation of Korea by the Japanese.

1601. Arrival of the Jesuit Father Ricci in Peking.

1604. First Dutch ships at Canton.

1622. Rebellion of the White Lotus sect in Shantung.

1624–62. Occupation of Formosa by the Dutch.

1637. First English ships at Canton.

1644–1911. Ts'ing (Manchu) dynasty. Westward expansion of the empire. The age of classical learning and philology. Entry of Europeans into China.

1644–61. Shun-chï.

1655. Embassy of Dutch and Russians to Peking.

1662–1722. K'ang-hi. Zenith of porcelain manufacture.

1680. Beginning of trade with the East India Company.

1689. Treaty of Nerchinsk. Demarcation of the Russo-Chinese frontier.

1699. Leibniz, *Novissima Sinica.*

1715. First English factory in Canton.

1722–77. The philosopher Tai Chên.

1723–35. Yung-chêng.

1724. Expulsion of the Catholic missionaries.

1726. Reorganization of the land tax.

1727. Treaty of Kiakhta with Russia.

1729. First anti-opium edict.

1736–95. K'ien-lung.

1757. Restriction of foreign trade to Canton.

1758–81. Mohammedan risings in Central Asia.

1773. Commission for cataloguing the Imperial Library.

1780. The Panshen Lama comes to Court.

1792–95. Lord Macartney's embassy.

1793. Second rebellion of the White Lotus sect.

1796–1820. Kia-k'ing.

1816. Lord Amherst's embassy.

1821–50. Tao-kuang.

1821. Yüan Yüan proposes the prohibition of the opium trade.

1823. Last Jesuit Father leaves Peking.

1833. Abolition of the monopoly of the East India Company.

1839. Destruction of opium stocks in Canton.

1840–42. The Opium War (with England).

1842. Treaty of Nanking.

1844. American commercial treaty of Wanghia. French commercial treaty of Whampoa.

1850–64. T'ai-ping Rebellion.

1851–61. Hien-fêng.

1854. Establishment of the new Maritime Customs at Shanghai.

1855. Yellow River shifts its course to the Gulf of Pechili.

1857–60. The Lorcha War (with England and France).

A.D.

1858. Treaty of Tientsin.
1859–1862. Prussian Far East mission.
1860. The Emperor's flight to Jehol.
1861. The Empress-Dowager's first *coup d'état*.
1861–75. T'ung-chï.
1862. Prussian Treaty of Tientsin.
1867–78. Mohammedan rebellions.
1868–72. Richthofen's travels in China.
1869. Japanese embassy to China. Commercial agreement with Russia.
1871. Treaty with Japan.
1873. First audience of the foreign ambassadors with the Emperor.
1875. The Empress-Dowager's second *coup d'état*.
1875–1908. Kuang-sü.
1876. Chefoo Convention. First Chinese railway (Shanghai–Wusung) is constructed and torn up. Japanese insist on the opening up of Korea to the world.
1881. Treaty of St Petersburg.
1882. France occupies Tongking.
1886. England occupies Burma.
1889. Personal assumption of government by Kuang Sü.
1897. Beginning of the foreign policy of annexation.
1898. Reform edicts. K'ang Yu-wei. Liang Ki-ch'ao. Conclusion of the treaty of Kiaochau.
1900–1. The Boxer Rising.
1901. The International Protocol.
1902. Return of the Court to Peking. Establishment of a central authority for State reforms.
1904. The English expedition to Tibet. Treaty of Lhasa.
1904–5. The Russo-Japanese War.
1905. Edict abolishing the old-style examinations.
1909–11. Hüan-t'ung.
1910. Convening of the National Assembly.
1911. The Revolution. China becomes a republic.

BIBLIOGRAPHY

BLAND, J. O. P., and BACKHOUSE, E. *China under the Empress-Dowager* (London, 1910).

BÖHME, K. *Wirtschaftsanschauungen chinesischer Klassiker* (Hamburg, 1926).

BRUCE, J. P. *Chu Hsi and his Masters : An Introduction to Chu Hsi and the Sung School of Philosophy* (London, 1923).

CARTER, T. F. *Periods of Chinese History* (Boston, New York, Chicago, London, 1925).

—— *The Invention of Printing in China* (New York, 1925).

CHALFANT, F. A. " Early Chinese Writing," in the *Memoirs of the Carnegie Museum* (vol. iv, No. 1, September 1906).

CHAVANNES, E. *La Sculpture sur pierre en Chine* (Paris, 1893).

—— *Les Mémoires historiques de Se-ma Ts'ien, traduits et annotés* (5 vols., Paris, 1895–1901).

CONRADY, A. *Die chinesischen Handschriften und sonstigen Kleinfunde Sven Hedins in Lou Lan* (Stockholm, 1920).

—— " China," in *Ullsteins Weltgeschichte*, 1910.

CORDIER, H. *Histoire générale de la Chine et de ses relations avec les pays étrangers* (4 vols., Paris, 1920).

COUVREUR, S. *Tch'ouen Ts'iou et Tso Tchouan* (Ho Kien Fou, 1914).

—— *Li Ki* (2 vols., Ho Kien Fou, 1899).

—— *Chou King* (Hsien Hsien Fou, 1916).

—— *Cheu King* (Hsien Hsien Fou, 1916).

—— *Les Quatre livres* (Ho Kien Fou, 1895).

DUBS, H. H. *Hsüntze, the Moulder of Ancient Confucianism* (London, 1927).

—— " Did Confucius study the *Book of Changes* ? " in *T'oung Pao*, Nos. 1 and 2, 1927.

ERKES, E. *Chinesische Literatur* (Breslau, 1922).

FABER, E. *Chronological Handbook of the History of China* (Shanghai, 1902).

FORKE, A. *Wang Ch'ungs Lun Hêng* (2 vols., Berlin, 1907 and 1911).

—— *Mê Ti und seiner Schüler philosophische Werke* (Berlin, 1922).

—— *Der Ursprung der Chinesen* (Hamburg, 1925).

—— *Die Gedankenwelt des chinesischen Kulturkreises (Handbuch der Philosophie)* (Munich and Berlin, 1927).

FRANKE, O. " Der Ursprung der chinesischen Geschichtsschreibung," in *Sitzungsberichte der Preussischen Akademie der Wissenschaften*, 1925.

—— *Über die chinesische Lehre von den Bezeichnungen* (Leyden, 1906).

—— " Die prähistorischen Funde in Nordchina und die älteste chinesische Geschichte," in *Mitteilungen des Seminars für Orientalische Sprachen* (Berlin, 1926).

HISTORY OF CHINESE CIVILIZATION

FRANKE, O. *Studien zur Geschichte des konfuzianischen Dogmas und der chinesischen Staatsreligion : Das Problem des Tsch'un-ts'iu und Tung Tschung-schu's Tsch'un-ts'iu-fan-lu* (Hamburg, 1920).

——— " Die Chinesen," in *Lehrbuch der Religionsgeschichte*, by Chantepie de la Saussaye, 4th edition (Tübingen, 1924).

——— "Ackerbau und Seidengewinnung als ethische und religionsbildende Elemente," in *Kêng Tschi Tu* (Hamburg, 1923).

——— *Ostasiatische Neubildungen* (Hamburg, 1923).

——— *Die Grossmächte in Ostasien von 1894–1914* (Brunswick and Leipzig, 1923).

——— *Die Rechtsverhältnisse am Grundeigentum in China* (Leipzig, 1903).

FRIES, S. VON. *Abriss der Geschichte Chinas* (Hong-Kong, Vienna, and Shanghai, 1884).

GILES, H. A. *A Chinese Biographical Dictionary* (London and Shanghai, 1898).

GRANET, M. *La Religion des Chinois* (Paris, 1922).

——— *Danses et légendes de la Chine ancienne* (2 vols., Paris, 1926).

GROOT, J. J. M. DE. *The Religious Systems of China* (unfinished ; Leyden, 1892–1912).

——— *Universismus* (Berlin, 1918).

——— *Die Hunnen in vorgeschichtlicher Zeit* (Berlin and Leipzig, 1921).

——— *Chinesische Urkunden zur Geschichte Asiens* (Berlin and Leipzig, 1926).

GRUBE, W. *Die chinesische Volksreligion und ihre Beeinflussung durch den Buddhismus* (s.l., 1893).

——— *Geschichte der chinesischen Literatur* (Leipzig, 1909).

——— *Religion und Kultus der Chinesen* (Leipzig, 1910).

HACKMANN, H. *Der Buddhismus* (Halle, 1906).

——— *Laien-Buddhismus in China* (Gotha, 1924).

——— *Chinesische Philosophie* (Munich, 1927).

HENKE, F. G. *The Philosophy of Wang Yang-ming* (London and Chicago, 1916).

HERMANN, H. *Chinesische Geschichte* (Stuttgart, 1912).

HIRTH, F. *The Ancient History of China* (New York and London, 1923).

——— *Chinesische Studien* (Munich and Leipzig, 1890).

HU SHIH. *The Development of the Logical Method in Ancient China* (Shanghai, 1922).

KARLGREN, B. *On the Authenticity and Nature of the Tso Chuan*, No. 32, 1926, of *Göteborgs Högskolas Arsskrift* (publications of the University of Gothenburg, Sweden).

KRAUSE, F. E. A. *Geschichte Ostasiens* (Göttingen, 1925).

——— *Ju Tao Fo, die religiösen und philosophischen Systeme Ostasiens* (Munich, 1924).

KU HUNG-MING. *Chinas Verteidigung gegen europäische Ideen* (Jena, 1911).

——— *Der Geist des chinesischen Volkes* (Jena, 1924).

BIBLIOGRAPHY

LEGGE, J. *The Chinese Classics* (5 vols., Oxford, 1865, etc.) (comprising the *Shï King*, the *Shu King*, the *Works of Mencius*, etc.).

—— *The Sacred Books of the East* (ed. by Max Müller): "The Sacred Books of China," vol. xvi, the *Yï King* [*I. King*] (Oxford, 1899); vols. xxvii and xxviii, the *Li Ki* (Oxford, 1885); vols. xxxix and xl, the *Texts of Taoism* (Oxford, 1891).

McGOVERN, W. M. *Manual of Buddhist Philosophy* (London and New York, 1923).

MASPERO, G. *La Chine* (Paris, 1925).

—— *La Chine antique* (Paris, 1927).

MUSSO, G. D. *La Cina ed i Cinesi* (2 vols., Milan, 1926).

PUINI, C. *Le Origini della civiltà secondo la tradizione e la storia dell' Estremo Oriente : Contributo allo studio dei tempi primitivi del genere umano* (Florence, 1891).

REICHWEIN, A. *China und Europa : Geistige und künstlerische Beziehungen im 18 Jahrhundert* (Berlin, 1923).

RICHTHOFEN, F. VON. *China* (Berlin, 1877, etc.).

ROSTHORN, A. *Geschichte Chinas* (Stuttgart and Gotha, 1923).

RUSSELL, B. *The Problem of China* (London, 1922).

SCHINDLER, B. *Das Priestertum im alten China* (Leipzig, 1919).

SCHÜLER, W. *Geschichte Chinas* (Berlin, 1912).

SHEN YI and STADELMANN, H. *China und sein Weltprogramm* (Dresden, 1925).

SUN YAT-SEN. *The International Development of China* (New York and London, 1922).

—— *The Three Principles of the People.* Translated into English by F. W. Price (Shanghai, 1928).

WANG KING KY. *La Voix de la Chine* (Brussels, 1927).

WIEGER, L. *Textes historiques : Histoire politique de la Chine depuis l'origine jusqu'en 1912* (2 vols., Hien-hien, 1922–23).

—— *La Chine à travers les ages* (Hien-hien, 1924).

—— *Histoire des croyances religieuses et des opinions philosophiques en Chine* (Paris, 1922).

WILHELM, R. *Chinesische Lebensweisheit* (Darmstadt, 1922).

—— " Die Religion und Philosophie Chinas " (Jena). Already published : *I Ging, Das Buch der Wandlungen* (2 vols., 1924); *Kungfutse, Gespräche (Lun Yü)* (1910); *Mong Dsï (Mong Ko)* (1916); *Laotse, Das Buch des Alten vom Sinn und Leben* (1923); *Lia Dsï, Das wahre Buch vom quellenden Urgrund* (1911); *Dschuang Dsï, Das wahre Buch vom südlichen Blütenland* (1923); *Frühling und Herbst des Lü Bu We* (1928).

—— *Die Seele Chinas* (Berlin, 1925).

—— *Chinesische Literatur* (Wildpark-Potsdam, 1925–27).

—— *Ostasien, Werden und Wandel des chinesischen Kulturkreises* (Potsdam, 1928).

—— *Lao Tse und der Taoismus* (Stuttgart, 1925).

HISTORY OF CHINESE CIVILIZATION

WILHELM, R. *Kung Tse, Leben und Werk* (Stuttgart, 1925).
—— *Konfuzius und der Konfuzianismus* (Sammlung Göschen, 1928).
ZENKER, E. V. *Geschichte der chinesischen Philosophie* (2 vols., Reichenberg, 1926).

CHINESE WORKS ALSO CONSULTED

CHANG T'AI-YEN. *Kuo Hüe Kiang Yen Tsi (Lectures on Sinological Studies)* (Shanghai, 1923).

CHANG YIN-LIN. " Ming Ts'ing Chï Tsi Si Hüe Shu Ju Chung Kuo K'ao Lüe " (" History of the Penetration of European Science into China at the Time of the Ming and Ts'ing Dynasties "), in the *Ts'ing Hua Journal*, vol. i, Part I (Peking).

CHAO WÊN-JUI. " T'ang Tai Shang Ye Chï T'ê Tien " (" The Peculiarities of Trade in the T'ang Dynasty "), in the *Ts'ing Hua Journal*, vol. iii, Part II (Peking).

CH'ÊN WÊN-PO. " Chung Kuo Ku Tai T'iao Wu Shï " (" History of Ancient Chinese Dancing "), in the *Ts'ing Hua Journal*, vol. ii, Part I (Peking).

CH'ÊN YÜAN. " Huo Yao Kiao Ju Chung Kuo K'ao " (" History of Zoroastrianism in China "), in the *Kuo Hüe Ki K'an*, vol. i, Part I (Peking).
—— " Mo Ni Kiao Ju Chung Kuo K'ao " (" History of Manichæism in China "), in the *Kuo Hüe Ki K'an*, vol. i, Part II (Peking).
—— " Yüan Si Yü Jên Hua Hua K'ao " (" Research on the Sinicization of the Western Tribes in the Yüan Dynasty "), in the *Kuo Hüe Ki K'an*, vol. i, Part IV (Peking).

CHU HI-TSU. " Chung Kuo Shï Hüe Chï K'i Yüan " (" Origin of Chinese Historical Science "), in the *Social Science Quarterly*, vol. i, Part I.
—— " Wên Tsï Hüe Shang Chï Chung Kuo Jên Chung Kuan Ch'a " (" Philological Researches into the Origin of the Chinese People "), in the *Social Science Quarterly*, vol. i, Part II.

CHU SHï. " Chung Kuo K'ao Shï Chï Tu " (" The Chinese Examination System "), in the *Eastern Miscellany*, vol. xxiv.

HU SHï. " Ts'ï Ti K'i Yüan " (" On the Origin of the Ts'ï "—*i.e.*, a certain form of poetry), in the *Ts'ing Hua Journal*, vol. i, Part II (Peking).
—— *Chung Kuo Chê Hüe Shï Ta Kang (Outline of the History of Chinese Philosophy)* (Shanghai, 1919).
—— Article in *Kuo Hüe Ki K'an*, vol. ii (see p. 178 *n.*)

KU KIE-KANG. *Ku Shï Pian (On Ancient Chinese Historical Works)* (Peking, 1926).

KU KIE-KANG and WANG CHUNG-KI. *Pên Kuo Shï (Chinese History)* (Shanghai, 1926).

LI KI-HUANG. *Ku Shu Yüan Liu (The Sources of Chinese Classical Literature)* (Shanghai, Commercial Press, 1926).

LI T'AI-FÊN. *Chung Kuo Shï Kang (Outlines of Chinese History)* (Peking, undated).

LIANG K'I-CH'AO. *Chung Kuo Li Shï Yen Kin Fa (Methods of Research into Chinese History)* (Shanghai, 1926).

270

BIBLIOGRAPHY

LIANG K'I-CH'AO. *Ts'ing Tai Hüe Shu Kai Lun* (*Science in the Ts'ing Dynasty*) (Shanghai, 1921).

LIU TA-KÜN. " Chung Kuo Ku Lai T'ien Chï Yen Kiu " (" Research into the Ancient Agricultural System of China "), in the *Ts'ing Hua Journal*, vol. iii, Part I (Peking).

LU MAO-TÊ. " Chung Kuo Ti I P'ien Ku Shï Shï Tai K'ao " (" Research on the Date of the Oldest Chinese History "), in the *Ts'ing Hua Journal*, vol. i, Part II (Peking).

—— " Yu Kia Ku Wên K'ao Kien Shang Tai Chï Wên Hua " (" The State of Civilization in Shang Times judged from Oracular Inscriptions on Bones "), in the *Ts'ing Hua Journal*, vol. iv, Part II (Peking).

TING WÊN-KIANG. " Li Shï Jên Wu Yü Ti Li Ti Kuan Hi " (" Connexions between Historical Personalities and Geography "), in *Science*, vol. viii, Part I.

WANG KUO WEI. " Ta Ta K'ao " (" Research, on the Tatars "), in the *Ts'ing Hua Journal*, vol. iii, Part I (Peking).

YUNG KENG. " Kia Ku Wên Tsï Chï Fa Kien K'i K'ao Shï " (" The Discovery and Deciphering of Oracular Inscriptions on Bones "), in the *Kuo Hüe Ki K'an*, vol. i, Part IV (Peking).

Chou Li (*Chou Ritual*).
Han Shu, " I Wên Chï."
Huang Ts'ing King Kie.
I Li (*Ceremonial Customs*).
Kia Yü.
Lü Shï Ch'un Ts'iu.
Pan Ku Lou I K'i Kuan Shï.
Po Hu T'ung.
Sui Shu, " King Tsi Chï."
Ta Tai Li.
Topography of Lao Shan.
Tsui Kin Chï Wu Shï Nien of the last fifty years (Shanghai, *Shen Pao*).
Wên Hien T'ung K'ao.
Yü Shï.

INDEX

INDEX

Confucius, temple of, 45
Conrady, A., 110 *n.*, 183 *n.*
Conversations (Lun Yü), 115 *n.*, 117 *n.*, 143, 175, 244, 251
Cor Hydræ, 66 *n.*
Cosmogony, 67–69, 177–178
Court life, in the Yin dynasty, 93–94 ; in the Chou dynasty, 100 ; in the Han dynasty, 186 *et seq.*
Ctesiphon, 182 *n.*
Cycle of sixty, 65

DEATH, understanding of, 110 ; life beyond, 112, 151
Devil's Country (Kuei Fang), 24
Divination, 52, 85, 120
Divine Husbandman (Shên Nung, *q.v.*)
Doctrine of the Mean (Chung Yung), 171–172, 244, 251
Domestic life, in antiquity, 77 *et seq.* ; in the Chou dynasty, 95–96, 102 *et seq.*
Dragon-boat Festival, 62, 80 *n.*
Dragons, 41 (Fig. 2) ; power of, 80
Drama in the Yüan dynasty, 255
Duality, principles of (*yin* and *yang*), 172, 197, 249
Dubs, Homer H., 143 *n.*
Duke of the Hundred Clans (Po Sing), 61
Dynastic histories, 27 *et seq.*

EASTERN SEA, 176
Eclipse of the sun, 82, 121 *n.*
Education in feudal times, 118
Elixir of life, 211, 225, 248
Emigration, a punishable offence in Ming times, 258
Encyclopædias, 30 *et seq.*, 233, 243
Êr Ya (dictionary), 175
Eunuchs, 186 *et seq.*, 194 *et seq.*, 202, 228–229, 256
Europe, influences of, 35 ; art influences of, 46
Examination system, 215 *et seq.*, 240, 258

FA HIEN (pilgrim), 56
Fabrics, preservation of ancient, 40
Falling into Trouble, 171
Fan Tsü (Ts'in general), 156 *n.*
Feather Mountain, 58 *n.*

Federation of states, 135
Fêng Tao (promoter of printing), 230–231
Fengtien, 49
Ferghana, 182
Filial piety, 71
Financial reforms of Wang An-shï, 236 *et seq.*
Fish-bladder design in Gothic art, 249
Five elements, principle of the, 197
Forke, A., 178 *n.*
Former Han dynasty, 167 *et seq.*, 194, 201
Former heaven, doctrine of a (*sien t'ien*), 67 *n.*, 249
Four great ' criminals,' 58 *n.*
Four Mountains, 70
Four quadrants, 67
Franke, O., 22 *n.*, 24 *n.*, 49 *n.*, 177 *n.*, 208 *n.*
Franks, 217
Frescoes, 38, 39 *n.*
Fu Hi (Pao Hi), 24, 31, 60
Fu Shêng (Confucian scholar), 23, 35
Fu Yüe, 84
Fukien, 179, 184–185

General Institutions, 31
Geography of ancient China, 89 *et seq.*
Getæ, 181, 182
Giles, Dr Lionel, 31 *n.*
God, 82 *et seq.*, 116 *n.*, 151, 193, 205, 209 ; the Supreme, 72, 100, 116 *n.*
Gothic art, 249
Grand Astrologer, 64
Grand Temple (at Lo-yang), 38
Grape-vine, introduction of, into China, 182
Grass character, 207 (Fig. 14). *See also* Script
Grave-thieves, 37
Great Institutions of the Yung-lo Period, The (Yung Lo Ta Tien), 31
Great Learning (Ta Hüe), 144, 244, 251
" Great Plan," 85 *et seq.*
Great Treatise (*Ta Chuan*), 24, 59. *See also Book of Changes*
Great Wall, 36, 163, 179, 215, 236, 256
Greater Seal character (*Ta Chuan*), 142
Greece, 205, 221, 255 ; civilization of, 201 ; art influences of, 245
Greeks, 183

275

INDEX

INDEX

INDEX

Tripods of Chou, 41, 130
Ts'ai Lun (inventor of paper), 201
Ts'ai state, 124
Tsao (hearth-god), 78
Ts'ao state, 124
Ts'ao Ta Ku (Pan Chao, *q.v.*)
Ts'ao Ts'ao (father of first Wei ruler), 203
Tsi river, 90
Tsi Shï, Mount, 92
Ts'i state, 124 *et seq.*
Tsï Ch'an (Chêng statesman), 152
Tsï Chï T'ung Kien—see *Universal Mirror of Aids to Government*
Tsï Chï T'ung Kien Kang Mu—see *Root Causes and Effects of Affairs recorded in the " Universal Mirror "*
Ts'ien river, 91, 92
Ts'ien-fu Shan, sculpture at, 46
Tsin dynasty, 203, 210 *et seq.* ; bronzes of, 41
Tsin state, 124 *et seq.* ; great families of, 119 *n.*
Tsin shi examination, 219
Ts'in dynasty, 53, 155 *et seq.*, 169 ; bronzes of, 42 ; monuments of, 45
Ts'in Kuei (rival of Yo Fei, *q.v.*), 242
Ts'in Shï Huang Ti (first Ts'in emperor), 22, 24, 35, 36, 43, 53, 136, 142, 156 *et seq.*, 169 *et seq.*, 196, 211
Ts'in state, 111, 124 *et seq.*, 147, 150 *n.*, 152, 154, 197
Tsinan, reliefs at, 45
Tsing-chou Fou, 37
Ts'ing-t'ien—see Well system
Ts'ing Chou (province), 90
Ts'ing dynasty, 33, 39, 234 ; historical researches in, 23 *n.* ; records of, 55 ; novel-writing in, 223 ; renaissance under, 251
Tsingtau, 44 *n.*
Tso Chuan (Tso's Commentary), 24 *n.*, 25, 29, 122 *n.*, 175, 219
Tso K'iu (historian), 24–25, 33, 122 *n.*
Tsou (home of Mencius), 144
Tsou Yen (philosopher), 16
Ts'ui Shu (philosopher), 178
Tsung (deities), 69
Tu Fu (T'ang poet), 55, 219, 221
Tu-küe tribes, 93, 218. See also Turkic tribes
Tu Yu (historian), 30–31, 33
T'u Shu Tsi Ch'êng, 31

T'u Wu, 195
T'u-an Ku, 131
Tun-huang, 38, 56 ; literary remains in, 55
Tung Cho (Han general), 43, 53, 202
Tung Chung-shu (Han philosopher), 172, 177, 197, 208
T'ung Chï (Complete Chronicles), 31, 33
T'ung Kien Ki Shï Pên Mo—see *Root Causes and Effects of Affairs recorded in the " Universal Mirror "*
T'ung Tien, 30 *n.*
Tungusic tribes, 241
Turcomans—*see* Turkic (Tu-küe) tribes
Turkestan, 260
Turkic (Tu-küe) tribes, 95, 96, 206, 218
Twelve Pastors, 70
Twenty-four Historical Works, The, 27

UIGHURS (Hui-ho), 218, 224, 226
Underground tendencies of religion, 63, 83 *et seq.*, 99–100, 111
Uniformity, theory of economic, 160 *et seq.*
Universal Mirror of Aids to Government, 29 *n.*, 31
Upward, Allen, 117 *n.*
Urban civilization, 93, 95–96, 169
Uriatubo, 182

VEGETATION rites, 62–63, 79

WALL-PAINTINGS—*see* Frescoes
Walnut, introduction of, into China, 182
Wang (Han empress), 189
Wang An-shï (Sung minister and social reformer), 29 *n.*, 236 *et seq.*, 246, 251, 254
Wang Ch'ung (philosopher), 178, 208
Wang family, 213
Wang Kuo-wei, 23 *n.*, 41, 55 *n.*
Wang Mang (founder of the Sin dynasty), 53, 189 *et seq.*, 196, 197 *n.*, 202 ; reforms of, 190 *et seq.*
Wang Pi (philosopher), 209 *et seq.*
Wang Wei (painter and poet), 219
Wang Yang-ming (philosopher), 251, 258
Warring States, period of the, 133 *et seq.*, 160, 163, 196
Weaving maiden, legend of the, 80

283

DATE DUE

DEMCO 38-297